Scsi: Understanding The Small Computer System Interface

NCR Corporation

Prentice Hall, Englewood Cliffs, New Jersey 07632

Editorial/production supervision: BARBARA MARTTINE
Cover design: LUNDGREN GRAPHICS
Manufacturing buyer: RAY SINTEL

Published by Prentice-Hall, Inc.
A Division of Simon & Schuster
Englewood Cliffs, New Jersey 07632

Printed in the United States of America

10 9 8 7 6 5 4 3 2 1

ISBN   0-13-796855-8

Prentice-Hall International (UK) Limited, *London*
Prentice-Hall of Australia Pty. Limited, *Sydney*
Prentice-Hall Canada Inc., *Toronto*
Prentice-Hall Hispanoamericana, S.A., *Mexico*
Prentice-Hall of India Private Limtied, *New Delhi*
Prentice-Hall of Japan, Inc., *Tokyo*
Simon & Schuster Asia Pte. Ltd., *Singapore*
Editora Prentice-Hall do Brasil, Ltda., *Rio de Janeiro*

Contents

What Is SCSI? Understanding The Small Computer System Interface

FOREWORD

In an industry dominated by the newest bells and whistles, it may not be stylish to admit that the *Small Computer System Interface* is not new. SCSI, named in 1982, was based on SASI (Shugart Associates System Interface) which was two years old at that time.

But people are still quite excited by what SCSI has to offer — often for divergent reasons. Some see SCSI as offering true device independence. Others see a true peer-to-peer I/O interface permitting multiple processors to share peripherals. Most would agree that it is an inexpensive way to put a high-performance disk, tape, or optical disk on a computer system. In fact, they are all right.

The word "Small" has caused no end of grief for me. Many people would rather die than put anything *small* on their computer. Especially if it means low performance. It's true some early SCSI devices stressed cost above performance, but the current third-generation SCSI products have excellent performance. And, to the dismay of some suppliers, they are still inexpensive.

I used to be annoyed at the common pronunciation of the SCSI acronym, "Scuzzy". It seemed, and perhaps was intended to be, derogatory. But I have come to believe that "Scuzzy" has been a great asset. Do you know of any engineers who would not want to know more about a "Scuzzy" interface?

The term is, at times, deserved. SCSI certainly has some aspects that are indeed Scuzzy. Many of these result directly from attempts to avoid burning bridges. Planned migration has always been important to the SCSI Committee (X3T9.2). Occasionally this results in less than pristine solutions.

What is SCSI? is a welcome tutorial. I certainly would not recommend the SCSI standard to those who are interested in simply learning about SCSI. Standards are meant to be precise, legal documents. They are rarely easy to read. This book is.

Reading this book will not make you an expert although you will understand SCSI's terminology and concepts. If you want to become an expert on SCSI, this book is a good starting point. If you don't, that's okay. Besides, you should see the strange looks my wife gets when she tells acquaintances that her husband is a Scuzzy Guru.

John B. Lohmeyer
Standards Architect, NCR Corporation
Chairman X3T9.2

PREFACE

This book provides an overview of the Small Computer System Interface (SCSI). It is intended for people who want to understand what SCSI is, how SCSI operates, and what systems support SCSI. For more detailed information about the SCSI bus, refer to the ANSI SCSI specification. To obtain a copy of the specification, see the following information.

Title:

Small Computer System Interface (SCSI) Specification (ANSI X3.131-1986)

Available from:

American National Standards Institute
1430 Broadway
New York, New York 10018

Sales Department: (212) 642-4900

This book was reviewed by :

John Lohmeyer, Chairman of the ANSI X3T9.2 Subcommittee.

List of contributors:

Text	Stanley E. Relf
Cover Illustration	Douglas W. Trowbridge
Editing and Production	Computer Aided Publications department, Engineering & Manufacturing – Wichita, NCR Corporation
Marketing Consultation	Cynthia J. Morey

What Is SCSI?
Understanding The
Small Computer
System Interface

What Is The Purpose Of This Book?

As a pioneer in defining and implementing the Small Computer System Interface (SCSI), NCR Corporation recognizes the need for a concise but thorough overview of this multifaceted, flexible, peripheral interface. This book was written to address that need. It provides an overview of SCSI for first time implementors and other people who need to know basically what SCSI is and how the SCSI bus operates.

This book answers some of the most commonly asked questions about SCSI. It provides a brief history and general overview of SCSI. It then explains some of the general concepts of SCSI and builds upon those concepts to provide a detailed overview. After explaining what SCSI is, this book provides a glimpse of the future of SCSI and NCR's commitment to future enhancements of SCSI.

Understanding SCSI — Background

What Does SCSI Mean?

SCSI is the acronym for Small Computer System Interface. SCSI is a specification (ANSI standard X3.131-1986) for a peripheral bus and command set. The SCSI specification defines a high performance peripheral interface that distributes data among peripherals independently of the host, thereby freeing the host computer for more user-oriented activities.

What Is The History Of SCSI?

In 1981, NCR Corporation joined forces with Shugart Associates to develop an intelligent interface for disk drives. The new interface was called SASI for Shugart Associates Systems Interface. In December of 1981, NCR Corporation and Shugart Associates convinced the X3T9 standards committee to adopt SASI as a working document for an ANSI interface standard. In April of 1982, with NCR's representative leading the technical working groups, subcommittee X3T9.2 began work on the new standard. The subcommittee named the proposed I/O standard the Small Computer System Interface (SCSI). Extensive work within the X3T9.2 subcommittee resulted in many enhancements and revisions to SCSI. In April 1984, the X3T9.2 subcommittee forwarded SCSI Revision 14 to the X3T9 Standards Committee to begin the approval process. This process included more revisions until in June 1986, ANSI accepted SCSI Revision 17b as an ANSI standard.

About the same time SCSI was receiving final approval from ANSI, an industry group defined a Common Command Set (CCS) that was accepted by the X3T9.2 subcommittee as part of the basis for the proposed SCSI-2 standard. With NCR's representative serving as chairman, the subcommittee continues to develop the SCSI-2 standard and has proposed an SCSI-3 standard project to begin upon completion of SCSI-2. These new standards pave the way for the future of SCSI by providing enhancements that permit SCSI to take advantage of new technologies as they become available.

Why Use SCSI?

Before SCSI, adding a new peripheral to a host computer meant "teaching" the host to work with the new peripheral by adding new hardware and/or software modules. By the time the host computer "learned" how to work with the new peripheral, more advanced peripherals were available, and the host computer was unable to take advantage of them. No matter how much development effort was spent, the peripherals that could be used on a host system were usually at least a generation behind current technology.

SCSI is designed to keep computers in step with advancing technologies. SCSI enables host computers to connect with virtually any peripheral device — even those just off the drawing board — without always having to overhaul system hardware and/or software. The host computer does not have to "learn" a new way to communicate every time a peripheral device is added.

SCSI works by masking the internal structure of the peripherals from the host computer. It uses an eight-port bus that can accommodate either single or multiple-host systems. Its impressive transfer rate of up to 5 Mbytes per second allows direct copying between devices. This frees the host for additional activity, and also gives the host power for considerable I/O data transfers.

SCSI gives original equipment manufacturers (OEMs), systems integrators, and value-added resellers (VARs) a cost-effective way to personalize product offerings without sacrificing compatibility. Equally important is the upward mobility provided by the SCSI I/O bus. As new storage, printing, and communications technologies move into the mainstream of systems design, integrators can quickly incorporate them into their existing systems with only minimal hardware engineering and software development.

What Systems Support An SCSI Bus?

The function of the SCSI bus is to integrate all the parts of a computer system so that they can communicate with each other. Some computers such as the Apple MacIntosh directly support SCSI. Other computers indirectly communicate with SCSI peripherals using an SCSI host adapter.

Today there are about as many buses as there are applications. Below is a list of some of the buses that are supported on systems today. SCSI can be adapted to computers that use these buses.

- S-100 bus

- STD bus

- G64 bus

- Multibus I/II

- IBM PC, PC/AT, and Micro Channel buses

- I-Bus

- X-Bus

To adapt SCSI to a computer that uses one of these buses, a host adapter is installed in the computer. The adapter communicates SCSI on one end and communicates with the host computer's bus on the other end.

To adapt a peripheral to the SCSI bus, an SCSI bus controller is used. The controller communicates SCSI on one end and communicates with the peripheral on the other end. The following illustration shows an SCSI host adapter and controller with the necessary connections.

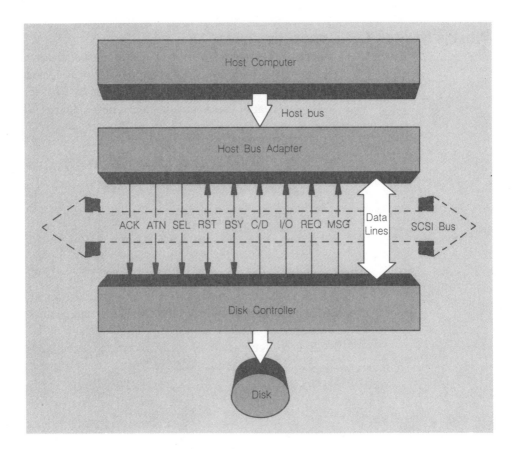

What Is NCR's SCSI Connection?

NCR and SCSI are well connected. Besides being instrumental in the development of the SCSI standard and the ongoing development of the Common Command Set, SCSI-2, and SCSI-3, NCR Corporation has been a leader in developing SCSI products.

- The first SCSI protocol chip (5385)

- The first SCSI single-chip disk controller

- A high performance SCSI host adapter

- The first SCSI 24 MHz SMD disk controller

- The first SCSI printer controller

- A family of SCSI host adapters, controllers, and subsystems

NCR continues its leadership role in the market place by offering SCSI chips, host adapters, and controllers that communicate with a wide range of host computer system buses and peripherals. NCR also offers a selection of SCSI storage subsystems that use these SCSI chips and boards. Following are brief descriptions of these products.

NCR's SCSI Host Adapters

NCR Corporation offers a variety of SCSI host adapters such as PC bus to SCSI bus, and Multibus I to SCSI bus.

NCR's SCSI Controllers

NCR Corporation's SCSI controller boards operate with such peripheral devices as the ESDI Caching and SMD disk drives. NCR's controller boards also operate with flexible disk drives, printers, half-inch Pertec type tape drives, and STC tape drives.

NCR's SCSI Chips

NCR Corporation offers a variety of SCSI chips. These chips can be used on both host adapter and controller boards. These chips can also be embedded into peripheral devices such as disk drives. Following is a list of some of the NCR SCSI chips.

- NCR 5380 — Standard SCSI (NMOS)

- NCR 5381 — Standard SCSI with control signals for differential-transceivers (NMOS)

- NCR 53C300 — Standard SCSI with integrated buffer controller (CMOS)

- NCR 53C80 — Standard SCSI (CMOS)

- NCR 53C81 — Standard SCSI with control signals for differential-transceivers (CMOS)

- NCR 53C90 — Enhanced SCSI Processor (CMOS)

- NCR 53C90A — Enhanced SCSI Processor with SCSI-2 support (CMOS)

- NCR 53C90B — Enhanced SCSI Processor with SCSI-2 support and parity (CMOS)

- NCR 53C94 — 18-bit DMA bus, 8-bit processor bus (CMOS)

- NCR 53C95 — 18-bit DMA bus, 8-bit processor bus, differential-transceivers (CMOS)

- NCR 53C400 — PC AT bus to SCSI, 8-bit chip (CMOS)

NCR's SCSI Subsystems

NCR Corporation offers a variety of SCSI storage subsystems. These subsystems come in three basic types: desktop, deskside, and large-capacity deskside. For each type of storage subsystem there is a range of storage capacities and peripheral devices. Data storage capacities range from hundreds of megabytes to multiple gigabytes.

Understanding SCSI — General Overview

SCSI is an eight-bit, parallel I/O bus that provides a host computer with device independence within a class of devices. This means that different disk drives, tape drives, printers, and even communication devices can be added to a host computer without major modifications to the system hardware or software.

The SCSI bus uses logical rather than physical addressing for all data blocks. For direct access devices, each logical unit may be interrogated to determine how many blocks it contains. A logical unit may coincide with all or part of a peripheral device.

The SCSI bus provides two electrical specifications: single-ended and differential.

The single-ended driver and receiver configuration uses TTL logic levels and is primarily intended for applications within a cabinet. The single-ended version uses cable lengths of up to 6 meters (19.68 feet).

The differential driver and receiver configuration uses EIA RS-485 signals and is primarily intended for applications requiring longer cable lengths. The differential version uses cable lengths of up to 25 meters (82.02 feet).

The SCSI bus provides two handshaking protocols: asynchronous and synchronous. Asynchronous requires a handshake for every byte transferred. Synchronous transfers a series of bytes before the handshake occurs. This increases the data transfer rate. SCSI operates at data transfer rates of up to 5 megabytes per second.

The SCSI bus supports up to eight devices, including the host(s). The bus protocol includes provision for the connection of multiple hosts, usually referred to as initiators. Initiators are SCSI devices capable of initiating an operation. SCSI host adapters are initiators but can be targets in multiple-host configurations. The interface protocol also includes provision for connection of multiple peripherals, usually referred to as target devices. SCSI target devices are capable of responding to a request from an initiator to perform an operation. All peripherals are targets but some peripherals can act as initiators by initiating operations such as the Copy operation.

The SCSI architecture has optional arbitration (bus-contention) built into it. Arbitration is a priority system that awards interface control to the highest priority SCSI device that is contending for use of the bus. The time to complete arbitration is independent of the number of devices that are contending.

All activity on the SCSI bus occurs in phases. SCSI specifies a series of eight bus phases. These phases are listed below.

- Bus Free

- Arbitration

- Selection

- Reselection

- Message

- Command

- Data

- Status

The SCSI specification defines commands according to device types. These device types are listed below.

- All device types

- Direct-access devices (typically disk drives)

- Sequential-access devices (typically tape drives)

- Printer devices

- Processor devices

- Write-once read-multiple devices

- Read-only direct-access devices

The SCSI specification also defines different sets of commands. Each vendor is also free to define their own vendor-unique commands.

Understanding SCSI — Basic Concepts

This section provides an overview of the SCSI bus signals and their functions in transferring information. It also provides an overview of the SCSI bus operations necessary to transfer data over the bus.

A maximum of eight SCSI devices can be attached to the SCSI bus. Of these eight, only one pair of devices can communicate at one time. Each SCSI device has an SCSI ID bit assigned to it. The SCSI Device ID is a bit-significant representation of the SCSI address, referring to one of the signal lines DB7-0. DB7 has the highest priority.

When two SCSI devices communicate on the SCSI bus, one acts as an initiator (host), and the other acts as a target (controller). The initiator originates an operation, and the target performs the operation. Most SCSI devices usually have a fixed role as an initiator or a target, but some devices are able to assume either role.

The SCSI bus has a total of eighteen signals. Nine are used for control and nine are used for data (eight data lines and one parity line). The data lines are bi-directional and transfer data, commands, status, and message information. The control signals and the bus phases determine when and in what direction data is transferred.

What Configurations Are Available?

SCSI was designed to be a flexible bus. It permits the host computer to communicate with peripherals and other hosts. It also permits peripherals to communicate with other peripherals. There are four distinct SCSI I/O system configurations. As indicated in the following list, host computers are usually initiators on the bus, and device controllers are usually targets.

- Single Host (Initiator) / Single Controller (Target)

- Single Host (Initiator) / Multiple Controllers (Targets)

- Multiple Hosts (Initiators) / Single Controller (Target)

- Multiple Hosts (Initiators) / Multiple Controllers (Targets)

The configuration of the SCSI bus is determined by the number
of hosts and peripherals on the bus. Each configuration adds a
level of complexity and offers a significant increase in I/O
performance. The following sections of this book provide
illustrations of the four distinct configurations.

Single Host / Single Controller

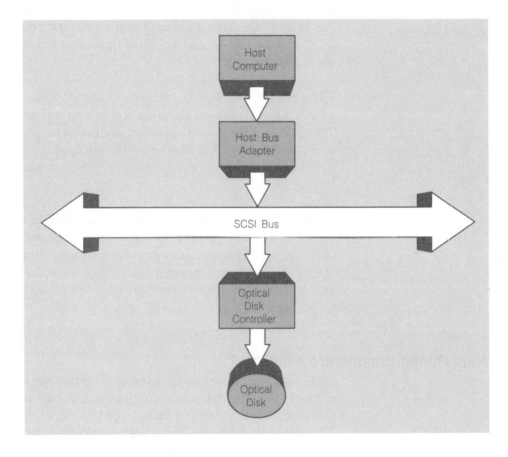

Single Host / Multiple Controllers

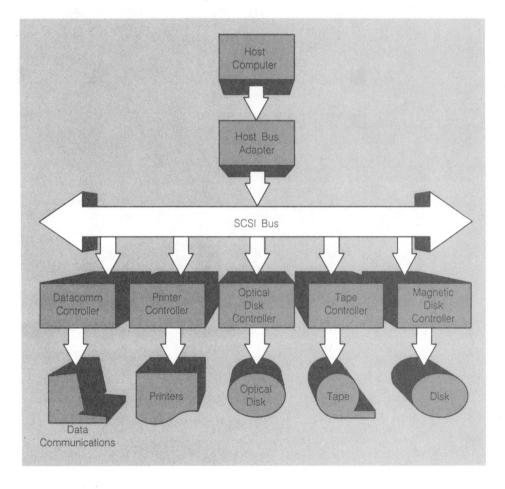

Multiple Hosts / Single Controller

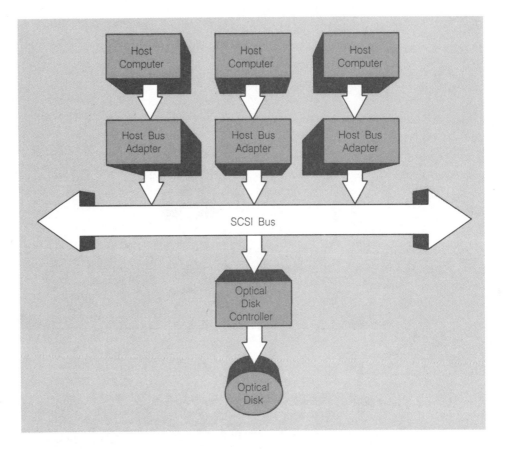

Multiple Hosts / Multiple Controllers

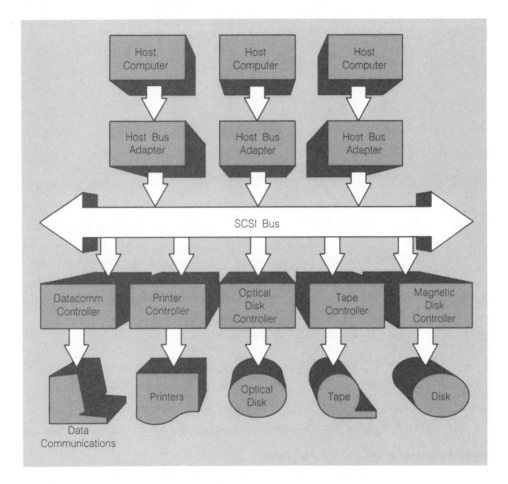

How Is Bus Activity Controlled?

All activity on the SCSI bus occurs in one of eight phases.

- Bus Free

- Arbitration

- Selection

- Reselection

- Command

- Data

- Status

- Message

These phases determine what type of information is on the data lines and in what direction it travels. The eight SCSI bus phases are determined by the configuration of the control signals. Certain control signals are driven by the initiator and others are driven by the target. RST and BSY may be driven by either the initiator or the target.

All SCSI bus operations begin and end with the Bus Free phase. The Bus Free phase is also entered after initial power-up or a bus reset.

What Control Signals Are Used?

The initiator drives the following five control signals:

- RST — the initiator uses the RST signal to reset the bus

- BSY — the initiator declares the bus busy with the BSY signal

- SEL — the initiator selects a target device with the SEL signal

- ACK — the initiator acknowledges a request from a target with the ACK signal

- ATN — the initiator uses the ATN signal to inform the target it has a message

The target drives the following seven control signals:

- RST — the target uses the RST signal to reset the bus

- BSY — the target declares the bus busy with the BSY signal

- C/D — the target uses the C/D signal to indicate whether information on the data bus is control information or data

- I/O — the target uses the I/O signal to define the direction of data movement on the data bus with respect to an initiator

- MSG — the target uses the MSG signal to indicate to the initiator that a message is being transferred

- REQ — the target uses the REQ signal to request a data information transfer

- SEL — the target uses the SEL signal to reselect an initiator

How Is A Connection Established?

For a command operation, the initiator arbitrates for the bus and then selects the target device. In some older single-host configurations, the initiator does not arbitrate for the bus. It merely selects the target device it wants to communicate with. After selection is complete, the target controls the sequence of phases and the transfer of information to and from the initiator.

Except in the older single-host configurations, a target device can disconnect from the bus to perform an operation that consumes time (such as a disk seek). After the operation is complete, the target can reconnect itself to the bus by reselecting the initiator.

How Is The Communication Mode Established?

The mode and speed of communication (asynchronous or synchronous) is established between the initiator and the target, usually at the start of day or after a bus reset. This agreement is established in a synchronous data transfer negotiation procedure using messages. The data transfer agreement remains in effect until changed, usually as a result of a bus reset.

Understanding SCSI — Detailed Overview

The following illustration provides an overview of the SCSI bus. The illustration shows the signals and bus phases that are explained later in this section.

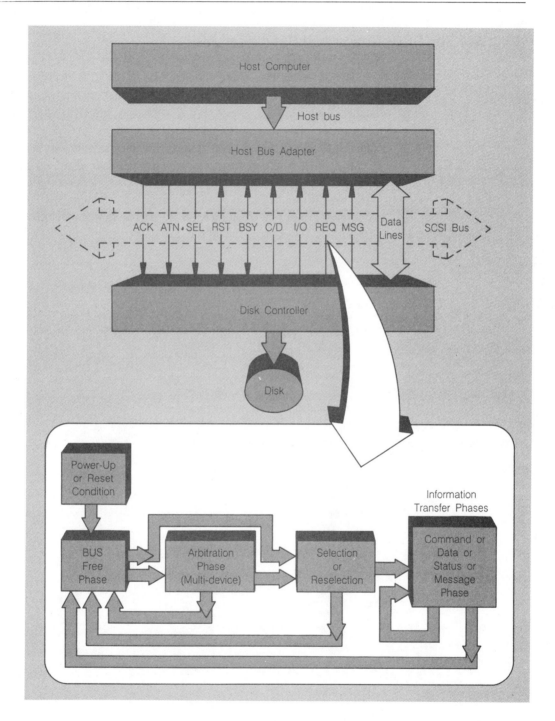

What Are The SCSI Bus Signal Specifications?

The SCSI bus supports two electrical specifications: single-ended and differential. The single-ended version uses TTL levels, while the differential version uses EIA RS-485 signals to allow longer cables.

The SCSI bus is made up of 50 lines. The bus uses nine data signals (including parity) and nine control signals. The following tables contain the pin assignments for the single-ended signals and the differential signals. On the single-ended signals, all odd numbered lines plus 20, 22, 24, 28, 30, and 34 are connected to ground on the controller and pin 25 is left open.

SINGLE-ENDED SCSI BUS SIGNALS			
Pin	Mnemonic	Signal	Driven by
2	-DB0	Data Bus Line 0	Initiator/Target
4	-DB1	Data Bus Line 1	Initiator/Target
6	-DB2	Data Bus Line 2	Initiator/Target
8	-DB3	Data Bus Line 3	Initiator/Target
10	-DB4	Data Bus Line 4	Initiator/Target
12	-DB5	Data Bus Line 5	Initiator/Target
14	-DB6	Data Bus Line 6	Initiator/Target
16	-DB7	Data Bus Line 7	Initiator/Target
18	-DBP	Data Bus Parity	Initiator/Target
26	TERMPWR	Terminator Power	Any device
32	-ATN	Attention	Initiator
36	-BSY	Busy	Initiator/Target
38	-ACK	Acknowledge	Initiator
40	-RST	Reset	Any device
42	-MSG	Message	Target
44	-SEL	Select	Initiator/Target
46	-C/D	Control/Data	Target
48	-REQ	Request	Target
50	-I/O	Input/Output	Target

DIFFERENTIAL SCSI BUS SIGNALS				
Pin	**Mnemonic**	**Pin**	**Mnemonic**	**Driven by**
1	Shield Gnd	2	Ground	
3	+DB(0)	4	-DB(0)	Initiator/Target
5	+DB(1)	6	-DB(1)	Initiator/Target
7	+DB(2)	8	-DB(2)	Initiator/Target
9	+DB(3)	10	-DB(3)	Initiator/Target
11	+DB(4)	12	-DB(4)	Initiator/Target
13	+DB(5)	14	-DB(5)	Initiator/Target
15	+DB(6)	16	-DB(6)	Initiator/Target
17	+DB(7)	18	-DB(7)	Initiator/Target
19	+DB(P)	20	-DB(P)	Initiator/Target
21	DIFFSENS	22	Ground	Active high
23	Ground	24	Ground	
25	TERMPWR	26	TERMPWR	Any device
27	Ground	28	Ground	
29	+ATN	30	-ATN	Initiator
31	Ground	32	Ground	
33	+BSY	34	-BSY	Initiator/Target
35	+ACK	36	-ACK	Initiator
37	+RST	38	-RST	Any device
39	+MSG	40	-MSG	Target
41	+SEL	42	-SEL	Initiator/Target
43	+C/D	44	-C/D	Target
45	+REQ	46	-REQ	Target
47	+I/O	48	-I/O	Target
49	Ground	50	Ground	

How Are The SCSI Signals Terminated?

The SCSI signals must be terminated at both ends of the SCSI bus.

Termination for single-ended devices.

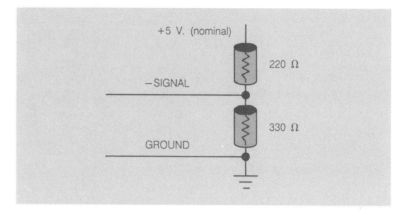

Termination for differential devices.

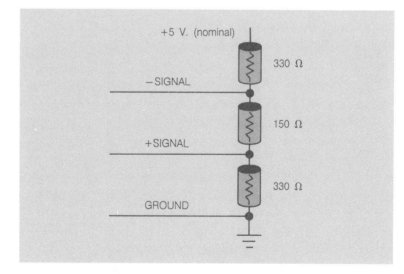

SCSI devices that supply terminator power do so through a diode
or similar semiconductor that prevents the backflow of power to
the SCSI device. The following illustration shows a differential
driver protection circuit.

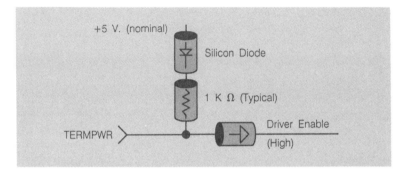

How Are The Signals Used?

Data Signals (DB7 - DB0)

The initiator and target use this bi-directional, eight-bit, parallel bus to transfer data. This bus not only transfers data, commands, status, and messages but also transfers SCSI Device ID codes during Selection and Reselection phases. The SCSI Device ID is the bit-significant representation of the SCSI address, referring to one of the signal lines DB7-0. DB7 has the highest priority.

Data Bus Parity (DBP)

Parity is an SCSI bus option. If an SCSI bus uses parity, the parity must be odd and must be supported by all devices on the bus. Parity is valid for all information transfer phases, the Selection phase, and the Reselection phase.

Control Signals

The nine bus control signals fall into three functional groups.

- Group one — includes the SEL and BSY signals that permit an initiator to select a target. They are also used for reselection.

- Group two — includes the C/D, I/O, and MSG signals, along with the REQ and ACK signals, that define the information transfer phases and provide handshake signals for the information transfer phases.

- Group three — includes the ATN and RST signals, that define the two asynchronous bus conditions.

SEL (Select) — The initiator uses this signal to select a target to perform a command. If the disconnect option is supported, the target uses SEL to reselect the initiator from which it disconnected. After reselection, command execution continues. I/O differentiates between selection and reselection.

BSY (Busy) — This "wired or" signal indicates that the bus is in use (busy). The initiator uses the BSY signal during the Arbitration phase. The selected target uses the BSY signal to acknowledge selection and to indicate that it has bus control. The target also uses BSY to participate in arbitration.

C/D (Control/Data) — The target uses this signal to indicate if control or data information is being transferred. The asserted state (true) indicates command, status, or message information is being transferred. The negated state (false) indicates data is being transferred.

I/O (Input/Output) — The target uses this signal to define the direction of information transferred between the initiator and the target. Transfer direction is defined with respect to the initiator. The asserted state (true) indicates information is being transferred to the initiator from the target. The negated state (false) indicates that information is being transferred from the initiator to the target.

MSG (Message) — The target uses this signal to indicate to the initiator that the information being transferred is a message. The target sends a Command Completion message to the initiator after completion of each command.

REQ (Request) — The target uses this signal to initiate a request for a REQ/ACK data information transfer between the initiator and the target. In response to the assertion of REQ by the target, the initiator accepts data from the bus during an information-in phase or places information on the data bus during an information-out phase. The target continues to assert REQ until the initiator responds with ACK, except during synchronous data transfers.

ACK (Acknowledge) — The initiator uses this signal to respond to the assertion of the REQ signal by the selected target. Assertion of the ACK signal by the initiator indicates that it has placed information on the data bus during an information-out phase, or accepted data from the bus during an information-in phase. The REQ/ACK handshake is used for the transfer of all information between the initiator and the target.

ATN (Attention) — The initiator uses this signal to inform the selected target that a message is available. The target, at its convenience, requests the initiator's message, using the Message-Out phase. The initiator may assert the ATN signal during the Selection phase or at any time after the target assumes control of the bus.

RST (Reset) — This "wired or" signal is used by any device on the bus. Normally, RST is asserted only by the initiator during power-up. Targets may also assert RST during power-up or power-down.

How Is Communication On The Bus Controlled?

Communication over the SCSI bus is controlled by a sequence of bus states called phases. The bus has eight different phases.

- Bus Free

- Arbitration

- Selection

- Reselection

- Command

- Data

- Status

- Message

The last four phases in the preceding list are called information transfer phases because they transfer either command, data, status or message information. The SCSI bus can never be in more than one phase at any given time. These phases are controlled by SCSI bus control signals.

The state of the SEL, BSY, and I/O signals and the sequence of the phases determine when the Bus Free, Arbitration, Selection, and Reselection phases are entered. The Selection or Reselection phase can only be entered from the Arbitration phase. The Arbitration phase can only be entered from the Bus Free phase. The Bus Free phase can be entered from any of the other phases. Therefore, to know what the current phase is, the previous phase and the states of the signals are needed. The initiator and target drive these signals to change from one phase to another. For more information about phase sequences, see "What are the SCSI Bus Phase Sequences?" section of this book.

The SEL and BSY both being false (for at least 400 ns) indicates a Bus Free phase. After that point, SEL, BSY, and I/O are used to select the other phases (see the following table). A SCSI device arbitrates for the SCSI bus by asserting both BSY and its own SCSI ID. After waiting at least an arbitration delay (measured from the assertion of BSY), the device examines the data bus. If its SCSI ID is the highest, it has won the arbitration, and it asserts SEL. If I/O is false, the Selection phase is entered. But if I/O is true, the Reselection phase is entered.

PHASE SEQUENCE			
Phase	**SEL**	**BSY**	**I/O**
Bus Free	0	0	0
Arbitration	0	1	0
Selection	1	X	0
Reselection	1	X	1
NOTE: 0 = False, negated; 1 = True, asserted; X = Indicates that the signal is initially negated but is asserted when the target or initiator acknowledges selection.			

What Do The SCSI Bus Phases Do?

Bus Free Phase

This phase indicates that no SCSI device is actively using the SCSI bus and that it is available for use. This phase begins after SEL and BSY are both false for at least 400 nanoseconds. The SCSI devices immediately release all bus signals when the Bus Free phase is entered.

Arbitration Phase

This optional phase permits one SCSI device to gain control of the SCSI bus as either an initiator or a target.

When the SCSI device wishes to arbitrate for the bus in order to select a target or reselect an initiator, it performs the following procedure.

1. The SCSI device waits for the Bus Free phase to occur.

2. After a minimum of a bus free delay, it arbitrates for the SCSI bus by asserting both BSY and its own SCSI ID.

3. After at least one arbitration delay, the device examines the bus data lines in order to determine whether it is the highest priority device arbitrating. If it is, it continues with selection/reselection. Otherwise, the device either releases all bus signals or waits for the highest priority device to assert SEL.

4. The SCSI device that wins arbitration asserts SEL and waits at least a bus clear delay plus a bus settle delay before changing any signals.

Selection Phase

This phase permits a initiator to select a target to perform a function such as a Read or Write command.

Reselection Phase

This optional phase permits a target to reconnect to an initiator to continue an operation that was previously started by the initiator but was suspended by the target.

Information Transfer Phases

The Command, Data, Status, and Message phases are referred to as information transfer phases because they are all used to transfer data or information via the data bus.

The MSG, C/D, and I/O signals control the different information transfer phases and the direction of transfer during the phases (see the following table). The target drives these three signals and therefore controls the change from one phase to another. The initiator can request a Message-Out phase by asserting ATN. The target can cause the Bus Free phase by releasing all signals.

INFORMATION TRANSFER PHASES					
MSG	**C/D**	**I/O**	**Phase**	**Direction**	**Comment**
0	0	0	Data-Out	To target	Data phase
0	0	1	Data-In	From target	Data phase
0	1	0	Command	To target	Command phase
0	1	1	Status	From target	Status phase
1	1	0	Message-Out	To target	Message phase
1	1	1	Message-In	From target	Message phase
NOTE: 0 = False, negated; 1 = True, asserted; For these phases, SEL is negated and BSY asserted					

Command Phase — This phase allows the target to request command information from the initiator.

Data Phase — The Data phase refers to both the Data-In and Data-Out phases.

The Data-In phase allows the target to request that data be sent from the target to the initiator.

The Data-Out phase allows the target to request that data be sent from the initiator to the target.

Status Phase — This phase allows the target to request that status information be sent from the target to the initiator.

Message Phase — The Message phase refers to both the Message-In and Message-Out phases. Multiple messages may be sent during either phase. The first byte transferred in either of these phases is either a single-byte message or the first byte of a multiple-byte message.

The Message-In phase allows the target to request that message(s) be sent from the target to the initiator.

The Message-Out phase allows the target to request that message(s) be sent from the initiator to the target. The target may invoke this phase at its convenience in response to an Attention condition created by the initiator.

What Are The SCSI Bus Phase Sequences?

The order in which phases are used on the SCSI bus follows a prescribed sequence. In all systems, the Reset condition can abort any phase and is always followed by the Bus Free phase. Also, any other phase can be followed by the Bus Free phase. The bus phase sequence for non-arbitrating systems is different than arbitrating systems.

Non-Arbitrating Systems

In systems that do not implement the Arbitration phase, the allowable phase sequences are shown in the following flowchart. The normal progression is from the Bus Free phase to Selection, and from Selection to one or more of the information transfer phases (Command, Data, Status, Message) or back to the Bus Free phase.

There are no restrictions on the sequences between information transfer phases. A phase type may even be followed by the same phase type. For example, a Data phase may be followed by another Data phase.

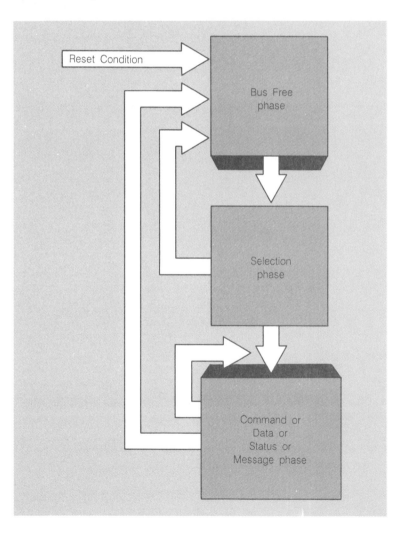

Arbitrating Systems

In systems that implement the Arbitration phase, the allowable
phase sequences are shown in the following flowchart. The
normal progression is from the Bus Free phase to Arbitration,
from Arbitration to Selection or Reselection, and from Selection
or Reselection to one or more of the information transfer phases
(Command, Data, Status, or Message). Any phase can return to
the Bus Free phase.

There are no restrictions on the sequences between information
transfer phases. A phase type may even be followed by the same
phase type. For example, a Data phase may be followed by
another Data phase.

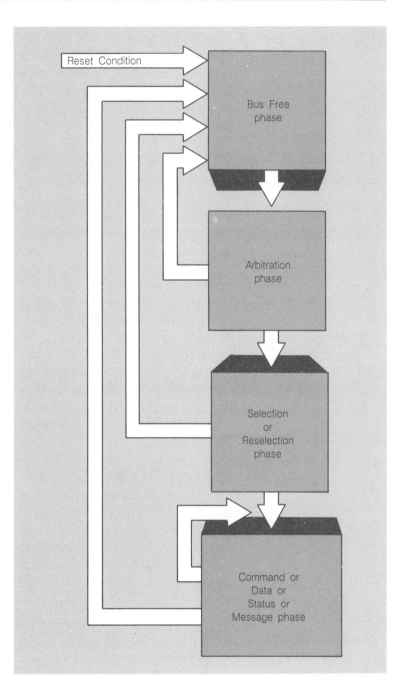

What Are The Data Transfer Options?

There are two handshaking protocols: asynchronous, which requires a handshake for every byte transferred, and synchronous, which allows a series of bytes to be transferred before the handshake occurs. This increases the data transfer rate.

How Is The Data Transfer Mode Selected?

The asynchronous data transfer mode is the normal mode. It does not have to be selected. All commands, messages, and status are always transferred asynchronously. However, a synchronous target can negotiate with the initiator for synchronous data transfer. To begin negotiation for synchronous data transfer, the target sends the initiator a Synchronous Data Transfer Request message that contains its minimum transfer period and its maximum offset allowed between a REQ and its corresponding ACK.

The initiator responds with either Message Reject (indicating that asynchronous data transfers are to be used) or with a Synchronous Data Transfer Request message in which it indicates its minimum transfer period and its maximum REQ/ACK offset.

At this point, Synchronous Data Transfer Mode has been established with the greater of the two minimum transfer periods and the lesser of the two maximum REQ/ACK offsets. The Synchronous Data Transfer Mode will remain in effect until either party requests a change (via another sequence of Synchronous Data Transfer Request messages) or until a Bus Device Reset message is received by the target or a Hard Reset condition occurs.

What Are SCSI Bus Conditions?

The bus has two conditions: Attention and Reset. These conditions can alter the bus phase sequence. They provide the only means the initiator has to force the target to alter normal command execution.

Attention Condition

The Attention condition allows the initiator to inform the target that the initiator has a message ready. The initiator creates this condition by asserting Attention (ATN) during any phase except Arbitration or Bus Free. The target retrieves the message, at its convenience, using a Message-Out phase.

Reset Condition

The Reset condition is used to clear all SCSI devices from the bus. It can be generated by any SCSI device that can assert Reset (RST) and can occur at any time. It forces the bus into the Bus Free phase. Reset takes precedence over all other phases and conditions. Upon receiving Reset, a target goes through a complete power-up diagnostic check and initialization. This immediately clears any current or pending operations.

A target asserts Reset immediately after power-up to avoid possible power-up noise on the SCSI bus. A target also asserts RST when it detects it is being powered-down. However, some targets can be set to never assert RST.

The effect of the Reset condition on uncompleted commands, SCSI device reservations, and SCSI device operating modes is determined by whether the SCSI device implements the Hard Reset option or the Soft Reset option.

Hard Reset Option — SCSI devices that implement the "Hard" Reset option, do the following upon detection of the Reset condition.

1. Clear all uncompleted commands.

2. Release all SCSI device reservations.

3. Return any SCSI device operating modes (MODE SELECT, PREVENT/ALLOW MEDIUM REMOVAL commands, etc) to their default conditions.

Soft Reset Option — SCSI devices that implement the "Soft" Reset option, do the following upon detection of the Reset condition.

1. Attempt to complete any uncompleted commands that were fully identified.

2. Preserve all SCSI device reservations.

3. Preserve any SCSI device operating mode (MODE SELECT, PREVENT/ALLOW MEDIUM REMOVAL commands, etc).

The Soft Reset option permits an initiator to reset the SCSI bus without disturbing the operation of other initiators in a multiple-host system.

What Is The Message Protocol?

The message system allows communication between an initiator and target for the purpose of physical path management. Messages are sent during the Message Phase. All SCSI devices must implement the Command Complete message, but the other messages are optional.

The initiator indicates it has the ability to accommodate more than the Command Complete message by asserting Attention (ATN) during the selection phase. The target responds with a Message-Out phase immediately after selection is complete if it can accommodate messages other than the Command Complete message. The initiator or target responds to any unimplemented message with Message Reject.

What Are The Messages?

The following table shows the messages that are defined.

SCSI MESSAGES		
Message Description	**Hex Code**	**Direction**
Command Complete	00	In
Extended Message	01	In/Out
Save Data Pointer	02	In
Restore Pointer	03	In
Disconnect	04	In
Initiator Detected Error	05	Out
Abort	06	Out
Message Reject	07	In/Out
No Operation	08	Out
Message Parity Error	09	Out
Bus Device Reset	0C	Out
Identify	80 to FF	In/Out
NOTE: In = Target to initiator; Out = Initiator to target		

Command Complete (00)

The target sends this message to the initiator to indicate that the execution of a command has terminated and that a valid status has been sent to the initiator. This message is mandatory for all SCSI devices.

Extended Message (01)

The initiator or the target sends this message as the first byte of a multiple-byte message. A value of one in the first byte of a message indicates the beginning of a multiple-byte extended message. The minimum number of bytes for an extended message is three.

Save Data Pointer (02)

Upon receiving this message from the target, the initiator saves a copy of the present active data pointer for the currently attached logical unit. The target sends this message before transmitting a disconnect message.

Restore Pointers (03)

The target sends this message to direct the initiator to restore to the active state the most recently saved pointers for the currently attached logical unit.

Disconnect (04)

The target sends this message to the initiator to indicate that the present physical path is going to be broken and that a later reconnect will be required to complete the current operation. The target then disconnects by negating BSY.

Initiator Detected Error (05)

The initiator sends this message to inform the target that an error, such as a parity error, has occurred that does not prevent the target from retrying the operation. Although present pointer integrity is not assured, a Restore Pointers message or a disconnect followed by a reconnect, causes the pointers to be restored to their defined prior state.

Abort (06)

The initiator sends this message to the target to clear the present operation. If a Logical Unit Number (LUN) has been identified, all pending data and status for the issuing initiator is cleared, and the target goes to the Bus Free phase. If a logical unit has not been identified, the target simply goes to the Bus Free phase. No status or ending message is sent for the operation.

Message Reject (07)

The initiator or target sends this message to indicate that the last message it received was inappropriate or has not been implemented.

No Operation (08)

The initiator sends this message to the target when the target is requesting a message and the initiator does not have any other valid message to send.

Message Parity Error (09)

The initiator sends this message to the target to indicate that one or more bytes in the last message it received had a parity error.

Bus Device Reset (0C)

The initiator sends this message to direct a target to clear all current commands. This message forces the target to an initial state with no operations pending for any initiator. The target then goes to the Bus Free phase.

Identify (80 to FF)

The initiator or target sends these messages to establish the physical path between the initiator and the target for a particular logical unit. Bit 7 is always set to one to distinguish this message from the other messages. Bit 6 is set to one by the initiator. When it is set to one, it indicates whether or not the initiator supports disconnection and reselection. Bits 2, 1, and 0 contain the logical unit number.

How Are The Commands Executed?

This section describes the information required by the target in order to execute a command. It also describes the status information it returns after executing the command. In some cases the structure of the data required or generated by a command is described.

Execution of a command by the target involves three steps:

- Acquiring and decoding command information

- Transferring data (not all commands require a data transfer)

- Generating and returning status information

Command Descriptor Block

The Command Descriptor Block (CDB) is a data structure within the initiator that contains the command code and supplemental information required to execute the command. When the target is ready to retrieve the information in the CDB, it uses the SCSI bus Command phase to read the CDB bytes from the initiator. The structure of the CDB is given for each command in the following section.

Command Codes

Group 0 commands are those from opcode 00 to opcode 1F. Group 1 commands are those from opcode 20 to opcode 3F. Group 0 commands have a six-byte CDB, and group 1 commands have a ten-byte CDB.

For read/write operations, the SCSI command format includes the logical starting address and the number of data blocks to be transferred. Group 1 commands are used with the extended functions for large-capacity peripherals that require greater addressing capabilities.

Following is an illustration of the two CDBs.

GROUP 0 COMMAND DESCRIPTOR BLOCK								
BIT	**7**	**6**	**5**	**4**	**3**	**2**	**1**	**0**
BYTE **00**	0	0	0	Command Opcode				
01	Logical Unit Number			Logical Address (MSB)				
02	Logical Address							
03	Logical Address (LSB)							
04	Transfer Length (Number of blocks)							
05	Control Byte							

GROUP 1 COMMAND DESCRIPTOR BLOCK								
BIT	**7**	**6**	**5**	**4**	**3**	**2**	**1**	**0**
BYTE **00**	0	0	1	Command Opcode				
01	Logical Unit Number			Reserved				
02	Logical Address (MSB)							
03	Logical Address							
04	Logical Address							
05	Logical Address (LSB)							
06	Reserved (00)							
07	Transfer Length (Number of blocks) (MSB)							
08	Transfer Length (Number of blocks) (LSB)							
09	Control Byte							
Reserved fields are always set to zeros.								

Pointers

The SCSI architecture provides for two sets of three pointers within each initiator. The first set of pointers is known as the current (or active) pointers. The second set of pointers is known as the saved pointers. The three pointers in each set are the command, data, and status pointers.

The initiator's device-driver software initializes these pointers before target selection. After target selection, the pointers are conceptually controlled by the target. The target selects the desired pointer by using the MSG, C/D, and I/O signals to establish one of the information transfer phases and increments the selected pointer by REQ/ACK handshakes.

Current Pointers — The current pointers point to the next command, data, or status/message byte to be transferred between the initiator's memory and the target. There is only one set of current pointers in each initiator. The target currently connected to the initiator uses the current pointers.

Saved Pointers — There is one set of saved pointers for each command that is currently active. The saved command pointer always points to the start of the command descriptor block (CDB) for the current command. The saved status pointer always points to the start of the status area for the current command.

At the beginning of each command, the saved data Pointer points to the start of the data area. It remains at this value until the target sends a Save Data Pointer message to the initiator. In response to this message, the initiator stores the value of the current data pointer into the saved data pointer.

The target may restore the current pointers to their saved values by sending a Restore Pointers message to the initiator. The initiator moves the saved value of each pointer into the corresponding current pointer. Whenever a device disconnects from the bus, only the saved pointer values are retained. The current pointer values are restored from the saved values upon the next reconnection.

Save Data Pointer Message — The target sends this message to direct the initiator to save a copy of the present active data pointer for the currently attached logical unit.

A Single Command Example

One of the most common commands issued to a target is the Read command. Therefore, the Read command is used in the following example. The example is for a bus that supports arbitration. Following the example is a signal sequence diagram of the SCSI control and data lines in reference to each phase.

1.   Bus Free Phase

The initiator waits for the Bus Free phase before arbitrating for the SCSI bus. The Bus Free phase indicates that no SCSI device is actively using the SCSI bus. This phase is indicated by both the SEL and BSY signals being negated for at least a bus settle delay.

2.   Arbitration Phase

The initiator arbitrates for the SCSI bus by asserting both the BSY signal and its own SCSI ID. After waiting at least an arbitration delay, the initiator examines the data bus. If a higher priority SCSI ID bit is true on the data bus (DB7 is the highest), the initiator has lost the arbitration and the initiator releases its signals and returns to step 1. But, if no higher priority SCSI ID bit is true on the data bus, it has won the arbitration. It asserts the SEL signal.

3.   Selection Phase

The initiator asserts the data lines corresponding to the IDs assigned to the target and the initiator. After a delay, the initiator negates BSY. When the target detects SEL asserted, BSY and I/O negated, and its own ID present on the data bus, it asserts BSY and then latches the initiator ID in an internal register. When the initiator detects BSY asserted, it releases the data bus and negates SEL.

The following illustration is a signal sequence diagram of the SCSI control and data lines in reference to each of the phases.

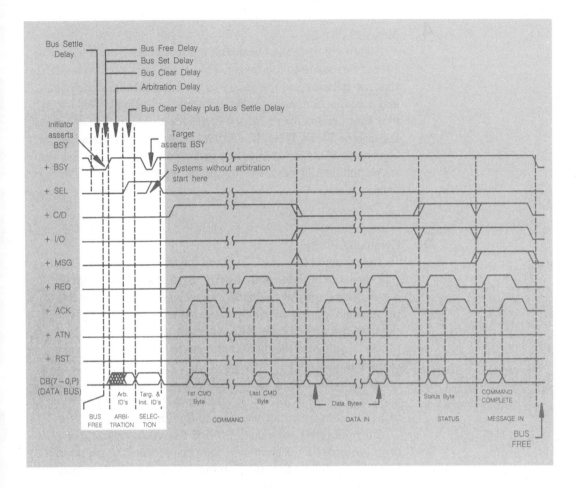

4. Message Phase

Before entering the Command phase, the initiator can send an Identify message to the target. This message is used to establish that the initiator has the ability to accommodate disconnection and reconnection, and specifies a target logical unit. This logical unit specification overrides the logical unit field in the Command Descriptor Block. If the Identify message is not sent before the Command phase is entered, it is assumed that messages are not supported. In this case, the logical unit specified in the CDB is used.

5. Command Phase

The target enters the Command phase and asserts REQ. In response, the initiator gets the first byte of the CDB from the initiator's memory at the address specified by the command pointer and asserts ACK. The target then accepts the byte from the data bus and negates REQ which is an indication to the initiator to release the data lines, negate ACK, and increment the command pointer. The first byte from the CDB is the command code, which the target uses to determine if the CDB contains an additional 5 or 9 bytes. These additional bytes are then transferred in a manner identical to the first byte.

After obtaining the complete CDB from the initiator, the target interprets the command code and locates the first data block requested on the specified logical unit. Once the requested data has been located, the target enters the Data-in phase.

The following illustration is a signal sequence diagram of the SCSI control and data lines in reference to each of the phases.

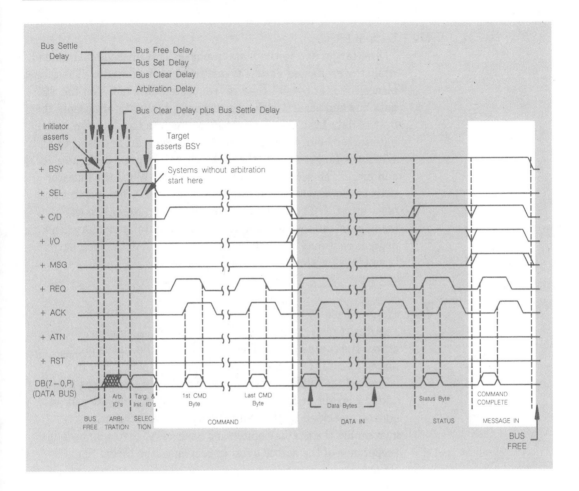

6. Data-in Phase

The target enters the Data-in phase. This phase is maintained while the requested data is transferred to the initiator. The target places the first byte of the first requested data block on the SCSI data bus and asserts REQ. In response, the initiator accepts the byte of data from the bus, transfers the data to a location in the initiator's memory specified by the data pointer, and asserts ACK. When the target detects the asserted ACK signal, it negates REQ and places the second data byte on the bus. When the initiator detects the negation of REQ, it increments the data pointer and negates ACK. The target asserts REQ again to initiate the transfer of the second data byte to the initiator's memory. This process continues until all bytes in the logical data block have been transferred to the initiator's memory.

7. Status Phase

After transferring all requested data to the initiator, the target enters the Status phase. The target enters the status phase, places a status byte on the data bus, and asserts REQ. In response, the initiator accepts the status byte and places it in a status register or transfers the byte to initiator memory at an address specified by the status pointer. The initiator then increments the Status pointer and asserts ACK to acknowledge acceptance of the status byte. In response, the target negates REQ.

8. Message-in Phase

After transferring the single status byte to the initiator, the target enters the Message-in phase. The target enters the message phase and places a Command Complete message on the data bus and asserts REQ. In response, the initiator accepts the message byte and places it in a register. The initiator then asserts ACK to acknowledge acceptance of the message byte. In response, the target negates REQ and releases the data bus. The target then negates BSY and releases all SCSI bus signals to create the Bus Free phase thereby completing execution of the Read command.

This information is an overview of the Read operation. For complete details see the ANSI SCSI standard.

The following illustration is a signal sequence diagram of the SCSI control and data lines in reference to each of the phases.

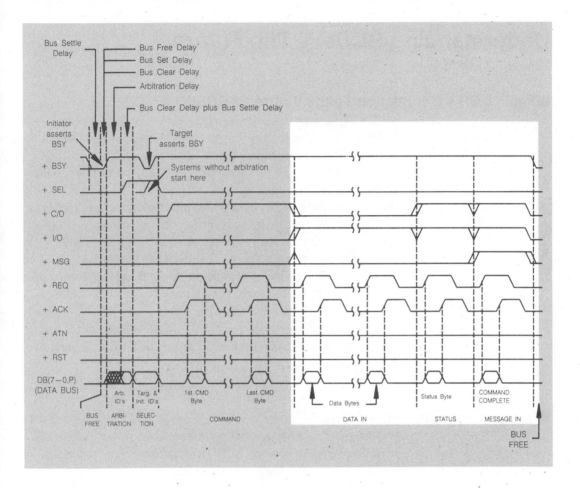

Understanding SCSI — The Future

What Is NCR's Connection To the Future Of SCSI?

NCR's SCSI connection already extends well into the future. NCR is committed to providing technical expertise and leadership to the X3T9.2 subcommittee and to the industry. Their commitment to the SCSI subcommittee is emphasized by the fact that NCR's representative to the subcommittee has served in leadership functions since the subcommittee's inception, including serving as vice chairman and chairman. NCR's commitment to leadership in the industry is emphasized by their wide range of SCSI product offerings, from chips, to circuit boards, to subsystems. The inclusion of SCSI in all their major system platforms gives NCR a firm connection to the future of SCSI.

With its strong representation in the X3T9.2 subcommittee and its continuing development of SCSI products, NCR is helping to guide the future of SCSI.

What Is In The Future For SCSI?

The future of SCSI is in constant motion. As new technologies in peripheral devices develop, SCSI evolves to accommodate them and to minimize the impact on the computer systems that use them. While it maintains pace with new technologies, SCSI also maintains integrity by striving to provide compatibility. The SCSI emphasis on compatibility is reflected in such things as the SCSI Common Command Set, SCSI-2, and SCSI-3.

What Is The Common Command Set?

The Common Command Set (CCS) is a proposal before the X3T9.2 subcommittee. As such, it is subject to change. However, the following information provides some indication of the future direction of SCSI.

When SCSI became a standard, many of the commands and features were optional, and some were not defined. The SCSI standard provided for the addition of the undefined commands and features through vendor-unique commands. This ability to expand is good, but it can lead to incompatibility between SCSI products developed by different manufacturers. To solve this problem, many manufacturers of SCSI products adopted CCS. CCS is a subset of 18 commands within the SCSI command set. CCS also adds controls over device formatting and error recovery. A group of manufacturers have already adopted this set of commands to make their SCSI products compatible with each other. CCS is also proposed as a part of SCSI-2.

What Is SCSI-2?

SCSI-2 is a proposal before the X3T9.2 subcommittee; as such, it is subject to change. However, the following information provides some indication of the future direction of SCSI.

SCSI-2 evolved from the original SCSI standard and is now in development form. This evolution is occurring because of changing technology, new applications, and greater performance expectations. SCSI-2 consists of the basic SCSI standard with some additions and changes and some deletions.

The large number of options in the original SCSI specification can lead to compatibility problems. That is, one vendor's SCSI product might not "plug and play" with another vendor's SCSI product. Therefore SCSI-2 removes some of the design options that can lead to these compatibility problems.

Following is a list of some of the major SCSI-2 enhancements. These enhancements are explained in more detail in the following sections of this book.

- Common Command Set

- Wide SCSI

- Fast SCSI

- Command Queuing

- High-Density Connector

- Asynchronous Event Notification

- Extended Contingent Allegiance

- Command Set Enhancements

Common Command Set

The Common Command Set (CCS), explained earlier in this book, is a part of the proposal for SCSI-2. See page 52 for more information on CCS.

Wide SCSI

Wide SCSI is an option that adds a second SCSI cable of 68 conductors. This cable provides a data path for 16 or 32-bit data. This path has separate handshake signals and is for data transfer only. The transfer rate is two or four times the present transfer rate of original SCSI. With the second cable, SCSI-2 remains compatible with the 8-bit SCSI.

Fast SCSI

Fast SCSI is an option that doubles the synchronous data transfer speed. This feature has been tested only with differential drivers and receivers. The speed is achieved by removing excess margins from certain times and delays. To use the fast SCSI option, high quality cables are required. This option is compatible with normal synchronous SCSI.

Command Queuing

Command Queuing is an option that permits multiple commands
from the same initiator to the same logical unit. This option
permits up to 256 commands per logical unit for each initiator.
The initiator can specify the fixed order of the commands, the
target's order of the commands, and the head-of-queue
commands. Command Queuing is compatible with non-queued
devices.

High-Density Connector

A high-density connector with 50-thousandth center-line contacts
is proposed for SCSI-2. The low-density connectors will not fit the
IBM PS/2 form factor.

Asynchronous Event Notification

Asynchronous Event Notification is an option that allows a
peripheral device to notify a processor device of events, even if
there is no current command pending. These events include Unit
Attention conditions, Not-Ready to Ready, queue cleared by
another initiator, and so on.

Extended Contingent Allegiance

Extended Contingent Allegiance is an option that is most useful
for sequential-access devices. However, it may be used by any
device type. Extended Contingent Allegiance acts as an implied
device reservation whenever certain errors occur. It permits
extensive error recovery in multiple-host systems.

Command Set Enhancements

SCSI-2 provides command set enhancements for existing device
types and adds new device types (CD-ROMs, scanner devices,
optical memory devices, medium changers, and communication
devices).

What Is SCSI-3?

SCSI-3 is a proposal before the X3T9.2 subcommittee. As such, it is subject to change. However, the following information provides some indication of the future direction of SCSI.

Some of the features or functions that are being considered for SCSI-3 are as follows.

- Scatter Write — Gather Read
- Auto-Configuration
- More than eight devices per bus
- Longer cables
- Improved single-ended cable length and data transfer rates
- Fiber Optic option
- File Server command set

What Is The Trend In SCSI?

The trend in SCSI is to apply new technologies as quickly as possible while striving to maintain compatibility among the various SCSI products. Therefore, SCSI will continue to grow as new technologies are applied to computer systems and peripheral devices. SCSI will continue to be refined and improved so it will solve today's problems and anticipate tomorrow's.

Glossary

Accredited Standards Committee
A standards committee that operates under rules approved by the American National Standards Institute (ANSI).

AENC
Asynchronous Event Notification Capability.

ANSI
American National Standards Institute.

arbitration
The process of selecting one respondent from a collection of several candidates that request service concurrently.

assertion
The act of driving a signal to the true state.

asynchronous transmission
Transmission in which each byte of the information is synchronized individually, through the use of Request (REQ) and Acknowledge (ACK) signals.

backplane bus
A bus in the form of a set of rigid, adjacent connectors. Typically, computer modules connected to this type of bus are either circuit boards or are connected through circuit boards.

bus
A collection of unbroken signal lines that interconnect computer modules. The connections are made by taps on the lines.

CCS
Common Command Set. CCS is a subset of 18 commands within the SCSI command set. CCS also adds controls over device formatting and error recovery. CCS is not an ANSI standard. It is a proposal before the X3T9.2 Subcommittee.

CDB

Command Descriptor Block. A data structure used to
communicate requests from an initiator to a target.

CMOS

Complementary-symmetry Metal Oxide Semiconductor. A type
of integrated circuit.

command

An instruction transferred from initiator to target, typically
containing function codes and an address.

connect

The function that occurs when an initiator selects a target to
start an operation, or a target reselects an initiator to continue
an operation.

controller

A computer module that interprets signals between a host and
a peripheral device. Often, the controller is a part of the
peripheral device, such as circuitry on a disk drive.

control signals

The set of nine lines used to put the SCSI bus into its different
phases. The combinations of asserted and negated control
signals define the phases.

DASD

Direct Access Storage Device.

DBx

A data line used in the SCSI bus. "x" represents 0 through 7 or
P for parity.

device

A single unit on the SCSI bus, identifiable by an SCSI address.
It can be a processor unit, a storage unit (such as a disk or
tape controller or drive), an output unit (such as a controller or
printer), or a communications unit.

device identification

The process of determining the highest-priority device ready for service from among a set of multiple devices that have requested service.

differential configuration

An electrical signal configuration that uses a pair of lines to differentiate actual signals from noise. Each signal driver has two outputs and each signal receiver has two inputs. The advantages of a differential configuration (as compared to single-ended) are, first, comparatively large tolerance for common-mode noise, and second, little cross-talk when used with twisted pair cables. As compared to a single-ended configuration, this configuration is more expensive because of dual pins, chips, and board area. However, it allows much longer cable lengths.

disconnect

The function that occurs when a target releases control of the SCSI bus, allowing the bus to go to the Bus Free phase.

DMA

Direct Memory-Access. The ability of an I/O subsystem to transfer data to and from a memory subsystem without processor intervention.

driver

When used in the context of electrical configuration, "driver" is the circuitry that creates a signal on a line. When used in the context of software, "driver" is the program that translates commands between the initiator and target.

EIA

Electronic Industries Association.

ESDI

Enhanced Small Device Interface.

free

In the context of Bus Free phase, "free" means that no SCSI device is actively using the SCSI bus and, therefore, the bus is available for use.

gigabyte
One billion bytes; equal to one thousand megabytes.

H
A letter signifying that the preceding number is hexadecimal.

host
A processor, usually consisting of the central processing unit and main memory. Typically, a host communicates with other devices, such as peripherals and other hosts. On the SCSI bus, a host has an SCSI address.

host adapter
Circuitry that translates between a processor's internal bus and a different bus, such as SCSI. On the SCSI bus, a host adapter usually acts as an initiator.

initiator
An SCSI device that requests another SCSI device (a target) to perform an operation. Usually, a host acts as an initiator and a peripheral device acts as a target.

I/O
Input/Output.

logical unit
The logical representation of a physical or virtual device, addressable through a target. A physical device can have more than one logical unit.

LSB
Least Significant Byte.

LUN
Logical Unit Number. Used to identify a logical unit.

MHz
MegaHertz. Measurement in thousands of cycles per second. Used as a measurement of data transfer rate.

microsecond
One millionth of a second.

MSB
Most Significant Byte.

nanosecond
One billionth of a second.

negation
The act of driving a signal to the false state or allowing the cable terminators to bias the signal to the false state (by placing the driver in the high impedance condition).

NMOS
N-channel Metal Oxide Semiconductor. A type of integrated circuit.

OEM
Original-Equipment Manufacturer.

parity
A method of checking the accuracy of binary numbers. An extra bit, called a parity bit, is added to a number. If even parity is used, the sum of all 1s in the number and its corresponding parity bit is always even. If odd parity is used, the sum of the 1s and the parity bit is always odd.

peripheral device
A device that can be attached to an SCSI bus. Typical peripheral devices are disk drives, tape drives, printers, or communications units.

phase
One of the eight states to which the SCSI bus can be set. During each phase, different communication tasks can be performed.

port
A connection into a bus. The SCSI bus allows eight ports.

priority
The ranking of the devices on the bus during arbitration.

protocol
A convention for data transmission that encompasses timing, control, formatting, and data representation.

queue
A first-in, first-out (FIFO) structure.

receiver
The circuitry that receives electrical signals on a line.

RS-xxx
Recommended Standard, as in RS-485 or RS-232.

reconnect
The function that occurs when a target reselects an initiator to continue an operation after a disconnect.

release
The act of allowing the cable terminators to bias the signal to the false state (by placing the driver in the high impedance condition).

reselect
A target can disconnect from an initiator in order to perform a time-consuming function, such as a disk seek. After performing the operation, the target can "reselect" the initiator.

reserved
Bits, fields, and code values that are set aside for future standardizations.

SASI
Shugart Associates Systems Interface.

SCSI
Small Computer System Interface.

SCSI address
The octal representation of the unique address (0-7) assigned to an SCSI device. This address is normally assigned and set in the SCSI device during system installation.

SCSI ID (Identification) or SCSI Device ID

The bit-significant representation of the SCSI address referring to one of the signal lines DB0 through DB7.

single-ended configuration

An electrical signal configuration that uses a single line for each signal, referenced to a ground path common to the other signal lines. The advantage of a single-ended configuration is that it uses half the pins, chips, and board area that differential configurations require. The main disadvantage of single-ended configurations is that they are vulnerable to common mode noise. Also, cable lengths are limited.

synchronous transmission

Transmission in which the sending and receiving devices operate continuously at the same frequency and are held in a desired phase relationship by correction devices. For buses, synchronous transmission is a timing protocol that uses a master clock and has a clock period.

target

An SCSI device that performs an operation requested by an initiator.

termination

The electrical connection at each end of the SCSI bus, composed of a set of resistors.

TTL

Transistor-Transistor Logic.

us

Microsecond.

VAR

Value-Added Reseller.

vendor unique

Bits, fields, or code values that are vendor-specific and are not defined by the SCSI standard.

X3

An Accredited Standards Committee, entitled X3 Information Processing. It is one of the primary organizations developing computer-related standards in the United States.

X3T9

A Technical Committee of Accredited Standards Committee X3. The Technical Committee is entitled X3T9 I/O Interfaces. Its mission is to develop standards for moving bulk data in and out of central computers.

X3T9.2

A subcommittee of Accredited Standards Committee X3. X3T9.2 operates under Technical Committee X3T9 I/O Interfaces. The charter of X3T9.2 is Lower Level Interfaces. Its principal work is the Small Computer System Interface (SCSI). SCSI was published as ANSI Standard X3.131-1986 in 1986. X3T9.2 is currently working on enhanced SCSI (more commonly called SCSI-2).

Index

The Complete Scoliosis Surgery

Handbook for Patients

An In-Depth and Unbiased Look Into What to Expect Before
and During Scoliosis Surgery

By Dr. Kevin Lau D.C.
Foreword by Dr. Siddhant Kapoor M.D..

HEALTH IN
YOUR HANDS

ACA American Chiropractic Association

THE AMERICAN CHIROPRACTIC ASSOCIATION IS PLEASED TO GRANT THIS CERTIFICATE OF MEMBERSHIP TO

Kevin Lau, D.C.

I HEREBY CERTIFY THAT THIS DOCTOR OF CHIROPRACTIC IS A MEMBER OF THE AMERICAN CHIROPRACTIC ASSOCIATION, WHICH SUPPORTS PATIENTS' RIGHTS AND PATIENT TREATMENT REIMBURSEMENT, AND HAS PLEDGED TO ABIDE BY THE ACA CODE OF ETHICS, WHICH IS BASED UPON THE FUNDAMENTAL PRINCIPLE THAT THE PARAMOUNT PURPOSE OF THE CHIROPRACTOR'S PROFESSIONAL SERVICES SHALL BE TO BENEFIT THE PATIENT.

Keith S. Overland, DC
President

April 17, 2012
Date

ACA's PURPOSE
To provide leadership in health care and a positive vision for the chiropractic profession and its natural approach to health and wellness

ACA's MISSION
To preserve, protect, improve and promote the chiropractic profession and the services of Doctors of Chiropractic for the benefit of patients they serve

ACA's VISION
To transform health care from a focus on disease to a focus on wellness

SOSORT

INTERNATIONAL *SOCIETY ON SCOLIOSIS ORTHOPAEDIC AND REHABILITATION TREATMENT*

In recognition of his contributions to the care and conservative treatment of scoliosis

Kevin LAU, DC
Singapore, Singapore

is hereby declared
Associate Member of SOSORT in 2012

Stefano Negrini, MD, Italy
President

Patrick Knott, PhD, PA-C
General Secretary

HEALTH IN YOUR HANDS

Handbook for Patients

The Complete Scoliosis Surgery

About the Author

A graduate of RMIT University in Melbourne, Australia and Clayton College in Alabama, America, Dr. Kevin Lau D.C., combines university education with a lifetime of practicing natural and preventive medicine. His immensely successful holistic approach for treating scoliosis attempts to free your mind, body as well as the spirit from all the remnants of the disease.

Watch out for the most amazing array of books, journals, tools and devices to aid you on the road to recovery from scoliosis. Dr. Kevin Lau brings to you never-before, information-rich volumes and books on scoliosis, presented in an extremely reader-friendly manner. Look for some of the best natural forms of treatment in the Amazon bestseller 'Your Plan for Natural Scoliosis Prevention and Treatment'. Acting as a perfect accompaniment to this, 'Your Natural Scoliosis Treatment Journal' is just the companion you need on the path to treatment. To guide your way through the world of parenthood, Dr. Lau also brings to you 'An Essential Guide for Scoliosis and a Healthy Pregnancy', a path-breaking and pioneering compilation of practical knowledge on how to handle conception and pregnancy in scoliosis.

Being a man of the contemporary, Dr. Kevin Lau also perfectly combines technology with healthcare practices. The Scoliosis Exercises DVD is the most comprehensive compilation of correction exercises you could ever look for. Also try the innovative ScolioTrack, the top ranking iTune for Medical Apps and Scoliometer, the state of the art of app that can help you keep track of your deformity and monitor your progress.

After counseling hundreds of patients diagnosed with scoliosis and a host of other diseases, Dr. Lau discovered ground-breaking research that established, beyond a doubt, the clear merits of non-surgical treatment of scoliosis.

A firm believer in the ideology that health and sickness are within our control, Dr. Lau's main grounding has come from his own life experiences. His patients hail from all walks of life and have ranged in age from young children to ninety-year-olds. Dr. Lau was honored with the "Best Healthcare Provider Award" from the major newspaper publication in Singapore, Straits Time Newspaper.

Over the course of his career and based on his experiences, Dr. Lau has gained special expertise in treating patients with scoliosis, diabetes, depression, osteoarthritis, high blood pressure/hypertension, heart conditions, chronic neck and low back pain, and chronic tiredness, as well as several other "modern diseases".

Dr. Lau knows that the best medicine in the world comes straight from nature and it cannot be produced and mass marketed from a lab.

Dr. Kevin Lau's Mission Statement

The true cure for scoliosis lies in the eradication of its root cause. I, hereby reinforce my commitment to the research to unravel the factors that cause scoliosis. The current research is limited to the analysis of bracing and surgical techniques which only treat the symptoms and impact of the disorder. The research to identify and treat the core cause of scoliosis still offers a vast scope.

Towards this end, I promise to dedicate a portion of proceeds of my books to the research focused on understanding the root cause of scoliosis, which will help us protect our future generations from this widespread spinal deformity. .

Foreword

The human race is at its perplexing and unnerving best today. The scramble for the zenith was never that intense as it is now. With the mechanism as God has gifted, modern medicine and science continues to endeavor its way through the world of research, discoveries and amazing inventions. To be a befitting part of this scenario, contribute to it effectively and gain from it as desired, it is imperative for the mind and body to be in perfect form. Disease and infirmities are an integral part of our lifestyle, especially owing to the inadvertent, unhealthy constituents and boons of modern life.

When it comes to the impact of our occupational and lifestyle hazards on our existence, it is our body, the physical and biological mechanism created by God that perhaps takes the maximum impact.

And form thereon comes the disastrous toll on the component that literally holds up our body straight. Recent research showed that back problems including scoliosis are fast becoming the most oft-reported reason for fatal illnesses in the US.

The Complete Scoliosis Surgery Handbook for Patients is an effort to understand the mechanics of the human spine in a crystal clear fashion. It is a comprehensive volume on scoliosis, one of the most common deformities of the spine. The distortion and disruption caused by the deformity is discussed threadbare along with other related dimensions. The author has laid out all the essential aspects of the deformity in a step-wise method for the reader to understand and correlate with their own lives. From why does the curve happen in the first place, to assessing its severity, analyzing the modes of treatment and finally to the specifics of the spinal corrective surgery, the publication covers it all.

Dr. Siddhant Kapoor, M.B.B.S, D.N.B.
Orthopaedic Surgeon

Disclaimer

Aknowledgement

An ode to all my loved ones, my dear friends and above all for my wonderful patients, who've always had an unflinching support and faith in my work, advice and counsel.

'The Complete Scoliosis Handbook Surgery for Patients' is dedicated to all my associates who've helped me evolved my own unique theory of the workings of the human spine, its deformities and the treatments.

Additional Thanks and Credits

Nemanja Stankovic (*Graphic Designer, UK*) – Who gave it his best to design an extremely professional and creative front and back cover for the book, giving it a novel definition of its own.

Adriana Nicoleta Zamfir (*Graphic Designer, Romania*) – For giving the book an immensely reader-friendly layout, making it interesting as well as useful for the reader and lending the perfect artistic blend to the entire publication

Jasmin Pannu (*Masters in Journalism, India*) – For helping me dissect and find the latest and well designed research. Her gift as a word smith helped me convey difficult concepts in an easy to understand matter.

Jennifer Carter (*Editor, Physiotherapist, USA*) – For their meticulous and untiring efforts to provide a high quality, authentic information source for the reader and unwavering attention to details.

Dr. James Carter (*Editor, Medical Doctor, USA*) – For helping me edit and provide the most valuable information that patients most want to know.

Dr. Siddhant Kapoor (*Editor, Orthopaedic Doctor, Singapore*) – For fact checking the information contained in this book and lending his invaluable knowledge on surgery.

Jee Choi (*Model, Korea*) – For clearly demonstrating the exercises contained in this book.

Jericho Soh Chee Loon (*Photographer, Singapore*) – For all the professionally taken photos.

Ritwij Sasmal (*Illustrator, India*) – For all his creative expertise, conveying the subject matter and the concept through well-designed, descriptive images.

Table of the contents

PART ONE

Overview of the Disease

CHAPTER 1

What is Scoliosis?

Now that you are here and have understood the basic purpose of this book, , it is time to take you by the hand and show what this book is all about. In this chapter, we will tell you all about your spine, its basic structure and most importantly, various diseases and disorders affecting it. We will also give you a detailed introduction to scoliosis, one of the most common spinal deformities. You will understand why this spinal deformity is being seen as a condition requiring a multi-modal approach, including disciplines such as orthopedics, physiotherapy, surgical treatments, chiropractic care and so on, apart from the essential principles of nutrition, exercise and lifestyle modifications.

The Present Day Scenario

Every one of you must have experienced the rush in your daily routine at some point in your life. Like all other species, you must have also been tempted to pack in many more goals and activities in your daily regimen than you or your body can bear. In the pursuit to progress, achieve success and earn more, all of us tend to load our minds and bodies, beyond the permissible limits.

While it is true that action and mobility are imperative to life, pushing your body beyond a certain point actually works against nature. As a result, your physical energies are washed out, your mind loses its power and vigor and, most important of all, your physiological system begins to rebel.

When it comes to the human body, it is your spine, the backbone, that takes the brunt of the kind of life you live. Made up of complex structures, your spine virtually holds your body together, bearing all the stresses of your various day-to-day activities.

In the beginning of this section we will talk about one of the most important parts of your body, the human spine. We will give you a detailed look at what your spine looks like, what is it made of and, most importantly, what the problems are that your spine may develop.

1) Our Spine

Let us start with a look at what is our spine made up of. The human spine is a collection of bones known as the vertebrae, which are arranged in a columnar fashion. Your spine extends from directly below your skull to your tailbone, enclosing and protecting your spinal cord. It also provides support to your chest, abdomen and pelvis.

It is your spine that facilitates the physical mobility and flexibility of your body, allowing you to stand, sit, bend, arch and twist, whenever you wish to. In fact, it is interesting to know that your spine actually supports almost half of your body weight.

Let us have a closer look at the basic structure of your spine, after which we will see what problems your spine may give you, owing to a disease, malfunction or other issue.

Key Components of Your Spine

Your spine is comprised of five main sections or parts. Beginning at the base of the skull these parts are the cervical, thoracic and lumbar vertebrae, followed by the sacrum and coccyx at the tip. If you visualize it like this, your spine resembles a stack of 33 bones or vertebrae, placed on top of each other. Starting from the neck downwards, you will first have the 7 cervical or neck vertebrae, clinically referred to as C1-C7. Moving down, you will then have the 12 thoracic or upper back vertebrae, known as T1-T12. Finally, you have the 5 lumbar vertebrae, which are referred to as L1-L5. As you move down even further, you have the sacrum and coccyx, which are basically the fused bones at the base of your spine.

The table below will give you a clear description of location of each of the parts, and their role in your body.

Name	Location	Number of bones/ vertebrae	Clinical reference	Key role
Cervical vertebrae	Neck	7	C1-C7	To support your head, allowing you to shake, nod, bend, turn and extend your head.
Thoracic vertebrae	Chest	12	T1-T12	These attach to your ribs and provide the key framework for them.
Lumbar vertebrae	Lower back	5	L1-L5	To carry the majority of the weight of your upper body.
Sacrum	Pelvis	5 vertebrae, fused together	S1-S5	Constitutes the back of the pelvis
Coccyx	Base of the spine	4 vertebrae, fused together	NA	Evolutionary remnant of tails in other vertebrates

The Vertebra

As we have just learned, the vertebrae make up the most critical components of your spine, with the body of the vertebra being the primary area of weight-bearing. Let us now understand what they are made up of and how problems can be created by normal wear and tear or injury to its components.

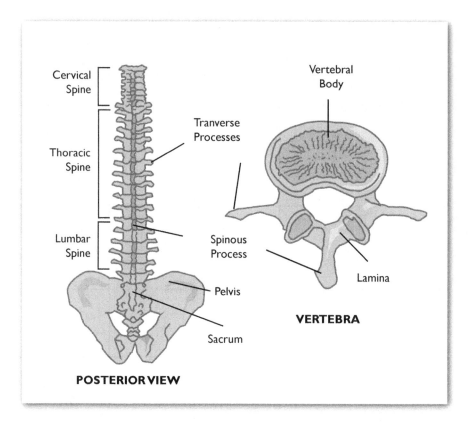

Each vertebra is made up of, and surrounded by, a series of parts and components. Let us understand each of them before we go any further:

- **Vertebral Body** – This is the large, block-like bony part of a vertebra, which bears the majority of the weight of your spine.
- **Spinal canal** - This is the large space in the centre of the vertebral column, which allows for the passage of the spinal cord.

- **Lamina** – This covers the spinal canal, extending from the body of the vertebra and forming a ring to enclose the spinal cord, offering it protection from the back.
- **Spinous process** – A part of the lamina that elongates like a beak over the back. This is the part of spine that you feel as you run your hand down your back.
- **Transverse process** – This structure is oriented perpendicular to the spinous process, providing attachment for the back muscles.
- **Pedicle** – This connects the lamina to the vertebral body.
- **Facet joints** – Similar to any other joint in your entire body, the facet joints are the spinal column joints. Each of the vertebrae has four facet joints attached to it. While one of the pair faces upwards, the other faces downwards. Each of the facet joint interlocks with the adjacent vertebrae which further lends stability to the spine.
- **Intervertebral discs** – These are small structures that separate the vertebrae, acting as soft, gel-like cushions between them. An intervertebral or a spinal disc is round in diameter and flat on the top and bottom, firmly attached to the vertebrae above and below them. These discs help absorb pressure and also prevent the bones from rubbing on each other. Each of these discs is made up of two parts, the annulus fibrosus and the nucleus pulposus. While the annulus is the hard, tougher, outer layer, the inner most core is known as the nucleus. A spinal or intervertebral disc is perhaps the strongest and most important shock absorber your body has. It bears all the stress and pressure of your lifestyle including exercise and other physical activities. In a normal, healthy adult, the intervertebral disk is well-hydrated with the nucleus consisting of 80% to 85% water and the annulus consisting of approximately 80% water. Through the normal process of aging and the associated biochemical changes in your body, the overall water content is likely to decrease to 70%. While this decrease in the amount of fluid is considered as a normal part of aging, it is the degeneration beyond this point that forms the ground for Degenerative Disc Disease.

A Word on the Spinal Cord

Your spinal cord is a big bundle of nerves that runs through the hollow cavity in the centre of your spinal column, attached to the brain, and is a part of the Central Nervous System (CNS). It is these nerves that perform the important function of relaying messages between your brain and the entire body. About 18 inches long, it extends from the base of the brain up to near your waist. These nerve fibers collectively contain two types of motor neurons, explained as below:

Upper motor neurons: These are the primary component of the nerve fibers located in your spinal cord.

Lower motor neurons: These are present in the spinal nerves that branch off the spinal cord at regular intervals in the neck and back.

2) Issues of the spine

By now, we know our spine is responsible for a huge series of functions we perform every day. In fact, we can safely assume that a healthy spine is the cornerstone of a healthy life. Hence, it is imperative that a problem in any one of the multitude of components of the spine, including the discs, vertebrae or joints can lead to a series of complications and disorders, ranging from birth defects, injuries and infections to tumors and other conditions like ankylosing spondylitis and scoliosis.

Spinal Disc Pain

Experts divide all forms of spinal disc pain and disorders into two broad categories, namely:

Axial pain: This is the pain which you feel when your spinal disc itself is the source of pain. It occurs when you have Degenerative Disc Disease, which is basically associated with the wear and tear that your spinal discs face due to the process of aging. The cushioning and space between your vertebrae shrinks, further leading to small tears in the outer part of the disc, resulting in spinal pain.

Radicular pain: This is a type of nerve root pain which travels along one of the nerves that exits the spine. You will experience radicular pain if the inner, soft nucleus ruptures or leaks out of the disc through tears in the annulus and comes in contact with the nerve root. This phenomenon is also known as disc herniation or rupture. The nucleus may rupture from either side of the disc and can eventually compress the nerve root, also known as a pinched nerve, causing radicular pain. In some cases, your pain might not be a result of a direct nerve root compression. Small fragments of the nucleus within the epidural space can trigger an inflammatory reaction which can cause irritation to the adjacent nerve root as well, as demonstrated by Jinkins in his study, where nerve root enhancement was observed in 5% of patients who complained of back or leg pain . Put in laymen terms, this research implies that a pinched nerve, as explained above can actually cause pain in the back or even the leg, though the two might sound unrelated.

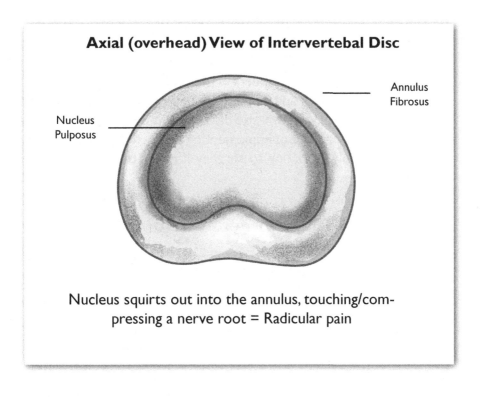

Axial (overhead) View of Intervertebal Disc

Annulus
Fibrosus

Nucleus
Pulposus

Nucleus squirts out into the annulus, touching/compressing a nerve root = Radicular pain

Types of Spinal Disorders					
Degenerative spinal disease	Vertebral fractures	Coronal plane deformity, Sagittal deformities	Inflammatory disease	Spinal cord injuries	Others
Herniated Disc (Cervical, Thoracic and Lumbar)	Compression fracture	Lordosis	Spondylitis	Tetraplegia	Spina Bifida and Spinal Dysraphism
Spinal Stenosis (Cervical, Lumbar, Foraminal)	Burst fracture	Kyphosis	Ankylosing spondylitis	Paraplegia	Spinal tumors (benign and malignant)
Spinal Instability	Flexion-distraction fracture	Scoliosis			Spondylolysis
Spondylosis	Fracture + dislocation	Hyperlordosis			Spondylolisthes
	Stable vs. unstable fracture				

The previous table gives you a detailed view of all the common diseases and disorders that can occur due to your spine.

For the purpose of selective study, here onwards we will only concentrate on the subject of scoliosis. We will present in depth information on the various aspects of the condition, from its historical background, categories and causative factors to the people it might affect the most. Finally, we will also discuss various treatment options, including the importance of implementing corrective measures early on, and eventually resorting to surgery if other treatment options are not effective.

3) Scoliosis – The Disorder of Deformity

Understanding Scoliosis

Scoliosis is defined as a musculoskeletal condition which has an abnormal lateral curvature of the spine as its primary characteristic. The spinal column of an individual with scoliosis bends laterally in a curve that may resemble the letter "S" or the letter "C".

Generally speaking, scoliosis can develop in either the thoracic (mid-back) or the lumbar (lower back) spine, with the curvature being prominent accordingly.

The condition can be further worsened by other related deformities such as lordosis, inward curvature or forward arch of the spine, or kyphosis, outward curvature or posterior rounding of the spine.

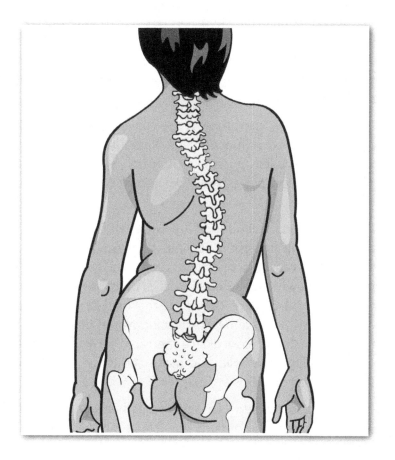

In simplified terms, scoliosis is a form of a spinal deformity, which means that it is a state in which the spine has deviated from its normal shape, .i.e. a straight line. This medical condition derives its name from 'skoliosis', the Greek word for 'crookedness'. Though it might have been addressed in a different manner, scoliosis has been recognized for a long time, with the condition being mentioned often in the earliest medical histories.

A fairly common musculoskeletal disorder, scoliosis is most commonly identified in the age group of 10-15 years, though it can affect adults and smaller children as well. Statistics show that at least 2-3% of the population of the United States suffers from scoliosis, which brings the number to a whopping 6 million people in the United States alone. As per the estimates of the International Scoliosis Society, one in nine females are likely to have the condition, while the number of males is likely to be lesser. In the next chapter, we will go into detail on the causes of scoliosis and will also talk about the factors that make a certain group of adults and children more prone to scoliosis.

In some cases, the curvature of the spine might actually develop as a reaction to another functional problem in the body. Common examples could be a spasm in the muscles of the back, a discrepancy in leg length or improper posture being observed over a very long stretch of time.

However, experts still ponder over whether scoliosis is primarily a spinal condition, at least in its initial stages. Though the actual mechanism that causes scoliosis is yet to be specifically defined, research has shown a possible lack of proper development in the automatic postural control centre of the hind brain or the brain stem. Due to this possible neuro-developmental deficit, the human mechanism is unable to coordinate the rapid growth that the body faces in adolescence. You will read more about the possible role of genetics in causing scoliosis in Chapter 2.

Refer to the diagram below for a generalized view on the progression of scoliosis and treatment options possible at various stages.

What Scoliosis Does to You?

When you have scoliosis, your physical appearance might give telltale signs of your condition, especially on a closer look. Since scoliosis is all about physical asymmetry and imbalance, the disorder manifests itself in the form of physical attributes.

So, what really happens to your appearance when you have scoliosis? Here, we've listed some of the most important changes and discrepancies in the symmetry of your body that you or others might notice:

- Difference between the length of your legs
- Difference between the height of your shoulders or hips
- Your head may not appear to be in the center of your body
- Prominence of rib cage or shoulder blade, especially when bending forward
- Apparent curve in the spine
- Trousers or even hemlines can hang unevenly at the bottom

Experts strongly believe that scoliosis eventually becomes a condition which affects the entire body. It encompasses your entire system and can have an impact on multiple bodily functions. In fact, idiopathic scoliosis is often referred to as a multifaceted disorder which can impact the 5 vital organ systems including digestive, muscular, hormonal, skeletal and neurological.

Some specific areas of impact could be:

- Any part of the skeletal system, including the ribs (rib deformity), spine and pelvis
- Brain and central nervous system (CNS)
- Hormonal and digestive systems
- Heart and lungs (shortness of breath)
- Chronic pain

The image on the next page depicts the curved spine more clearly.

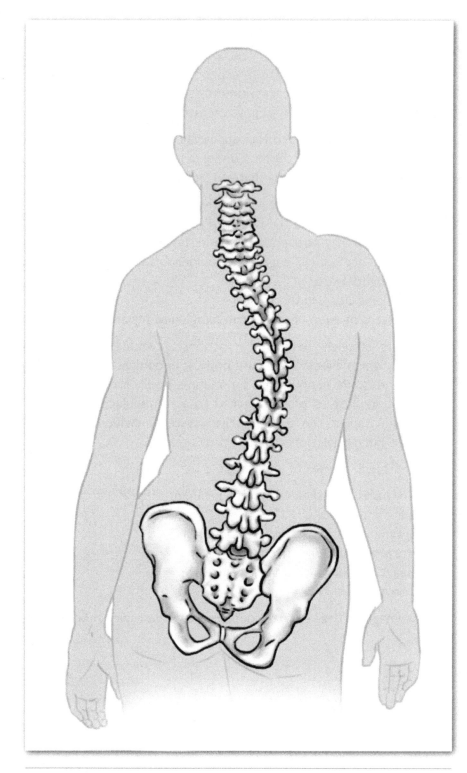

History of Treatment

The earliest mention of a condition similar to scoliosis is found in the annals of history by Hippocrates, way back in 400 B.C. A curvature in the spine was most often observed in young girls, especially ones with a delayed menarche.

Historically, scoliosis was often subjected to the conventional 'wait and watch' approach wherein the slowly progressing curvature was expected to halt or, better, reverse on its own. Unfortunately, scoliosis in young adolescents is often dismissed as a part of growing up and gains attention only when extreme pain, discomfort or inability begins to surface. Until a few years back, braces often used to be the first treatment option adopted at this stage to restrict the curvature. To be effective, braces have to be worn for a long period of time and can often restrict the activity level of the individual concerned.

Why is Early Prevention Important?

In further continuation of the above, science gives ample evidence to point out that scoliosis, until it progresses to a certain level, is still within the realms of prevention and reversal. Since the later stage of progression of scoliosis has a strong correlation to environmental factors, it might be possible to inhibit or even reverse the progression of the curve in the initial stages itself.

When a human being is born, the spine looks like a straight line. However, as this particular spinal deformity begins to set in, the straight line slowly begins to take the form of the English alphabet 'S' or 'C'. So, what would be easier? Will it be to prevent the straight line from turning into the 'S' or the 'C' curve as it is slowly changing? Or alternatively, will it be to change the shape of the 'S' or the 'C' curve once it has actually developed, as we try to do with the use of braces and eventual surgery? It is for this reason that modern science attempts to lay more stress on factors like early detection, physical manipulation, dietary modification, appropriate fitness regimen and of course lifestyle changes.

Here, let's take a quick look at 5 reasons why a holistic approach involving corrective measures might help much more than taking to braces or surgery for this disorder.

1. Braces can be very uncomfortable.
2. Braces do not assure you of full reversal of the condition.
3. Surgery can be complicated and carries an inherent risk.
4. In young adolescents, braces can affect the confidence level and can lead to the development of an inferiority complex.
5. Full reversal might not be possible with braces or at times, even surgery.

There is another important reason why early intervention and a holistic approach for treatment are called for. Since scoliosis is a progressive condition, the curvature can continue to advance even after full skeletal maturity has been achieved.

Research adequately demonstrates that whatever your age, extent of the curve or genetic history, early detection and initial corrective measures improve your chances of a cure to a great extent, if done in a systematic manner.

In the later part of this book, you will read about the various treatment options available and their pros and cons to help you decide the most suitable treatment option for you.

Interesting facts you must know!

Some people still believe that scoliosis might result from factors like carrying heavy items, involvement in athletic activities, incorrect postures or a minor inequality in the lower limb length. Though this might not be absolutely true, but research does show that these factors can increase the level of spinal misalignment, thereby aggravating the condition.

→ Young girls are more likely to have scoliosis than the boys.
→ Scoliosis existed and was even identified in the age of Hippocrates.
→ it happened to a golfer!

Real Scoliosis Stories: Surgery

Scoliosis is a fairly common condition and can affect individuals across age-groups and health backgrounds.

Tracy (name changed), an avid golfer, was merely 11 years of age when she was diagnosed with scoliosis in one of her school screening exams. It's quite amazing to know how Tracy, now a professional golfer and a star on the LPGA Tour has reached the pinnacle after going through a case of severe progressive scoliosis and an equally difficult surgery.

After being first screened, Tracy was put on to a brace for a long period of 7 ½ years to help straighten her curve. Though she wore the brace for around 18 hours every day, once she took it off at age 18, her curve continued to progress rapidly, leaving her with the lone choice of surgery. A corrective surgery was carried out in which a single rod and 5 screws were inserted into her spine. She was put on a brace for 3 months post-surgery and invested another 6 months into golf rehabilitation after her surgery.

With a balanced spine and a healthier body, Tracy today continues to play and excel in the sport of her choice, in spite of the odds which were once against her.

CHAPTER 2

What Causes Scoliosis?

Once you know what scoliosis is, it's now time to know why it occurs. In this chapter we will talk about why scoliosis happens and whether you stand a chance of being affected. You will also learn more about what kind of individuals are vulnerable to scoliosis and why.

Did you know that in the United States, about 1.5 per 1000 persons are said to be suffering from scoliosis or spinal curvature of more than 25 degrees?

By now, you know that scoliosis is the term used to define a deformity in the shape of your spine. Basically referred to as a 'crooked' shape, your spine will slowly begin to resemble the curved English letters 'S' or ' C', as opposed to a 'straight line', which it is supposed to look like. Here are some questions that may enter your mind. Is this something you are born with? Is it caused by your lifestyle? Do you inherit it from your parents or grandparents? Do your nerves have a role to play?

While these questions may make you anxious about scoliosis, read on further to have all your questions answered.

To begin with, first let us make an attempt to understand how scoliosis was viewed in historic times.. Back in the 18ᵗʰ and 19ᵗʰ centuries, scoliosis was thought to be caused by having improper posture or postural deformities.

The best way to understand why scoliosis occurs is to look at it in three different ways:

1. Physiological and degenerative reasons, such as aging, disease, trauma and the like
2. Neurological reasons, developed at birth (congenital) or later in life
3. Unknown and unidentifiable (idiopathic) reasons

Before we go any further into the reasons of why scoliosis might happen, it is first important to know that as many as 80% of scoliosis cases are idiopathic in nature, which implies that it has no underlying identifiable cause. The incidence of idiopathic scoliosis is so widespread that it can also be divided further into sub-categories, such as:

- Infantile idiopathic
- Juvenile idiopathic
- Adolescent idiopathic
- Adult idiopathic

Interestingly, idiopathic scoliosis is mostly found in young girls, especially during the growth spurt of puberty. You will read about each of these sub categories in the later chapters of this book.

In the sections that follow, we will discuss in detail, each of the possible causes of scoliosis, based on evidence gathered from patients with scoliosis, the medical history of their family members, pre-disposing environmental factors and so on.

Degenerative and Physiological Causes

Your body undergoes changes all the time. Factors like age, trauma, lifestyle and diseases are constantly altering your state of health. In this sub-section, we will discuss various physiological causes and diseases that can lead to an onset of scoliosis.

Degeneration and aging are one of the major examples of physical changes that can lead to scoliosis. A condition that mostly develops after the age of 50, it is characterized by disk degeneration and may be associated with further spinal deformity.

Some of the specific incidents, diseases and physical abnormalities that might be related to scoliosis include:

→ Spinal fracture or injuries
→ Osteoporosis
→ Abnormal growths or tumors in the spinal column. Syringomyelia, a disorder in which cysts develop along the spine is an example of how such abnormal growths can cause scoliosis.
→ An abnormal pattern of muscle growth or functioning, as demonstrated in the case of a disturbance in the growth of paravertebral muscles, could be a possible cause for idiopathic scoliosis.
→ Muscle paralysis and stress fractures.
→ In some cases, spinal cord and brainstem abnormalities may play a significant role in the progression of the curve.

There is also research to suggest that an imbalance in the muscles around the vertebrae may exist. Due to this imbalance, any spinal deformity or distortion which exists earlier in life is likely to progress considerably with age.

Meanwhile, there are other physiological causes that might lead to a temporary or non-structural scoliosis. In these types of scoliosis, the spine is normal and the curvature is a result of other reasons, such as a difference in the leg lengths, muscle spasms, appendicitis or other such conditions. You will read more about this type of scoliosis in the sections to come.

Neurological Causes

There is ample research to show that any form of disruption of the postural reflex system can lead to the development of scoliosis[1, 2]. Before you read any further, let us have a closer look at the concept of postural equilibrium. Scoliosis is believed to be associated closely with your body's natural postural alignment and pattern. Any abnormality or even a minor deviation from the normal and balanced postural pattern can be related to scoliosis at two different levels:

→ Initial postural imbalance can lead to an onset of scoliosis.
→ The extent of postural imbalance can determine the degree of curvature.

Often termed as the third leading cause after idiopathic and physiological, neurological causes can lead to what is termed as the neuromuscular scoliosis. A number of neurological disorders or diseases can cause this type of scoliosis to develop. More specifically, the diseases that might make you more vulnerable to develop scoliosis include:

• Cerebral palsy
• Muscular dystrophy
• Poliomyelitis (Polio)
• Myelomeningocele
• Myopathies
• Spina bifida

In addition, scoliosis can also develop due to various degenerative causes such as spondylosis. Other factors such as a spinal cord injury or traumatic brain injury can also be a related cause.

In the majority of such disorders, children actually have weak trunks that are unable to support the weight of their bodies, due to which their spine begins to buckle into a long 'C' shape curve. In children born with such disorders, initial signs of scoliosis might take time to develop, but they invariably do appear before they reach adolescence. For instance, almost 80% of children born with myelodysplasia will begin to show symptoms of scoliosis by the age of 10[3]. This is basically a term given to a group of disorders in which the bone marrow does not function in a normal manner. Due to this, it produces an insufficient number of blood cells in the body, thus leading to further complications.

In addition, even injuries to the brain can result in the development of a curvature of the spine. A typical example in case is the Kinematic Imbalance due to Suboccipital Strain (KISS)[4]. This is an injury to that part of the brain which is responsible for coordinating motor and sensory input. This defect is often found in newborns who have suffered from birth trauma from reasons like multiple pregnancies, multiple births, obstructed or prolonged labor, assisted deliveries, caesarean section and the like.

Do heredity and genes play a role?

Modern research has been placing an increasing amount of stress on how genetics can influence the development of scoliosis. The science of epigenetics suggests that an individual who is more vulnerable to scoliosis can reform his genetic code through a modified lifestyle, diet and exercise regimen.

Research now points out to concrete evidence that genes play an important role in the development of scoliosis. A study published in the journal, *Nature Genetics* indicates towards the possibility of a direct correlation of the gene GPR126 and the onset of adolescent idiopathic scoliosis[5]. In fact, experts have suggested there is a strong possibility for an individual to develop scoliosis if someone else in the family also has it, clinically referred to as the familial component.

Experts have also found a particular inherited defect which affects perception or coordination. In children suffering from scoliosis, this defect is likely to contribute to an unusual growth in the spine. As an example, Turner's syndrome, which is a genetic disease in females and is   known to affect physical and reproductive development, is likely to be associated with scoliosis.

There is strong evidence through multiple research studies that points towards the possible role of heredity in the cause of scoliosis. Wynne-Davies findings suggest a strong pattern of heredity, pointing towards either a single dominant gene or multiple genes collectively contributing to the development of the disorder[6]. On the other hand, Cowell et al suggests that the disorder is primarily linked to an inheritance, possibly linked to a sex-dependent gene[7].

However, equally perplexing is the observation that in the case of identical twins, one of the siblings may have the condition while the other remains unaffected[8].

Genetic Markers

Recent research hints at a probable role of a variation in the gene CHD7, which can make individuals more prone to idiopathic scoliosis[9]. In addition, the researchers at Texas Scottish Rite Hospital for Children also talk of the genes CHLI and DSCAM as the probable markers for idiopathic scoliosis[10]. According to the experts at the hospital, both of these genes participate in the process of nerve growth, guiding the direction in which the spinal cord is supposed to grow. A disruption of such mechanisms due to malfunctioning of the nerve pathways can be traced to the onset of scoliosis.

The researchers emphasize, that until recently, scoliosis has been viewed exclusively as a bone disease. But this perception is now quickly changing due to current research which indicates the presence of possible neurological pathways that are responsible for this spinal deformity.

Some of the genetic diseases that may induce physical abnormalities associated with scoliosis comprise of:

- Marfan's Syndrome
- Ehler's-Danlos Syndrome
- Neurofibromatosis
- Albers-Schonberg disease

- Friedreich's ataxia
- Rheumatoid arthritis
- Osteogenesis imperfecta
- Cushing's Syndrome

Amongst the total population affected by scoliosis, there is quite a high incidence of newborns that are born with spinal deformities. The condition is referred to as congenital scoliosis, which can develop a misshapen or malformed vertebral column. In such situations, there can be some problems with the formation of the vertebral column. Common examples are hemi-vertebra or wedge vertebra. In addition, it is also possible that the vertebrae are not joined together properly or are joined together in blocks. You will read more about congenital scoliosis in the chapters to come.

Hormones, Enzymes and Body Processes

Though the endocrine system is a different unit of the human body, there has been research which points at the possibility of hormonal abnormalities being a cause of scoliosis. Let us consider the case of melatonin, which is a hormone that is secreted by the brain and is related to the pattern of sleep and growth. Owning to a certain set of genetic factors, the levels of melatonin in the blood may decrease, which may in turn affect the muscle tone and development during sleep. Over time this is likely to have an aggravating effect on the curvature of the spine. In one such relevant study on chickens, it was observed that injections of melatonin administered within the body cavity, to the pineal-gland deficient chickens could actually prevent the development of scoliosis in the species[11].

In addition, it is also observed that a deficiency of melatonin can have an adverse effect on vestibulospinal activity. Moreover, such impaired signal transmission from brain to the posture-control centers can possibly lead to a deviation in the normal pattern of back muscle activities. On the other hand, research indicates a correlation between increased levels of the enzyme known as matrix metalloproteinase and both degenerative disc disease and scoliosis

Other deficiencies that can be associated with scoliosis are as discussed below:

→ Magnesium. Deficiency of vital nutrients like magnesium has been linked to Mitral Valve Prolapse (MVP) and further with the onset and progression of scoliosis.

→ Vitamin K. Deficiency of vitamin K can be linked to abnormally long bleeding times and osteoporosis and, eventually, with scoliosis.

→ Vitamin D. Deficiency of vitamin D can cause Rickets, which can further lead to pectus excavatum, the clinical term given to sunken chests which can be associated with scoliosis.

→ Lower levels of the hormone estrogen have often been linked to osteoporosis and osteopenia, both of which are associated with scoliosis.

Thus, we have seen that hormonal abnormalities, can also induce scoliosis in various patients, at least to some extent.

Ask Yourself

- Do you have constant, undiagnosed back pain or discomfort in your back?
- Do you suffer from any of the above physiological or neurological diseases?
- Does anyone in your family suffer from any of the discussed diseases?
- Did you have an accident or a fall in the recent past and the pain still remains?
- Does your physical appearance give tell tale signs of scoliosis (discussed further in Chapter 4)?

In the chapters to come, you will read more about each of these possible signs of scoliosis and how to identify them in yourself or your family members.

Point to Ponder

The study of the cause of scoliosis is quite multi-dimensional. Perhaps one of the main reasons for this fact is that even now idiopathic scoliosis remains the most prevalent form of this disorder. In fact, it is this non-clarity in the etiology of the disorder that causes the treatment to remain largely focused on measures such as bracing and surgery, while there are few preventive measures advocated.

It is also important to understand that due to the complex mechanisms of the human body, it may be a fallible task to draw a clear line between the various causes of scoliosis. An overlap of etiology from physiological to neurological and even to the genetic pathways can be possible and hence should not become a cause of ambiguity to the reader.

Interesting facts you must know

→ Scoliosis cannot be prevented, however, you can influence the progression of the curvature.

→ If you suffered from polio in your childhood, it is more likely that you may develop scoliosis or other deformities as you age.

→ Female athletes and ballet dancers are more likely to get scoliosis.

CHAPTER 3

Types of Scoliosis

K nowledge is indeed power. As you arm yourself to combat scoliosis, a comprehensive knowledge of your disorder is extremely crucial. Before you map out your path for treatment, your first step is to know the kind of scoliosis you have. That's exactly what you will learn in this chapter. We will talk about various kinds of scoliosis, their defining traits and how to demarcate one from the other.

Structural vs. Non-Structural Scoliosis

Scoliosis of different types and etiological backgrounds invariably ends in the key presentation of a spinal curvature. However, as the various modalities of treatments have evolved over the years, it has become evident that early detection of the disorder, along with the recognition of its basic type, can effectively influence the pattern of correction.

As we just studied in the previous chapter, the basic cause of the spinal curvature will determine the categorization for the type of scoliosis. For instance, scoliosis that occurs due to any spinal abnormality that may have developed prior to birth is termed congenital scoliosis.

Similarly, scoliosis having bony changes in the spinal column will be called structural scoliosis, while those arising out of non-spinal issues and without a bony change in the spinal column will be called non-structural scoliosis. A long-standing non-structural scoliosis may also give rise to structural scoliosis.

. Moreover, each one of these types will have further classifications based on different criteria.

The most important and prominent logic that differentiates between the structural and non-structural scoliosis is the presence of a rotational component. This element of rotation is present in an individual suffering from structural scoliosis and is absent in the case of functional or non-structural scoliosis.

In fact, here it is interesting to note that scoliosis can be defined in various ways, based on a number of criteria, which primarily include:

→ Cause of the condition
→ Age of the individual affected
→ Location of the curve

The charts at the end of this chapter will give you a clear list of the number of ways in which you can classify scoliosis.

Interesting to know...

Various sub-types of scoliosis can also be grouped under more than one category, which can lead to an overlapping in classifications. For instance, Juvenile Idiopathic Scoliosis that occurs in children is mainly categorized under idiopathic scoliosis. However, it can also be studied under the category of scoliosis, based on age. The same would be the case for Adult Idiopathic Scoliosis as well. This should not confuse you about the classification of scoliosis. Just keep in mind that scoliosis may be classified on the basis of various factors affecting the deformity.

For the purpose of a detailed study, we've given descriptions of each one of these types of scoliosis in the section below.

Structural Scoliosis

Structural scoliosis is the sideways curve of the spine along with a rotation of the vertebral column. A very typical example is that of degenerative scoliosis which occurs in adults due to the general aging process. Alterations in the structure and pattern of functioning of the various components of the spine can lead to this type of scoliosis. You have already learned about the different parts of the spine and the spinal cord in Chapter 1.

Since the spine curvature, caused in various types of structural scoliosis, has set in due to the issues of the spine itself, the deformity is usually irreversible. The condition can be treated and managed to control the progression of the curvature and encourage an appropriate lifestyle, but it is unlikely that the curvature will be reversed.

In the following section, we will discuss various key types of structural scoliosis, including:

→ Congenital Scoliosis
→ Idiopathic Scoliosis
→ Neuromuscular Scoliosis
→ Adult Scoliosis

Congenital Scoliosis

Congenital scoliosis is typically a sideways curvature of the spine that occurs due to a defect present at birth. A rather rare form of scoliosis, it occurs in only one out of every 10,000 newborns. However, the defects in the newborn usually do not become apparent until the infant reaches adolescence.

In an infant, three types of deformities can cause congenital scoliosis. Each of them has been explained below:

1. FAILURE OF SEPARATION/SEGMENTATION OF VERTEBRAE

In the early stages of the formation of the fetus, the spine forms as a single column of tissue. As the months progress, this column begins to segregate on its own and forms multiple tiny segments that eventually take the shape of the bony vertebrae. In some cases, this separation process remains incomplete, which can then result in a partial fusion of the spine. Eventually, a bony bar will be formed in which two or more vertebrae will be 'fused' or joined together. This bony bar will further disrupt the normal growth pattern, which will lead to a spinal curvature as the child grows.

Refer to the image at the end of this section to know more.

2. FAILURE OF FORMATION OF VERTEBRAL ELEMENTS

When the vertebral elements of one side fail to form, either partially or completely, congenital deformity appears known as wedge-vertebrae or hemi-vertebrae. A severe problem of growth can occur if a bony bar appears on one side of the spinal column and the hemi vertebra on the other. If left untreated, the curvature can grow at a rapid rate, causing serious growth issues in children.

3. COMPENSATORY CURVES

As your spine develops a curvature, it may try to balance the curve by creating other curves in the opposite direction, in an attempt to maintain an upright posture. The compensatory curve can develop either above or below the affected area.

In some cases, congenital scoliosis can also occur as a result of specific gender-based disorders such as the Mayer-Rokitansky-Küster-Hauser (MRKH) syndrome. Moreover, it has also been observed that newborns having congenital scoliosis are more likely to suffer from other congenital abnormalities, including anatomical anomalies of the genito-urinary tract or congenital heart defects.

In addition to all of the above, children having Rett Syndrome also often exhibit signs of scoliosis. A rare disorder associated with the mutation of 'X' chromosome, this disorder is mostly found in girls.

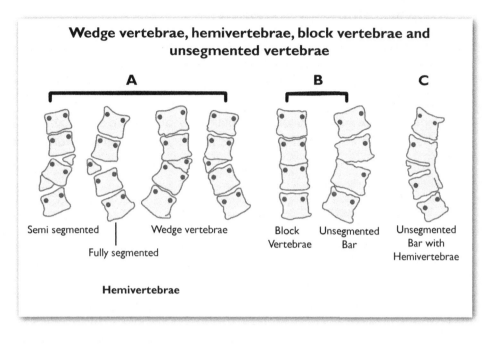

Wedge vertebrae, hemivertebrae, block vertebrae and unsegmented vertebrae

Semi segmented | Wedge vertebrae | Block Vertebrae | Unsegmented Bar | Unsegmented Bar with Hemivertebrae

Fully segmented

Hemivertebrae

Idiopathic Scoliosis

Perhaps the most common form of scoliosis, this category of the disorder has no explainable reason or cause. Any case of scoliosis that has no known reason or cause is basically termed as Idiopathic Scoliosis. Across the decades, research has analyzed various possible factors that may explain the etiology of idiopathic scoliosis, namely genetic, skeletal, chemical, neurologic and muscular factors. MRI studies conducted in a vast set of patients diagnosed with idiopathic scoliosis show approximately 4% to 26% of the patients to be also suffering from neurological abnormalities, such as syringomyelia and Arnold-Chiari malformation.

Though it can also occur in adults, the most common incidence of idiopathic scoliosis is observed in children, especially those who otherwise seem to have a normal skeletal growth.

When it occurs in children, idiopathic scoliosis is further divided into three sub-classifications, based on their age when the scoliosis appears. Here, we've given brief descriptions of each one of them.

Infantile Idiopathic Scoliosis

Scoliosis that develops at birth until the age of 3 years is typically called infantile idiopathic scoliosis. This type of scoliosis is usually painless and is observed much more in young boys than girls and accounts for almost 1% of all cases of idiopathic scoliosis. Though the reason may not be explainable, in infantile scoliosis the spine curves to the left side in most of the   cases and is predominantly thoracic in its presentation.

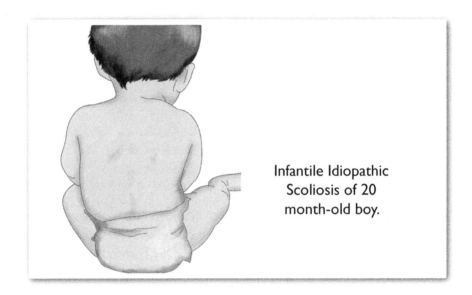

Infantile Idiopathic Scoliosis of 20 month-old boy.

However, research also points to the possibility that the curvature that arises in the first three years of life might actually resolve in due course of time. In 1965, Lloyd-Roberts and Pilcher reported that almost 92 percent of the cases of infantile idiopathic scoliosis could resolve within the first year of life.

It is also often observed that small children who develop scoliosis or a spine curvature before the age of 5 years might also have cardiopulmonary abnormalities.

Experts point out the following probable reasons that may cause infants to develop infantile idiopathic scoliosis and an 'S' shaped curvature of the spine:

→ In some cases, intrauterine molding has been linked to the development of the curve. In this case, the walls of the uterus in the mother's body exert abnormal pressure on one side of the fetus or position the fetus in an abnormal manner, which may actually result in the development of a curve.

→ Postnatal external pressures, which are exerted in situations where the infants are placed on their back or head in the cribs or beds for prolonged periods of time. In such cases, an abnormal level of pressure is put on the back, which could seriously impact its alignment levels. It is for such reasons that infantile idiopathic scoliosis is often associated with disorders like plagiocephaly or skull flattening in infants.

Although the above are suspected, the causes still remain largely hypothetical and further research is needed to validate the same.

Juvenile Idiopathic Scoliosis

Juvenile Idiopathic Scoliosis occurs between the ages of 3 and 9 years. Differing from infantile idiopathic scoliosis, this form of scoliosis affects more girls than boys and carries a major risk of rapid further progression of the curve, if not managed well in time. A controlled study conducted amongst 109 patients with juvenile idiopathic scoliosis showed that while the curve progressed at a rate of 1 to 3 degrees per year before the age of 10, it increased at the rate of 4.5 to 11 degrees per year after the age of 10 years. It has also often been observed that children with juvenile idiopathic scoliosis more frequently have left thoracic curves that are progressive and are associated with abnormal hairy patches and a somewhat higher incidence of intra-spinal pathology, including syringomyelia and diastematomyelia.

A bit more common than infantile idiopathic scoliosis, juvenile idiopathic scoliosis accounts for approximately 12-21% of all cases of idiopathic scoliosis observed. However, a distinct pattern does exist in the way juvenile idiopathic scoliosis affects boys and girls. In the age group of 3 to 6 years, almost an equal number of boys and girls are likely to develop the spine curvature. However, in the further age group of 6 to 10 years, more girls than boys are likely to become affected.

Prognosis in this type of idiopathic scoliosis is often positive, provided timely and accurate diagnosis and management are initiated.

Adolescent Idiopathic Scoliosis (AIS)

Idiopathic scoliosis develops in adolescents between the ages of 10 and 18 years, with a lateral spinal curvature of more than 10 degrees. The most important fact about AIS is its widespread incidence in young girls more than boys, perhaps due to the marked and early physical growth and progression during puberty in young girls. In fact, 60-80% of all cases of AIS are seen in young girls. AIS is also the most common form of scoliosis, occurring in at least 4 percent of all children between the ages of 9 to 14. Moreover, AIS is more commonly seen in children who have a family history of the deformity.

Here, it is also important to note that the spine curvature in AIS, if left untreated, can progress rapidly and lead to significant deformity. These deformities can further cause major psychological distress and physical disabilities in the adolescents. Moreover, due to the rotation of the vertebrae, the rib cage becomes affected which could eventually impact heart and lung function, leading to severe symptoms like shortness of breath.

Forms of Idiopathic Scoliosis – Key Facts

Infantile Idiopathic Scoliosis	Juvenile Idiopathic Scoliosis	Adolescent Idiopathic Scoliosis
Age: Birth to 3 years	Age: 3 to 9 years	Age: 9 to 18 years (adulthood)
More common in boys than girls	More common in girls than boys	More common in girls than boys
Accounts for 1% of all cases of Idiopathic Scoliosis	Accounts for around 12-21% of all cases of Idiopathic Scoliosis	Most common form of idiopathic scoliosis

Neuromuscular Scoliosis

Derived from the term 'neuro', which means nerves, this type of scoliosis, is one which occurs due to an abnormality in the development of the vertebral column owing to certain neurological disorders or any form of muscular weakness. In other words, neuromuscular scoliosis will result from a lack of control of the nerves and muscles which support the spine.

There is a specific pattern of muscle functioning that works to maintain adequate support to the spinal column for growth, alignment and balance. A vast range of such neuromuscular disorders exist that can alter this normal way of functioning, giving way to the spine curvature, either as an end result or as an allied outcome, which will usually be progressive in nature.

An abnormality in neuromuscular function which causes idiopathic scoliosis has two classifications:

→ Neuropathic – This is the term given to scoliosis that occurs due to an abnormal nerve function from diseases such as cerebral palsy.

→ Myopathic – This term refers to the curvature that develops due to an abnormal muscle function which occurs in diseases such as muscular dystrophy.

Here, we have listed some of the most common neuromuscular diseases that could cause scoliosis of this category:

• Cerebral palsy
• Spina bifida
• Spinal cord tumors
• Neurofibromatosis
• Muscular dystrophy
• Paralytic conditions

Important fact…

Most of these diseases cause neuromuscular changes during childhood. This is, incidentally, the time when the body and spine are growing and are adjusting themselves to meet the needs of physical growth. This is also the time when the maximum damage can be done to the spine.

Let us study a few important facts about neuromuscular scoliosis:

→ Children suffering from this type of scoliosis usually have poor coordination of their trunk, neck and head.

→ Kyphosis, an abnormal forward-bending of the spine, is also often found to be co-existent.

→ The chances of the progression of the curve are much higher if the curve has developed at an earlier age. Similarly, a curve that is already severe in initial diagnosis is likely to progress at a much faster rate.

→ The curves in neuromuscular scoliosis are usually longer, extending all the way down to the tail-bone.

→ Pelvic obliquity might also occur in children along with this form of scoliosis. In this condition, the pelvis is tilted, with one side positioned higher than the other one.

→ Larger thoracic curves (80° or more) and hyperlordotic curves, or a backward curve, might also add to pulmonary problems.

The curve progression in neuromuscular scoliosis is usually much more rapid than in idiopathic scoliosis. Although some of these children may be able to walk and perform some normal physical activities, most of these children will become wheelchair dependent in their adolescent years.

Adult Scoliosis

As your age progresses, the soft tissues of the spine and other components might experience some wear and tear, leading to the formation of a curvature in your spine. Experts define adult scoliosis as a spinal deformity in an otherwise skeletally mature individual, with a curve measuring more than 10° using the Cobb method.

For the purpose of study, we can classify degenerative scoliosis into three different types:

1. PURE DEGENERATIVE SCOLIOSIS

When individuals, having a perfectly straight and healthy spine, develop curvatures merely due to the aging process, the condition is referred to as pure degenerative scoliosis. Some experts also refer to the pure degenerative scoliosis as de novo ADS, literally implying adult degenerative scoliosis that has started afresh due to old age.

In adult scoliosis, deformity sets in as the intervertebral discs begin aging, leading to degeneration and ultimately ending in lack of competency of the posterior spinal elements, especially the facet joints . Eventually the expected axial rotation of the relevant spinal segments causes sideways spinal instability and subsequent laxity or increased give in the spinal ligaments.

2. IDIOPATHIC CURVES WITH DEGENERATION

In children diagnosed with infantile, juvenile or adolescent scoliosis, the curve further worsens due to the aging process. Though the curve had its origin during childhood, the degeneration associated with aging could further aggravate the curvature.

3. SECONDARY CAUSES

There are a number of causes in an adult's life that could lead to the development of a curvature, such as tumors, fractures, trauma or accidents.

Non-Structural Scoliosis

Non-structural or functional scoliosis is another type of the disorder. While structural scoliosis emanates from an underlying spinal disease or disorder, non-structural scoliosis stems from issues which might not be directly related to any spinal issue. Here, the curvature of the spine will result from a problem in another part of the body, a developing disease, lifestyle or any number of reasons.

We can broadly classify non-structural scoliosis into four different types, including:

→ Compensatory – The chief underlying cause of non-structural, compensatory scoliosis is due to a leg-length discrepancy. This form of scoliosis will occur as a result of your body's efforts to adjust to such discrepancies.

→ Sciatic – When your body tries to control and avoid the pain caused by a sciatic nerve issue by tilting to one side, you may gradually develop this form of scoliosis.

What is a Sciatic Nerve?

The sciatic nerve is the longest and largest nerve in the body. Pain along this nerve can cause severe discomfort and numbness or tingling, along the lower limb..

→ Inflammatory – This form of non-structural scoliosis is due to inflammatory conditions such as appendicitis or muscle spasms.

→ Postural – Improper postural habits observed over a long period of time can lead to this form of non-structural scoliosis, which might be corrected with specific management methods.

Differing from structural scoliosis, functional or non-structural scoliosis can be reversible. In other words, the spine can return to its normal alignment if the aggravating factors are able to be controlled.

Based on Site of the Curve

Apart from all the above criteria, the location and type of the curve can also be used to classify scoliosis. We can differentiate between three types of scoliosis based on these criteria.

1. Thoracic scoliosis: This type of scoliosis is seen when the thoracic region of the spine is curved. The curve will typically be seen towards the right side, somewhere in the middle of the back.

2. Lumbar scoliosis: As the name suggests, the majority of the scoliosis is concentrated in the lumbar or the lower back region. Meanwhile, the curvature is seen more on the left side of the spine.

3. Thoracolumbar scoliosis: In this case, the curve is predominant at the point where the thoracic and the lumbar spine meet.

Charts and Diagrams

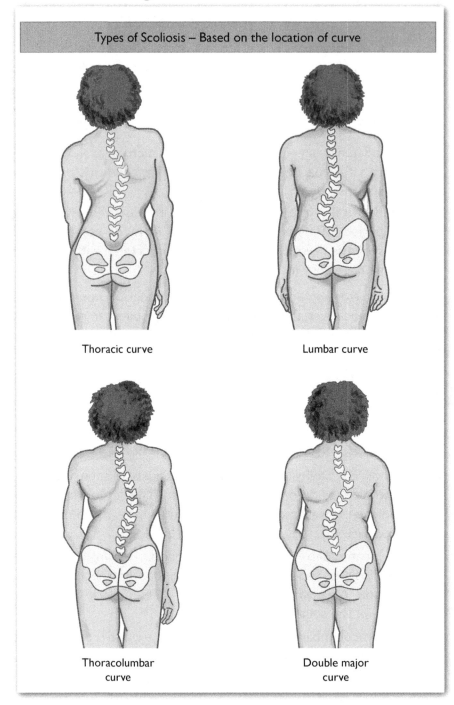

Thoracic curve

Lumbar curve

Thoracolumbar
curve

Double major
curve

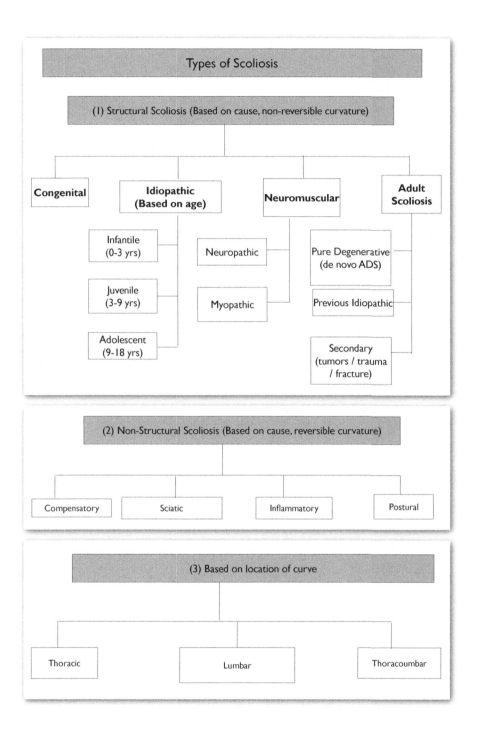

CHAPTER 4

Recognizing the Disease

In this chapter, we will talk about the most important signs of scoliosis, both common and rare.. We will teach you how to recognize the initial changes in physical appearance that will occur in scoliosis in children, as well as adults. We will also discuss the pain that is associated with scoliosis and the various forms it can take. You will read more about less common but critical signs such as shortness of breath and chest pain which indicate the need for immediate medical treatment.

Physical Abnormalities

Imbalance in physical appearance is the key sign of scoliosis, defined by an obvious change in posture and a curvature in the spine, both in children as well as adults. Experts call these changes, abnormal direction of the curve of the spine or imbalances that have a potential to have an impact on every part and system of our body.

Knowing how scoliosis can affect and change our body is the first step in recognizing the disease. Put simply, this spinal deformity has the potential to:

→ Change how you look
→ Change how you perform daily activities including sitting, standing and walking

→ Change the entire way you live life

In the sections that follow, we will give you a detailed and easy-to-follow guide you can use to recognize the condition, from its physical signs, characteristics of pain and other less common symptoms like shortness of breath and chest pain. Further in later chapters, you will also be able to analyze how bad your symptoms are and at what stage you should actually consider going in for a surgical correction of your deformity.

While the initial signs of scoliosis might be somewhat common across all age-groups, there are some skeletal changes that are more prominent and easy to spot in young children, adolescents and teenagers. Here, we've furnished a list of the top 10 signs of changes in physical appearance, specifically in the skeletal system, that might occur in the younger age group.

The Top 10 Changes in Scoliosis

1. One shoulder blade will be higher and more prominent than the other
2. Shoulders might look rounded
3. One hip may be more prominent than the other
4. One arm may appear longer than the other
5. One leg may appear shorter than the other, especially when lying down
6. Clothes may hang unevenly
7. Chest may appear sunken
8. Asymmetrical waistline
9. Rib cage may be more prominent on one side
10. Abnormal abdominal creases

Important notes

The entire body is connected directly or indirectly by the spine. Therefore, a change in the spine with alter the alignment throughout body and cause abnormalities, injuries, decreased function and pain in any joint.

Here, let us look at some of the above mentioned symptoms more closely:

→ Why do the shoulders appear uneven?

→ The shoulder on the convex side of the curve of the spine appears higher as compared to that on the concave side.

→ Why does the whole body look misaligned?

→ In the skeletal structure of a normal, healthy adult, the top of the skull should be in perfect alignment with the centre of the pelvic bone. This does not happen in scoliosis secondary to the lateral curve of the spine and hence creates misalignment throughout the body.

→ Why is one of the hips raised?

→ This especially happens when the curvature is prominent in the lower back and actually constitutes one of the most prominent physical signs of scoliosis.

→ What happens to the skin over the backbone?

→ A tell-tale sign of conditions like neurofibromatosis may be present on the skin over the backbone, with a small patch of skin turning red, scaly or more hairy than usual.

Did you know...

Since any physical changes brought on by scoliosis are first usually noticed by a family member or a friend, to mistake scoliosis with a muscle problem is a very common trap. Consult your physician the moment you notice any relevant symptom of scoliosis, failing which, you may experience quick and drastic deterioration of your condition!

In the following chapters, you will read more about specific tests that are performed to detect the presence of scoliosis, especially based on the changes that occur in the skeletal structure.

In addition to the above, in babies and newborns, scoliosis is specifically recognized as:

→ A visible bulge on one side of the baby's back or chest
→ The baby might lie down on one of its sides

Important to know...

Most often, early signs of scoliosis can go unnoticed in children, only to become more visible when the curvature worsens at a later stage. Hence, it is important to pay attention to any minor signs detected during a routine school physical screening and seek further medical advice. Early detection can actually help medical providers to halt or slow the progression the curvature.

Initial Signs in Adults

In addition to the above mentioned signs observed in the younger age group, there are also certain physical changes and abnormalities that appear in adults. These appear due to the bony spine compressing the nervous system. In this case, you might notice some of these symptoms:

- Urinary incontinence or loss of bladder control
- Bowel incontinence or loss of bowel control
- Weakness or numbness in legs, feet or toes
- In men, erectile dysfunction or an inability to maintain an erection

Some other symptoms that may be exclusive to adults will include:

- In women, unequal breast size
- Difference in rib cage height between sides

Visible difference in the texture or appearance of the skin, especially on the sides of the spine

All About Pain

Before we go any further into the relationship of scoliosis with pain, let us spend a few moments to understand what pain is.

You can feel pain, but is it just a sensation of discomfort? Is it simply something you can't tolerate or is it a sign of another abnormality in your body, or even a sign of a disease or injury that may occur in the near future?

Experts define pain as an unpleasant feeling, conveyed to the brain by sensory neurons. Besides being a mere sensation, it also includes the following three aspects:

→ Physical awareness of pain
→ Perception of the discomfort
→ Subjective/individualized perception of the discomfort

Scoliosis and Pain

As long as the curvature of your spine is in its initial stages, most times, scoliosis will not be painful, whatever the age of the patient might be. This is exactly the reason why scoliosis can go unnoticed in the beginning, until the point physical signs begin to appear, as explained above. However, in some cases, scoliosis also causes pain to set in, either due to abnormal muscle contractions or spasms or an ancillary problem created by the curvature.

Where does the pain of scoliosis come from? Is it from a bone or a muscle? Is it neuropathic pain or is it referred pain? It is all about the muscles, say the experts. Put simply, the pain of scoliosis comes from the muscles that surround the damaged area, which are constantly contracting and are never allowed to relax. These muscles, due to being in a contracted state, month after month, turn sore and finally lead to scoliotic pain.

Characteristics of pain

Back pain and constant muscle pain, usually appear as one of the first and most common signs of scoliosis. These types of pain may have one or more of the following characteristics:

- Pain is worse when you are sitting/standing and improves when you lie down on your back or side
- Constant pain, regardless of the position
- Pain that travels from your spine into the hip, legs or sometimes your arms, either while standing or walking

In specific conditions such as degenerative scoliosis, the accompanying pain has its own typical characteristics. Pain that comes along with degenerative scoliosis will generally have one or more of the following traits:

→ It develops over time and begins in association with physical activity.

→ It is worst in the morning and slowly reduces with activity.

→ It worsens during the latter half of the day.

→ It is more painful to stand or walk than to sit due to the pressure being exerted on the facet joints on the spine.

→ It is painful to stand or walk, with the legs being especially painful.

Interestingly, there is often a debate on whether scoliosis pain exists for real or is it just a discomfort perceived by the sufferer as ongoing or chronic pain? Well, research points out that the pain of scoliosis ranks approximately at an 8 on a 10 point pain scale, while a toothache usually measures up to a 6 at its worst stage.

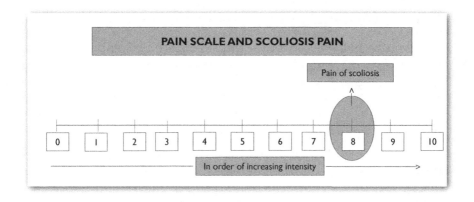

PAIN SCALE AND SCOLIOSIS PAIN

Pain of scoliosis

0   1   2   3   4   5   6   7   8   9   10

In order of increasing intensity

Forms of pain

All the pain felt by a patient with scoliosis is broadly discussed under two headings by experts. This covers the entire spectrum of the physical aspects of the disorder along with any related psychological factors.

Symptomatic pain

This form of pain is related to the causes that actually affect the spine. The pain will emanate from any of the components of the spine, muscles of the back or even from some internal organs. This pain might occur due to factors such as bone-to-bone contact, nerve compression or organ compression.

Psychosomatic pain

In some cases, a patient suspected of having scoliosis has a built-in fear of the diagnosis being positive. Owing to this fear, his/her brain begins to create painful symptoms merely on the basis of apprehension, while no actual biological cause for the pain is present. This type of pain emanates from and is propagated by the mind as opposed to from the body such as with symptomatic pain. Pain arising from such psycho-emotional causes is likely to respond much better to knowledge and behavioral therapy than to actual clinical treatment.

Pain and location of the scoliotic curve

How much pain a patient with scoliosis will experience also depends on a set of other factors, such as age and, most importantly, the location of the curve.

For instance, in most of the cases, thoracic or upper back curves do not cause much pain, even if it is a 90-100° curve. On the other hand, lumbar curves that of more than 45° are likely to cause pain most of the time.

Abnormal Pulmonary Function and Chest Pain

There are a number of issues that can impact any cluster of organs and their related functions throughout the body, including breathing passages, heart, lungs or blood vessels. Just for reference purposes, while shortness of breath is clinically referred to as dyspnea, hyperventilation is the term experts give to excessive, rapid breathing.

When you have a thoracic scoliosis of about 70° or more, the abnormal curvature can actually begin to impinge on the space that holds your heart and lungs. If this process continues over a period of time, then actual lung and heart capacity can be compromised, leading to shortness of breath and chest pain.

Research shows that when left untreated, as many as 0.2 to 0.5% cases of scoliosis can eventually reach a point where space becomes restricted within the ribcage, impacting optimal heart and lung function, At this stage, your lungs will be forced to work much harder than required, which will present itself in the form of shortness of breath and even chest pain.

Shortness of breath is primarily a stage 3 symptom of scoliosis (see table below). This implies that it will not develop immediately as the spine curvature sets in. Instead, it will begin to develop only when the curve worsens, often affecting your chest or lungs. When your spinal curvature worsens, it actually causes your rib cage to twist. This movement can then put major pressure on your heart and lungs, leading to a prominent shortness of breath or dyspnea. In other words, owing to this phenomenon, your chest is actually losing space, inhibiting your ability to breathe freely.

Did you know...

On average, a normal, healthy adult weighing around 70 kilograms (150 pounds) breathes at a rate of 14 breaths per minute at rest.

There has been research that shows another linked mechanism between the location of the curve and shortness of breath. For instance, for patients with a 50 degree or greater thoracic curvature, the risks of shortness of breath and even death are relatively higher.

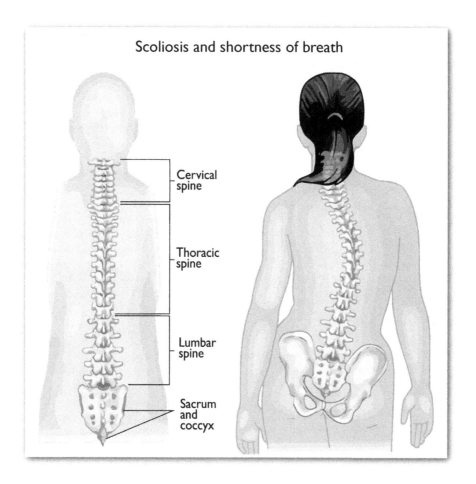

Scoliosis and shortness of breath

Cervical spine

Thoracic spine

Lumbar spine

Sacrum and coccyx

At this point, it also helps to know that shortness of breath and chest pain can even present themselves as a symptom or outfall of scoliosis years after the initial diagnosis has been made. Youngsters who were diagnosed with scoliosis earlier in life have often reported sudden shortness of breath and chest pain 10-12 years later, after assuming the curvature had halted its progression.

SIGNS OF SCOLIOSIS – 3 STAGES

Stage 1	Initial Onset		
	Mild change in posture	Immediately visible	No
	Spinal curvature	Causes pain	No
	Imbalance/misalignment in the body	Can be detected	Yes, on screening
		Medical attention	Can be controlled

Stage 2	Progression		
	Apparent tilt in posture	Immediately visible	Sometimes
	Prominent spinal curvature	Causes pain	Onset of mild pain
	Progression of imbalance/misalignment in body	Can be detected	Yes, on screening
		Medical attention	Can be controlled

Stage 3	Acute/Severe curvature		
	Drastic change in appearance	Immediately visible	Yes
	Onset of physical disability	Causes pain	Chronic, constant
	Shortness of breath, chest pain	Can be detected	Yes
		Medical attention	Bracing, physical therapy, surgery

CHAPTER 5
Detection and Diagnosis

N ow that we know the initial tell-tale signs that might signal the presence of scoliosis, we will move on to the diagnostic tools that are used for screening. We will also talk about the various pros and cons of the concept of screening and discuss various aspects of different screening tools.

Screening – The Process, Aspects, Pros & Cons

Screening is a clinical term given to the group of processes carried out to detect the presence of a disease during a medical check-up. In terms of scoliosis, screening refers to the physical examination done to identify scoliosis in unrecognized cases from the masses.

The key purpose here is to confirm or contradict the assessment procured in the postural analysis and to relate the observed external deformity to the internal severity of the spinal distortion.

The American Commission on Chronic Illness defines the process of screening as, "Presumptive identification of unrecognized disease or defect by the application of tests, examination or other procedures which can be applied rapidly".

Important to know...

The process of diagnosis starts with recognizing the condition from initial physical signs. It then moves onto screening using physical movement tests and eventually goes onto measuring the curve.

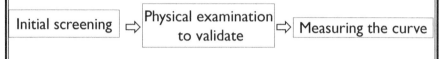

| Initial screening | ⇨ | Physical examination to validate | ⇨ | Measuring the curve |

While we've discussed the first part in the previous chapter, this chapter will focus on screening, while the next will talk about actually measuring the curve.

Screening for Scoliosis – The Purpose

Screening in scoliosis is primarily based on physical movements; it is most frequently carried out in schools, since they are the sites that are most likely to provide access to the majority of children.

At this point, it's helpful to ponder why such a screening is important for scoliosis. Experts point out that physical evaluation for a suspected case of scoliosis is primarily meant to exclude any other possible causes of spinal deformity. Basically a diagnosis of exclusion, the initial screening will help the clinician to rule out any other secondary causes of the curvature and associated symptoms. As an example, a few of these secondary causes which need to be ruled out through the screening process will include:

- Inherited disorders of the connective tissue, such as Ehlers-Danlos Syndrome and Marfan Syndrome
- Neurologic Disorders such as Syringomyelia, Tethered cord syndrome and cerebral palsy
- Musculoskeletal issues such as developmental dysplasia of the hip, Klippel-Feil syndrome and the like

Screening in Schools – The Aspects

A number of states in the U.S. have set guidelines for mandatory or voluntary school-based screening programs for scoliosis. In the sections below, we will discuss in detail the various aspects of the screening process and also highlight key points of research. In addition, we will also discuss the various aspects of efficiency, pros and cons and the need for such screening programs, especially in schools.

It is an established fact that the incidence of Adolescent Idiopathic Scoliosis (AIS) is much higher than the other forms of the disorder. This further reflects on the need to diagnose and screen school children when they are in the adolescent age group.

Historically, school children have normally been screened for scoliosis based on different age groups, including:

→ First Scenario - 10-15 years of age, boys and girls
→ Second Scenario - 10-12 years in girls and 13-14 years in boys

Here, we've discussed each one of these a bit more closely.

First Scenario

When the children are screened in the age group of 10-15 years, it makes it possible to detect spinal curves at a very early stage. This further saves the children from many health complications that might occur. However, this process often proves to be expensive and very time consuming.

Second Scenario

Screening in such a selective manner will help the healthcare team to concentrate only on the high-risk children. However, the possibility of missing out on probable cases of scoliosis also remains high.

Meanwhile, in situations where no screenings are done, there is an enormous savings of time and resources. However, this can prove to be costlier in the longer run in terms of further health complications and progression of the curve.

Interesting....

With such rampant and widespread screening programs, isn't it still a wonder that so many children go undiagnosed? Well, experts attribute it to the style of clothing and fashion. With so many youngsters wearing such loose and fashionable clothing, especially in their teenage years, a curvature that is progressing slowly is most likely to go unnoticed!

A Discussion

In the past few decades, screening for scoliosis has become almost an integral part of routine medical check-ups in schools, especially to check for the presence of adolescent idiopathic scoliosis. In the previous chapters, we showed you how important it is to have an early detection of scoliosis in this age group to avoid further progression of the curve.

Periodic research reports and guidelines issued by various government agencies have supported the need for regular screening for scoliosis and reporting of curvatures for further treatment. The American Academy of Orthopedic Surgeons recommends regular screening for girls in the age group 11 to 13 years and for boys in the age group 13 to 14 years. Similarly, a directive issued by the U.S. Preventive Services Task Force in 1996 instructs clinicians to remain alert for the presence of prominent curvatures in adolescents during their routine medical screening.

However, there is another downside to such a high-alert and enormous stress being laid on regular screening. This aspect presents itself in the form of over-referrals coming in from schools, due to the detection of insignificant curves in adolescents. However, there are a series of studies which show that over-referrals occur even in cases where a number of diagnostic tools are used, thereby implying that physical screening alone is not accountable for such surplus cases of referrals.

Likewise, contradictions also exist amongst such directions and guidelines. For instance, the American Academy of Pediatrics stipulates that the Adam's Forward Bend Test be performed during normal health check-up visits at ages 10, 12, 14 and 16. However, as per the contradictions we just mentioned, these recommendations are not supported by any existing evidence.

Regular examinations of children at vulnerable ages are also advised outside the school settings. The American Academy of Pediatrics suggests yearly well-child visits from ages 10 through 18, both for boys as well as girls. This well-child visit is ideally expected to include a physical examination involving a routine inspection of the back, with special attention being given to any abnormal curvature.

Physical Examination

In the previous chapter, we read how the initial signs of scoliosis can signal the presence of a spinal deformity. An obvious change in the posture or apparent imbalance in the skeletal structure will further point towards the need of a more systematic and result-oriented method of screening for scoliosis.

Towards this end, a detailed physical examination, along with neurological testing is the first step to be taken after the postural analysis has been done. When performed in suspected cases of scoliosis, a physical examination is likely to look for the following:

- Apparent imbalance issues
- Movement limitation
- Muscle weakness
- Pain or discomfort
- Extremity reflexes
- Sensation issues

For such physical examinations, the clinician will assess you from all three key views, including the:

- Anterior view

- Posterior view
- Lateral view

The examination should be done with complete exposure (to an acceptable limit) and will note the presence of any of the below:

→ A visible spinal asymmetry

→ Asymmetry in shoulder height, waist level, thoracic cavity, ribcage and levels of nipples

→ Signs of truncal decompensation which might occur as a result of the trunk not being centered on the pelvis

→ Palpation for asymmetric paraspinal prominences, which implies that the examiner would try and locate any abnormal levels or structures within the muscles that run along or parallel to the spine

→ Apparent leg-length discrepancy

In addition, your clinician might also ask you to walk on your toes and heels, which will reveal existing signs of even a slight motor weakness in the lower extremity muscle groups.

Further, any pattern of physical examination for scoliosis should ideally include an assessment of the Tanner stage. This is critical owing to the fact that real curve progression usually occurs during Tanner stage 2 or 3.

What is Tanner Stage?

The Tanner stages or the Tanner scale is a scale of physical development in children, adolescents and adults (see image below). It defines the physical measurements of development based on external primary and secondary sex characteristics, such as development of pubic hair, size of breast and genitalia, etc.

In addition to the above, you are also likely to be checked for neurological disorders which will include being tested for reflexes, muscle function and nerve sensation.

Following the above, you will then be subjected to the Adam's Forward Bend Test and be measured using a scoliometer for further validation and quantification of the results.

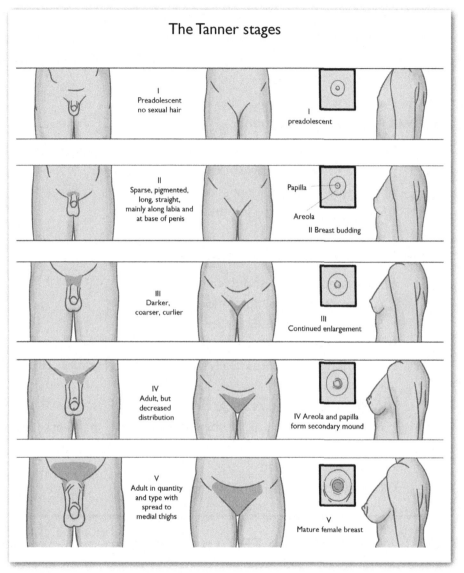

The Tanner stages

I
Preadolescent
no sexual hair

I
preadolescent

II
Sparse, pigmented, long, straight, mainly along labia and at base of penis

Papilla

Areola

II Breast budding

III
Darker, coarser, curlier

III
Continued enlargement

IV
Adult, but decreased distribution

IV Areola and papilla form secondary mound

V
Adult in quantity and type with spread to medial thighs

V
Mature female breast

Adam's Forward Bend Test (FBT)

The Adam's Forward Bend Test is usually the first proper diagnostic technique performed after any initial signs of scoliosis are noticed from the posture or even a slight visible curve. It is also the most common screening test used in schools and by pediatricians to look for the presence of a spinal curve, especially after an initial postural analysis shows probability of scoliosis.

Usually conducted during the middle school years, the Adam Forward Bend Test is meant to coincide with the rapid adolescent growth phase. It is based on the examination of surface topography of your back.

How the test happens

1. Bend the trunk forward at 90°, with both the arms dangling.
2. Feet are to be kept together, with knees locked.
3. The whole of the patient's back needs to be exposed, the spine being fully visible for the examination.

What will the examiner look for?

→ Asymmetry in the shoulder height

→ Asymmetry in the hip-to-floor distance

→ Unequal arm-to-floor length

→ An imbalance in the level of ribcages, commonly referred to as a 'rib hump', basically caused by the rotation of the vertebra

→ Asymmetry of the scapular prominence

→ Prominent unilateral lumbar (lower back) paravertebral muscles

→ Non-centered head

→ Overall lateral deviation of the spine

What is the FBT to the layman...

For a layperson, the FBT is an easy-to-use, convenient and quick method to look for concrete signs of scoliosis. While it will not measure the degree of curvature, it will give you a partially confirmed diagnosis of scoliosis if the listed signs are observed during the test.

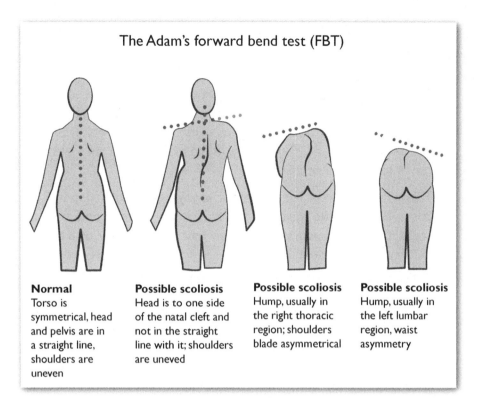

The Adam's forward bend test (FBT)

Normal
Torso is symmetrical, head and pelvis are in a straight line, shoulders are uneven

Possible scoliosis
Head is to one side of the natal cleft and not in the straight line with it; shoulders are uneved

Possible scoliosis
Hump, usually in the right thoracic region; shoulders blade asymmetrical

Possible scoliosis
Hump, usually in the left lumbar region, waist asymmetry

What Research Says

Controversies and debates abound over the use and efficiency of the Adam's Forward Bend Test. The most typical points of debate are:

- Does this test accurately rule out other conditions being present?
- Does it take into account all other possible abnormalities as well, in addition to an apparent curvature or tilt in posture?
- Does the test take into account a curve that might exist in all parts of the spine, especially lumbar and cervical spine?

Let us look at these controversial aspects in a detailed manner.

Generally viewed as the next step in a simple postural analysis, the Adam's Forward Bend Test is mostly regarded as being quite accurate as well as sufficiently reliable.

Moreover, it is also considered to be one of the easiest screening tools to use, one that even a parent or teacher can perform on the child without the assistance of any devices or instruments. Research also shows FBT to be a relatively inexpensive, quick and easy-to-perform form of screening.

Historically, the FBT has almost always enjoyed a dependable status as a diagnostic measure for scoliosis. A study conducted by Karachalios et al. reports the FBT to have a sensitivity of 84% and specificity of 93%. Meanwhile, the first argument that is presented against the use of the Adam's Forward Bend Test is that it misses out on the correct diagnosis for around 15% of the cases. It might also not take into account a curve in the lumbar spine or the lower back. Considering the fact that it is a fairly common location for the curve, this often proves to be a costly misdiagnosis. Moreover, it has also been reported that the Adam's test might not be able to detect a curve in obese children.

Using the Scoliometer

Once positive signs have been noted on the Adam's Forward Bend Test, a practitioner may use a scoliometer to achieve two objectives:

→ To validate the results found by the FBT and quantify the right and left-sided asymmetries found by the test
→ To measure the actual degree of curvature

A scoliometer is basically a device that is used for further screening of scoliosis after the FBT. It quantifies the measure of trunk rotation.

Also known as an inclinometer, it is a non-invasive and easy-to-use, hand held device which measures the degree of trunk asymmetry.

A result that gives a reading of more than 5 degrees at any paraspinal prominence (lumbar/thoracic) is generally considered as being positive

How does it Work?

The scoliometer, basically a version of a carpenter's level, gives you a reading known as the Angle of Trunk Rotation (ATR). A clinician, using the scoliometer, will generally follow the below steps:

→ The child bends over, parallel to the floor, with the shoulders level with the hips, hands almost touching the toes.

→ The examiner adjusts the height of the student's bending position to a level where the deformity is most pronounced, which will vary in individually. This deformity is often referred to as a 'hump' in the thoracic or lumbar area.

→ The examiner keeps his eyes focused at the same level as the back.

→ Gently, he lays the scoliometer across the deformity at a right angle to the body, measuring the reading corresponding to the highest point of the deformity (apex), first over the mid-thoracic area and then over the mid-lumbar area.

→ The entire process of measurement is repeated twice, with the patient being asked to return to a standing position between the repetitions.

Numbered mark on the instrument = Difference in angular degrees in height between each side of the thorax, owing to apical trunk rotation= ATR

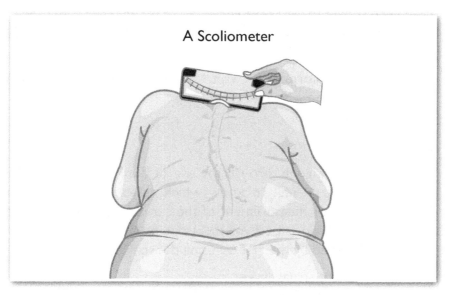

A Scoliometer

Interestingly, there is a possibility of scoliosis which is undetected using the Adam's Forward Bending Test being diagnosed later using a scoliometer. A study examined 954 sixth grade students and found 136 to show abnormal reading when using a scoliometer, though they had earlier appeared normal with the FBT screening. Similar research also shows the possibility of a correlation between the ATR and the Cobb Angle, which can be used to document the degree of progression of the curve. However, there is also evidence to prove that though the scoliometer has a higher rate of accurate diagnosis, it cannot be used as an alternative to axial CT scans for measurement of the vertebral rotation.

Another trait that probably supports the use of the scoliometer is that, apart from being convenient to use, it also provides guidelines for referrals, thereby standardizing the entire process of screening for scoliosis.

For this purpose, you might find the use of the following mobile applications like ScolioTrack and Scoliometer Apps convenient and helpful for home monitoring. Created by myself with a team of programmers, these have been especially designed to bring the functions of a scoliometer onto either an iPhone, iPad and Android device. While the Scoliometer App helps in measuring the curve, the ScolioTrack App also has other functions like such as graphing and saving the photo records of the users back. In fact, such applications have been shown to be a reliable and accurate enough to be used in a clinical setting and as one of the safest and most innovative ways to track one's scoliosis condition.

For more information visit: www.HIYH.info for video demonstrations and where to download.

Referrals

Once you have gone through the use of the FBT as well as the scoliometer, it is helpful to know which cases will qualify for a further referral for measurement of the curve. You will be advised to consult with a specialist if you meet one or more of the criterion below, as observed by the FBT or using the scoliometer:

→ Apparent spinal curve

- → One of the sides of the upper or lower back being prominent in the FBT
- → Scoliometer reading of 7 degrees or more at any level of the spine
- → Round back that you can cannot flatten, even during hyperextension of the head and neck
- → Other relevant signs such as uneven shoulders, hips or waist creases

Genetic Testing

Genetic testing is widely seen as the first step towards the use of prognostic technology as a method to manage scoliosis as compared to measures such as bracing and surgery.

Medical research has now made immense progress and has offered the world of diagnosis, concrete genetic markers that are able to predict a child's genetic pre-disposition for developing a strong spinal curvature.

In the year 2009, there were reports of scientists and experts identifying specific genetic markers that can predict the state of the scoliosic curve in a particular patient after some years. Through a series of genome-based studies, the geneticists working on the subject have pin-pointed single nucleotide polymorphism markers in the DNA which are likely to be significantly related to the development and progression of adolescent idiopathic scoliosis (AIS).

Interestingly, using this form of genetic testing to predict the progression level of scoliosis holds great potential to transform the entire methodology of the treatment of scoliosis. Amongst all others, it is likely to have a large impact on the extent to which bracing and even surgery is carried out for scoliosis patients.

Point to remember

While research does indicate that your genes might make you vulnerable, yet there is no concrete evidence of a direct correlation. Hence, having been diagnosed with these genetic markers might not essential mean that you are sure to have scoliosis.

What does this mean for the layman?

For a layperson, the breakthrough in the genetic testing for scoliosis makes it easy for the curve to be detected. However, we need to note that this genetic testing is not used as a basic screening tool to diagnose the presence of scoliosis. Instead, once it has been confirmed that a child has scoliosis, specific DNA markers are used to predict the extent to which this curve can progress in the future.

Scoliscore™ – The Breakthrough

Now that we know the basics of genetic testing for scoliosis, let us talk about the specific test in more detail.

A genetic test, known as the Scoliscore™, a DNA-based molecular test has been developed by Axial Bio-Tech and claims to be able to predict whether a particular child is vulnerable to develop scoliosis and to what extent. Apart from providing psychological relief for scoliosis patients, the test is also seen as a major money-saver, as it is likely to save on the cost of treatment and unnecessary clinic visits as well. However, there is a downside to this as well. Experts point out that, as of now, the test might be useful only for Caucasian adolescents, in the age group of 9 to 13 years, having a curve of 25 degrees or less. As it might be obvious, the test cannot be applied to patients with infantile or juvenile idiopathic scoliosis.

Scoliscore™ can be used by young boys and girls between the age group 9 to 14 with spinal curves measuring 10-25 degrees. Following the test, patients with scoliosis are categorized into three main groups:

- Those with a low risk of progression
- Those with a moderate risk of progression
- Those with a curve that is highly likely to progress beyond 45 degrees

To conduct the test, the patient's saliva is taken as a sample, which is then tested against the listed DNA markers. Once obtained, the results are ranked between 1 to 200, with 50 being identified as the point of low risk and 180-200 being considered high risk, increasing their possibility of surgery in the future.

Imaging Tests

Imaging tests are used to detect the extent of curvature in an individual being screened for scoliosis.

Your healthcare provider might suggest a different form of image testing in various situations. For instance, options such as an X- ray are suggested to gauge the extent of the curve once you are found to be positive on the basic screening tests such as the FBT or the scoliometer.

Similarly, an MRI scan will be suggested to patients likely to be having left thoracic curves, unusual pain, abnormal neurological symptoms or other signs that might signal the affection of the spinal cord due to the presence of tumors, spondylolisthesis or syringomyelia.

Some common forms of such tests include:

- X-rays
- CT scan
- MRI
- Myelography
- Discograms

Read further as we give you a brief insight into some of the most important tests.

X-rays

Once the child has been initially screened and found to be a likely case for scoliosis, he will then be referred for an x-ray, which remains the most economical and common imaging test used. Basically a painless and non-invasive imaging test, an x-ray imaging constitutes absorption of electromagnetic radiation on a photographic film after being passed through the body. Having a relatively shorter wavelength of less than 100 angstroms, an x-ray has the ability to penetrate solid masses of varying thicknesses. These images are then used to diagnose and identify the curve and its extent.

A typical x-ray of scoliosis

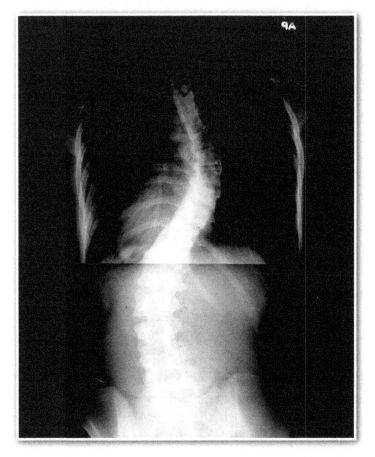

In addition to identifying the degree as well as the extent of scoliosis, an x-ray will also help in identifying other spinal deformities, such as kyphosis and hyperlordosis. In adolescents, an x-ray also helps in determining the skeletal maturity which tells the doctor a lot about how much the curve is likely to progress.

How is it done?

For scoliosis, you will be made to stand straight, while an x-ray machine is set just in front of you. You will be asked to stay still as the x-ray image is being taken. Using low doses of electromagnetic energy with short wavelengths, the machine takes the images which are then analyzed.

Magnetic Resonance Imaging (MRI)

An advanced imaging test, an MRI is usually not suggested for an initial diagnosis, it is performed after the initial x-ray has been done. For patients with scoliosis, it has the ability to identify spinal cord and brain stem abnormalities.

An MRI in progress

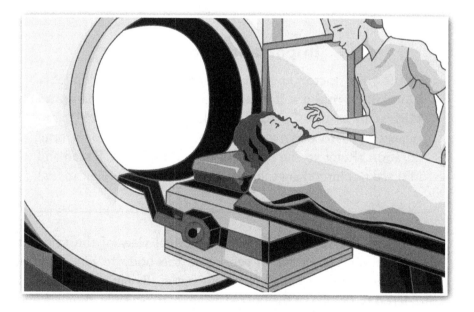

One of the reasons why an MRI scan is often preferred for scoliosis is the fact that, apart from bones, it can also provide clear images of the soft tissues. Hence, any spinal deformity owing to this factor can clearly be recognized and addressed suitably.

How is it done?

In an MRI scan, you will be instructed to lie down on a narrow table, which is then made to pass through a tunnel-like structure. Using magnetic waves, the machine takes images of the spine which are then clinically examined. Depending upon the level of structures to be scanned, an MRI scan is likely to take anywhere between 20 to 90 minutes.

Computed Axial Tomography Scan

Also known as a CT Scan, this imaging test is clinically referred to as the computed axial tomography scan and uses a computer to produce a detailed, 3-dimensional view of the body structures. It basically combines x-rays with computer technology to offer a much more reliable and detailed analysis for scoliosis.

Important to know...

Let your doctor know if you suffer from claustrophobia. **You might make a better case for a CT scan than an MRI scan** as the CT scan is wide open and the MRI scan requires you to endure tunnel-like surroundings for a brief duration. (Refer to the bold line within the box: CT scan and MRI are not interchangeable, both have their own indications)

Since the CT scan gives a cross-sectional view of the spine, it will enable your physician to see inside the body to pinpoint the presence and extent of any spinal deformities. By far, the CT scan is considered to be one of the best imaging tests available, having a fine ability to produce descriptive images of the bone.

How is it done?

You will be instructed to lie on a table which will then move slowly through the CT scanner, which is a large donut-shaped machine. The process produces three-dimensional images of the spine using thin x-ray beams which are then used for analysis.

Pros and cons of various imaging tests

	PROS	CONS
X-rays	Economical, can be done quickly, less exposure to radiation	Cannot detect soft tissue and spinal cord changes
MRI SCAN	Gives detailed images of bones and soft tissues, including spinal cord	Expensive, difficult for claustrophobic patients
CAT SCAN	Can be combined with other tests such as myelograms and discograms to give accurate results, less exposure to radiation, can be done for claustrophobic patients	Might be less descriptive than an MRI scan at times, not advisable for expecting mothers

Other Tests

A) BLOOD TESTS

Though blood tests for scoliosis might still be in their infancy and hence quite uncommon, they do exist and definitely form an ancillary option. To perform a typical blood test for scoliosis, a blood sample, approximately to the tune of 10 ml is taken from which blood cells are obtained.

The basic logic of the blood test lies in the way our cells respond to melatonin. Research has shown that in individuals diagnosed with idiopathic scoliosis, the pattern in which melatonin signals are transmitted is quite different.

B) BIOCHEMICAL TEST

This particular test has a biochemical base, wherein there is a blood test done to measure the levels of two proteins in the blood, namely Osteopontin (OPN) and soluble CD44 (sCD44). Research indicates that the level of OPN in the blood is associated with onset of idiopathic scoliosis. In fact, surgical cases (with Cobb angle ≥ 45°) exhibit the highest values as compared to patients of mild scoliosis.

Similarly, sCD44 is a protective molecule that can prevent OPN from triggering scoliosis or spinal deformity progression by binding free OPN. It is for this reason that the surgical cases have the lowest sCD44 values.

Levels of Screening – At a Glance

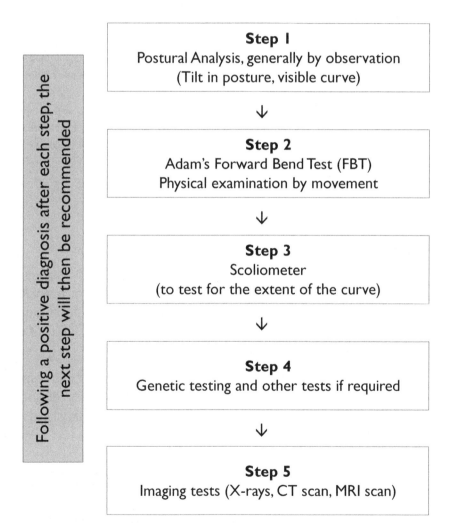

Following a positive diagnosis after each step, the next step will then be recommended

Step 1
Postural Analysis, generally by observation
(Tilt in posture, visible curve)

↓

Step 2
Adam's Forward Bend Test (FBT)
Physical examination by movement

↓

Step 3
Scoliometer
(to test for the extent of the curve)

↓

Step 4
Genetic testing and other tests if required

↓

Step 5
Imaging tests (X-rays, CT scan, MRI scan)

CHAPTER 6
Degree of Severity

You will learn in detail about the single-most important unit of measurement of the curve of scoliosis, which is the degree of the curve. You will learn about the various degrees of scoliosis, how to measure it using the Cobb Method and finally, how to classify the curve. Both the process of measuring as well as classifying the curve are done with the objective of deciding on the treatment modalities to be used.

By now, we know how a spinal curvature begins and makes you notice an apparent tilt in the posture of the person affected, reflected mainly in the level of shoulders and pelvis. You may also start appreciating a change in his or her appearance, and the manner in which they walk, move or sit. Scoliosis is all about how your spine develops a curvature due to various reasons that can be clinically analyzed and identified. A visible imbalance in the physical evaluation then leads to an elaborate pattern of screening and employment of an array of clinical tools along with various forms of imaging. Each of these steps, as we just read in the previous chapter, is meant to provide a greater level of validation to confirm the positive diagnosis of scoliosis.

Once the diagnosis is confirmed, the focus of medical attention then shifts to the accurate and quantifiable measurement and classification of the curve. At this stage, it is the degree of the curve that becomes the epicenter of medical attention. While initially the focus laid on a confirmation or negation of scoliosis through screening, here it shifts to the quantification of the curve. The direction in which the entire treatment plan shall be devised is based upon the result of this measurement of the curve. The fact that early screening, detection and quantification of the curve of scoliosis can largely influence the treatment outcomes further accentuates the critical role of measuring the degree of the curve.

Hence, the sole objective of the process of measuring and classifying the curve is to develop a plan of care and choose from the numerous treatment modalities available.

All About Degrees

Once it has been screened and confirmed to be existent, scoliosis is then all about degrees, classification and progression, thereon…

The entire treatment plan of scoliosis is based on the following three facts:

→ The original cause of the curvature (congenital, idiopathic, trauma, degenerative etc.)
→ Present degree of the curve
→ Scope of progression of the curve (based on various clinical features as well as genetic and other testing)

You can refer to chapters 2 and 3 to learn more about how the cause and origin of the curvature can impact the treatment modalities. The degree of the curve is the single most important factor that will decide the treatment plan. The treatment plan will also be influenced by how much the curve is likely to progress in the future (scope of progression). In the following section, we will explain all about the degree of a curve, along with the ways to measure and quantify the curve.

Before we offer any clinical analysis, it is helpful to know that degree of the curve forms the basis on which the medical community defines scoliosis.

What is the degree of a curve in scoliosis?

In scoliosis, degree is a term given to the unit of measurement that defines the extent of the curvature of your spine. The degree of curvature will identify the stage of your scoliosis, which will give you a clearer indication of the next course of treatment required.

Study groups like The Scoliosis Research Society define scoliosis as a lateral curvature of the spine greater than 10 degrees, as measured on a standing radiograph using the Cobb method. You can read about the Cobb Method in detail in the following sections.

Since scoliosis can range from a mild and negligible curve to a very severe curve of the spine, understanding all about the degree of spinal curvature is important in knowing the exact status of your health.

Measuring the Curve

A number of tools, statistical methods and geometrical techniques are employed to measure the degree to which a curve exists in the spine. X-rays of the spine are taken, onto which these tools are applied to assess the degree. The most critical objective of this procedure is to form a basis for the future treatment modalities used, based on the assessment of the extent to which the curve might progress.

The Cobb Method and the Harrison Posterior Tangent Method are two methods that might be used for the measurement. While the Cobb Method will be used for both, the sagittal as well as coronal deformity, the latter is only used for measuring the sagittal deformity.

In addition to measuring the curvature, there are methods available which use the rotation of the spine as a measurement of the degree of curve. To do this, the pedicles of the vertebra at the apex of the curve are observed to assess how far they are from the midline. The midline is basically a hypothetical vertical line drawn through middle of the vertebral body. Ideally, the two pedicles in a non-rotated vertebra should be at equal distances from the midline. Here, a scale of 0 to 4 will be used to describe the relative proximity of the pedicles to such a midline.

The Cobb Method

The Cobb Method remains the universally followed and most widely accepted standardized procedure for measuring the degree of curvature in scoliosis. Named after the orthopedic surgeon who invented it, the Cobb angle is measured by identifying the end vertebrae of the portion of the vertebral column that is curved. A set of straight and perpendicular lines are drawn to measure the angle of the curve. In 1935, Lippman introduced this procedure by drawing perpendiculars to the vertebral body endplate lines to analyze scoliotic curves on anteroposterior radiographs. This was eventually popularized by Cobb by 1984.

Here, we've listed the steps that are followed to measure the Cobb angle.

Steps for Cobb Method

It takes an expert to use the Cobb method to measure how severe your curve is. To use the Cobb method, the following steps will be generally taken.

STEP 1

A full-length standing x-ray of the spine is taken from PA view, which is the posteroanterior view, with the radiation being passed from the back to the front of the body. To have this kind of an X-ray, your doctor will ask you to stand absolutely straight, with your back facing the x-ray machine. The picture will cover your entire back, extending from the top of the neck to your pelvis. In some cases, your doctor might decide to take an AP X-ray as well, which is from the anteroposterior view, i.e. with you facing the X-ray machine.

STEP 2

The end vertebrae of the curve are identified. These are the vertebrae at the start and end of the curve.

STEP 3

Your doctor will then draw two straight lines by hand, on the x-ray film. The first will be above the superior plate of the highest vertebra in the structural curve while the second will be at the bottom of the lowest vertebra.

Step 4

Perpendicular lines will then be drawn to both the lines drawn above. This line will intersect at a particular angle.

Step 5

Your doctor will then measure the degree of this angle, which is the actual reading by the Cobb Method. The degree measured thus will be called the Cobb angle. It will then be documented in the radiographic report, which will be a concise summary of each of the findings.

The Cobb Angle

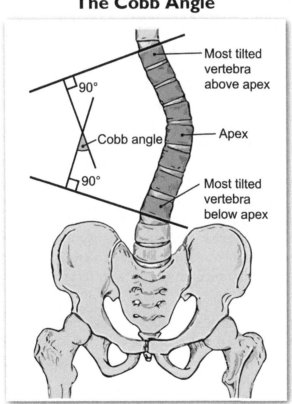

Interpretation

The results of the Cobb Method are usually interpreted as below:

- Less than 20 degrees = Mild scoliosis
- Between 25 and 70 degrees = Moderate scoliosis
- Over 70 degrees = Severe scoliosis
- Over 100 degrees = Very severe scoliosis

Variations and Scope of Errors

Though the Cobb method remains one of the most common methods for measuring the extent of the curve, experts point out that it might not be able to fully represent the three-dimensional aspect of the deformity of the spine. There are studies related to the Cobb method that demonstrate multiple sources of error and subsequent intraobserver variability, which ranges from 2.8 to 10 degrees. Experts warn that every time an X-ray is taken for this purpose, the body positions might vary slightly. Hence, it is important to keep a 3 to 5 degree margin of error when using the Cobb method. According to the Scoliosis Research Society (SRS), the differences in measurement by a particular orthopedic surgeon of the same X-ray over time (intraobserver difference) might go up to 5 degrees, while the differences in measurement between two orthopedic surgeons (interobserver difference) might vary up to as much as 10 degrees, as explained below.

As suggested, there are various other factors that govern the range of variability .i.e. the scope of error or how much reading the same patient might give when the curve is measured by the Cobb method repeatedly:

- By the same observer many times
- By different observers for the same patient

There is already sufficient research to show that factors like skeletal immaturity, incomplete ossification and anomalous development of the end-vertebrae can cause a higher amount of variability in the measurement of angles in patients with adolescent idiopathic scoliosis. One such study reported an intraobserver variability of +/-9.6 degrees and an interobserver variability of +/- 11.8 degrees amongst various readings.

The Vertebral Centroid Measurement

Interestingly, recent research also discusses the reliability of the vertebral centroid measurement in measuring the degree of deformity, though further research is needed to validate the same.

We know how the Cobb method measures the vertebral endplates to assess the status of your curve. However, the vertebral surface angle can be difficult to measure due to the variations in the architecture of the endplates. The vertebral centroid measurement of lumbar lordosis (CLL) attempts to address this problem. In this technique, the contours of the L1, L2 and L5 vertebral bodies form the basis for determining the angle of lordosis. This method is seen as an effective approach for measuring the angle of lordosis in the patient·

The Verterbral Centroid Measurement Method

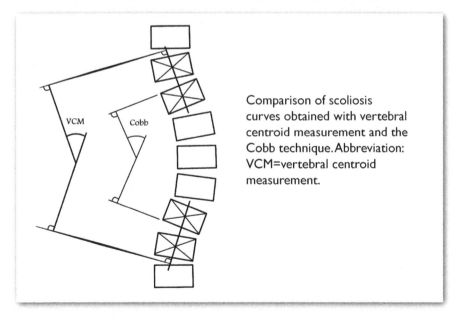

Comparison of scoliosis curves obtained with vertebral centroid measurement and the Cobb technique. Abbreviation: VCM=vertebral centroid measurement.

Classifying the Curve

Once the initial screening, diagnosis and measurement of the curve have been completed, you can prepare for your curve to be classified. A scoliotic curve can be classified based on a number of criterion and in a number of ways.

In this section, we will give you an outline of some of the most commonly used ways that are used by spinal deformity surgeons to classify a scoliotic curve, once the measurement of the curvature is over.

The first and most commonly used way to classify the curve is that based on the degree obtained by the Cobb method. As we mentioned earlier, we can classify the degree of scoliosis into four types:

→ Mild scoliosis: At 20 degrees or less, this is not a serious deformity and might not require more than basic monitoring.

→ Moderate scoliosis: Measured between 25 and 70 degrees, though there is no immediate risk it can cause serious health complications later.

→ Severe scoliosis: When the curvature is over 70 degrees, , restrict your breathing and also deplete your oxygen levels. This basically happens due to the differences in sizes of the hemothorax caused due to the deformity of scoliosis.

→ Very severe scoliosis: Your lungs and heart can undergo remodelling due to shortage of space, if the curve goes beyond 100 degrees.

The Lenke Classification System

The Lenke Classification System basically gives a more complete picture by viewing scoliosis from a multi-dimensional perspective, which allows for more effective planning for curve correction. This method identifies six different primary curve patterns and includes additional factors that modify each of these curves (see image).

Let us have a closer look at how this system works. The physican will take standard radiographs or X-rays of your spine. If X-rays were previously taken when measuring for the degree of deformity using the Cobb method, these films may be used. Your X-rays done in each position are then evaluated. Once this is completed, each of the spinal curves is then classified on the basis of:

→ Region of the location of the curve in the spine
→ Degree of the curve
→ Deformity in the sagittal plane

The Lenke Classification System For Scoliosis

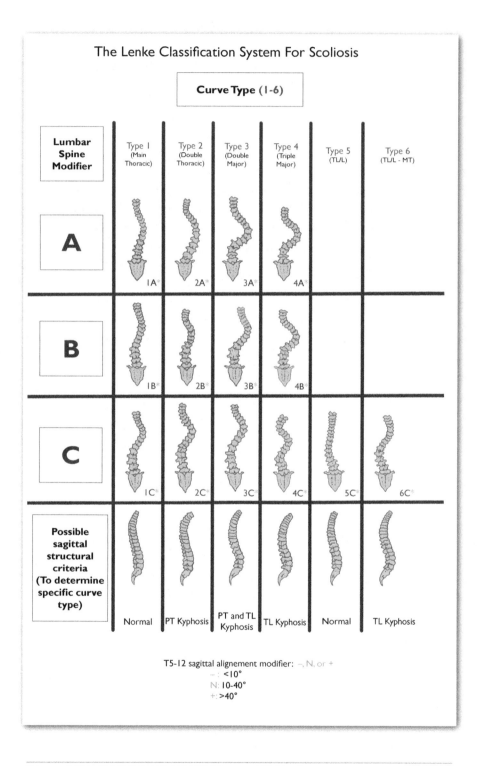

Lumbar Spine Modifier	Type 1 (Main Thoracic)	Type 2 (Double Thoracic)	Type 3 (Double Major)	Type 4 (Triple Major)	Type 5 (TL/L)	Type 6 (TL/L - MT)
A	1A*	2A*	3A*	4A*		
B	1B*	2B*	3B*	4B*		
C	1C*	2C*	3C*	4C*	5C*	6C*
Possible sagittal structural criteria (To determine specific curve type)	Normal	PT Kyphosis	PT and TL Kyphosis	TL Kyphosis	Normal	TL Kyphosis

T5-12 sagittal alignement modifier: −, N, or +
- − : <10°
- N: 10-40°
- + : >40°

Curve Types – Lenke's Classification System

Type	Proximal Thoracic	Main Thoracic	Thoracolumbar / Lumbar	Description
1	Non-Structural	Structural (Major)*	Non-Structural	Main Thoracic (MT)
2	Structural	Structural (Major)*	Non-Structural	Double Thoracic (DT)
3	Non-Structural	Structural (Major)*	Structural	Double Major (DM)
4	Structural	Structural (Major)*	Structural (Major)*	Triple Major (TM)[5]
5	Non-Structural	Non-Structural	Structural (Major)*	Thoracolumbar / Lumbar (TL/L)
6	Non-Structural	Structural	Structural (Major)*	Thoracolumbar / Lumbar-Main Thgoracic (TL/L-MT)

*Major = Largest Cobb measurement, always structural
Minor = All other curves with structural criteria
Type 4 - MT or TL/L can be major curve

STRUCTURAL CRITERIA
(Minor Curves)
Proximal Thoracic - Side Bending Cobb≥25°
- T2-T5 Kyphosis ≥ +20°

Main Thoracic - Side Bending Cobb≥25°
- T10-L2 Kyphosis ≥ +20°

Thoracolumbar / Lumbar - Side Bending Cobb≥25°
- T10-L2 Kyphosis ≥ +20°

LOCATION OF APEX
(SRS Definition)

CURVE	APEX
Thoracic	T2-T11/12 Disc
Thoracolumbar	T12-L1
Thoracolumbar / Lumbar	L1/2 Disc L4

Modifiers

Lumbar Spine Modifier	CSVL to Lumbar Apex			Thoracic Sagittal Profile T5+T12	
A	CSVL between pedicles			- (Hypo)	<10
B	CSVL touches apical body(ies)			N (Normal)	10°-40°
C	CSVL completely medial			+(Hyper)	>40°

Curve Type (1-6)+ Lumbar Spine Modifier (A, B, C)+ Thoracic Sagittal Modifier (–, N, +)
Clasification (e.g. 1B+): ....

The above table gives a detailed listing of the classification of scoliosis based on Lenke's method.

The King classification system

The King classification method, classifies the curve of scoliosis as one of five patterns, which is used to help determine the surgical treatment.

As per the Kings Classification system, idiopathic scoliosis is classified into 5 different types, using the following 2 parameters to define the severity of the curve:

- Readings from the Cobb method
- Readings of the flexibility index obtained from the bending radiographs

The classifications are as follows:

Type 1 – An S-shaped curve that crosses the midline of the lumbar and thoracic curve

Type 2 – An S-shaped curve where the thoracic and lumbar curve cross over the midline

Type 3 – A thoracic curve where the lumbar curve does not cross the midline

Type 4 – A long thoracic curve where the 5th lumbar vertebra is centered over the sacrum. The 4th lumbar vertebra will be angled in the direction of the curve

Type 5 – A thoracic double curve where the 1st thoracic vertebra (Th1) will angle into the convex shape of the upper curve

There are two main disadvantages associated with the use of this method. These include:

- Sagittal profile remains excluded at the time of evaluation
- The system doesn't take into account the double and triple curves

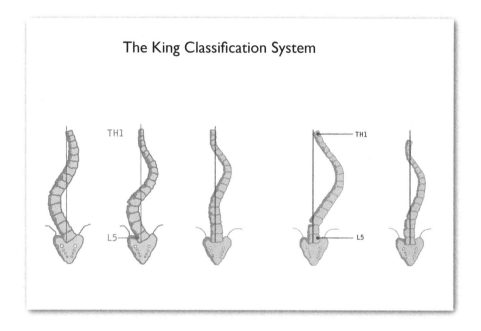

The King Classification System

What Your Doctor Might Not Tell You...

→ That the Cobb Method might be a popular and common method to quantify the deformity, but the curve assessment requires other classification methods too.

→ That the degrees do matter, even if it tells you that no intervention is needed right now except observation.

→ That the degrees can always help you choose a treatment option to halt the curvature, if measured correctly.

→ That errors can exist in the measurement of readings. So, think twice before feeling a sense of panic if your degree turns out to be quite high.

CHAPTER 7
March of the Curve

Once your curve has been measured and classified, you will be just one step away from knowing the exact form of treatment you need for your scoliosis. In this chapter, we will examine the factors that will be considered by your doctor in estimating how far your curvature is likely to progress. We will also discuss the eventual risk factors of having progressive scoliotic curves.

About Curve Progression

Appropriate knowledge of how much your curve is likely to progress is essential, since the curve is likely to progress at a rapid rate until the point when full skeletal maturity is reached at adolescence. Collective research over decades demonstrates that the way a scoliotic curve progresses is strongly correlated to factors like magnitude and pattern of the curve, the patient's age, the Risser sign and, in females, the stage of menarche.

So, when do you say that your curve of scoliosis has progressed? Experts define progression as an increase of 5 degrees or more in the Cobb angle. Here, let us begin by understanding a bit in detail about curve progression.

Important to know

When trying to understand what scoliosis is all about, there is a very thin line between the causes of the curve and the factors responsible for curve progression. While the former talks about the reasons why an individual will develop a curve, the latter talks about the factors that are responsible for any further progression of the curve.

Being screened and diagnosed with scoliosis is merely the first step towards treatment. Before your doctor can begin any forms of treatment, he needs to know exactly how far your curve is likely to deteriorate. Towards the end of this diagnostic period, your doctor will use certain indicators which will give him an estimate of how much your curve is likely to aggravate. Extensive research shows that the factors which define the risk of progression most accurately are the growth potential and the magnitude of the curve, though other factors do exist .

While this estimate is merely an approximate one and cannot predict progression to the fullest accuracy, it gives a tentative view of how the curve might behave in the near future. In the following sections, we will tell you about the 4 main indicators or predictors used by doctors to identify the future of the curve.

Factors – the correlation

Each of the factors we will be discussing is both a factor independently and also in correlation. For instance, though age is a crucial factor indicating whether the curve will progress further, progression will also depend on whether you are male or female and what is the current measurement of your curve. Hence, each of the factors matter individually as well as have a combined impact on deciding how much further the curve will progress.

Curve Progression – The 4 Most important factors

Read on for a detailed explanation and insight into the four main factors or indicators that point towards the possible scope of curve progression.

The Curve – Location and Severity

Research clearly points towards the fact that the initial Cobb angle magnitude is one of the most important indicators in the long-term progression of the curve. The Cobb angle measurement also indicates whether the curve is likely to progress beyond skeletal maturity. There is ample research to show that a Cobb angle of 25° is an important threshold magnitude for long-term curve progression. Hence, an individual detected with scoliosis of greater than 25° is much more likely to experience further progression. In fact, here the factors such as age, gender or skeletal maturity at the time of curve measurement might be less important than the Cobb angle reading.

Let's look at a few important facts here.

Degree/Extent of curve

→ If the curve is less than 30 degrees at the age of skeletal maturity, it is not likely to progress much.

→ If the curve is between 30 to 50 degrees, it is likely to progress at a rate of 10 to 15 degrees across the entire lifespan.

→ If the curve is more than 50 degrees at the age of skeletal maturity, it is likely to progress at a rate of more than 1 degree every year.

→ Curves at 25 to 30 during years of adolescence (13 and 19 years old) are likely to experience rapid progression with further growth.

Location of curve

→ Thoracic curves are likely to progress more than thoracolumbar or lumbar curves.

→ Thoracic curves that are less than 50 degrees at detection are likely to progress at a slower rate than those greater than 50 degrees.

→ A curve with an apex above the T12 vertebrae is likely to progress much more than isolated lumbar curves.

→ Lumbar curves of more than 30 degrees at skeletal maturity will progress much more than the curves of a lesser degree

→ Double curve patterns are more likely to progress than single curve patterns.

Age at the time of diagnosis – Impending skeletal growth

The rule of thumb with scoliosis says the higher the age of the child, the less tendency there is for the curve to progress. For instance, if we compare two young girls (one age 13 years and one older than 15 years) diagnosed with a curve of less than 19 degrees; the curve is likely to progress at a whopping rate of 10% for the younger child, and only at 4% for the elder one.

When an adolescent is diagnosed with scoliosis, the risk of progression remains high if there is a major growth potential still left. There are various research reports which suggest that the rapid skeletal growth during adolescence is one of the major factors that influences the progression of a scoliotic curve.

Spinal column is expected to grow with age, and continue growing till skeletal maturity is fully achieved. Hence, the correlation between age and skeletal maturity is a strong one.

Let us understand the key underlying logic here. The rate at which the curve of a youngster might progress is dependent on the stage of skeletal maturity, which means an adolescent or a youngster who is still skeletally immature is likely to face a higher rate of curve progression than an individual who has already reached skeletal maturity.

What is skeletal maturity?

Skeletal maturity is the term we give to the process of growth in an individual's bone structure or the skeletal system. A person is said to have reached the point of skeletal maturity when his vertebral growth reaches the peak of expected progress. Since the pace of growth and development in human beings is never uniform and always has episodes of acceleration and deceleration, evaluation of skeletal maturity holds major significance in the field of medicine. It is on the basis of such assessment that the optimum methods for treatment can be suitably decided upon.

For the purposes of scoliosis, we can assess the skeletal maturity of an individual using one of the two methods:

→ Risser Method
→ Fusion of the epiphyses of hand and wrist

When an individual has reached the point of skeletal maturity, it is often measured through parameters like the ossification of the iliac apophysis and cessation of vertebral growth. Ossification of iliac apophysis happens when the bone development in the pelvic region is considered to be complete. This step usually indicates that full bone maturity has been achieved in the individual. This ossification during which the human bones are finally formed as solid structures, might not always serve as a sign of full skeletal maturity. Even if reported so by the Risser scale, there is often a possibility that the timing of complete ossification might not be same as that of the cessation of the vertebral growth.

Skeletal Maturity and Ossification

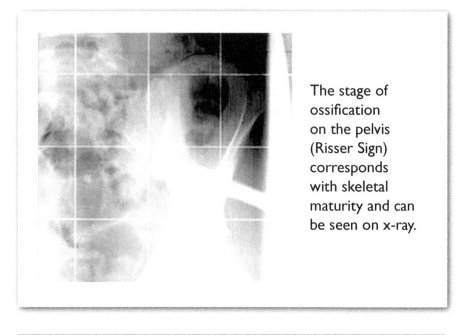

The stage of ossification on the pelvis (Risser Sign) corresponds with skeletal maturity and can be seen on x-ray.

The Risser-Ferguson Grade

The Risser-Ferguson grade is basically a scale of 0 to 5 that gives a useful estimate of how much skeletal growth is still remaining. This measurement is done by grading the progress of bony fusion of the iliac apophysis, where the area at the top of the hip bone is graded on the basis of the amount of bone fused. While a low grade on the Risser scale will indicate there is still a lot of skeletal growth pending, a high grade will mean that the skeletal growth is near maturity and that the spinal curve is not likely to progress much more. Read the section below to learn more about calculating the skeletal maturity by using the Risser method.

It is possible to use the Risser method for measuring skeletal maturity as the iliac apophysis ossifies in a very expected, standardized manner from front to back, alongside the iliac crest.

The Risser grade is categorized as follows:

- Grade 0 = No ossification
- Grade 1 = Up to 25% ossification
- Grade 2 = 26 - 50% ossification
- Grade 3 = 51 – 75% ossification
- Grade 4 = 76 – 100% ossification
- Grade 5 = Complete bony fusion of apophysis

Refer to the image below for a clearer view.

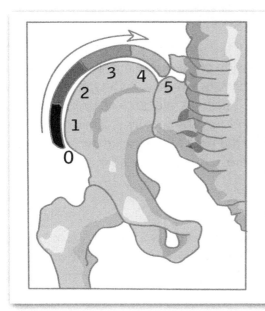

RISSER GRADE – 0 TO 5

The ossification of the iliac apophysis creates the Risser sign.

Risk of Curve Progression – Based on Cobb Angle and Risser Grade

Curve (degree)	Growth potential (Risser grade)	Risk*
10 to 19	Limited (2 to 4)	Low
10 to 19	High (0 to 1)	Moderate
20 to 29	Limited (2 to 4)	Low/moderate
20 to 29	High (0 to 1)	High
>29	Limited (2 to 4)	High
>29	High (0 to 1)	Very high

* **Risk of Progression:** Low risk = 5 to 15 percent; moderate risk = 15 to 40 percent; high risk = 40 to 70 percent; very high risk = 70 to 90 percent.

Progression beyond skeletal maturity

All of the above having been discussed, it is equally important to mention here that the progression of the curve might continue even when skeletal maturity has been fully achieved. As a typical example, lumbar curves of more than 30 degrees are quite likely to progress at a constant rate even beyond skeletal maturity. Similarly, curves diagnosed as 50-70 degrees at the time of skeletal maturity in adults may progress at the rate of almost 1 degree per year.

Progression in adults

Research shows that scoliotic curves show a tendency to progress even during adulthood, especially if the Cobb angle is over thirty degrees at skeletal maturity. Though a large amount of study is focused on curve progression in adolescents, there is also a specific pattern in which the curve progresses in adults, though the rate might be much slower, such as 0.5 to 2 degrees per year.

While curvatures that are less than 30 degrees in adolescents are unlikely to progress, those over 50 degrees are at the greatest risk of progression in adulthood. In fact, even a minor degree of scoliosis detected at age of 6 or 7 years can progress to a major curvature in the older adults, necessitating regular monitoring and management.

Talking of factors that might help an adult know how much his or her curve is likely to progress, the apical vertebral rotation can serve as a good measure which can predict the progression of the curve and even estimate whether and when the patient might need surgery for scoliosis.

CURVE PROGRESSION IN ADULTS

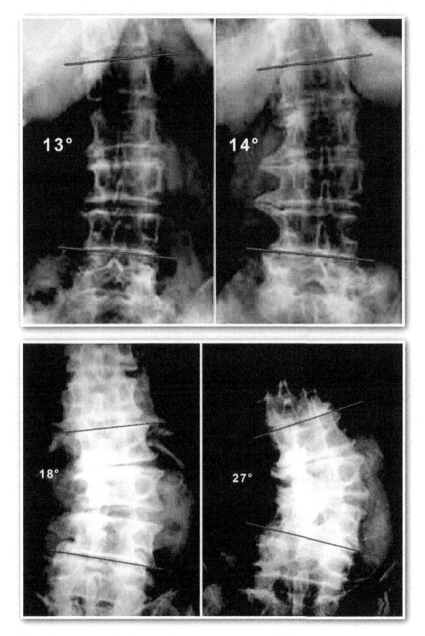

The above xrays depict the curve progression in two adults over 20 years of age. Here it depicts that the greater the initial degree of curvature at the time of screening leads to a higher chance of progression.

Conclusion

Whether age and the corresponding spinal growth actually contribute to the progression of your curve is a major matter of research and debate recently. In their study, Canadian researchers Hongfa Wu and his colleagues found age to be of the least significance as compared to other factors such as gender or curve magnitude and severity.

Gender

Research has often pointed towards the strong correlation that exists between the sex of the child and the chances of curve progression. This correlation is supposed to be even more significant than other factors like curve pattern, magnitude and skeletal maturity. As a general finding, scoliosis is likely to progress more rapidly in girls than in boys, with the gender difference being very prominent in the study of the incidence of the spinal deformity. Research even estimates that scoliosis is at least 10 times more common in girls than it is in boys, with the ratio coming out to be a drastic 11:1.

As another interesting finding, the curve is likely to progress less in girls who have scoliosis in their lower back and where there is spine is misaligned by 1 inch or more. Look at the image below to know more about how the type of curve in girls determines its scope of progression.

Types of curves most likely to progress in girls

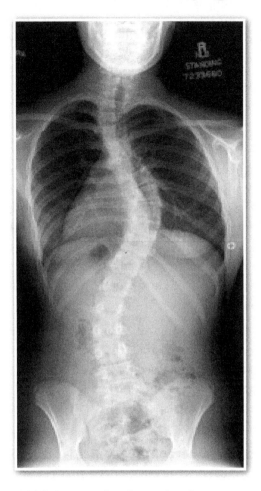

In girls, curve patterns most likely to progress are a right thoracic curve and a double major curve.

While in girls, the right thoracic curve and double major curve are likely to face maximum progression, the left lumbar curves in boys are likely to progress the most. Also, a scoliotic curve of more than 30 degrees in girls will face more progression than the same degree in boys.

Pubertal state/Stage of menarche

As a generalized observation, girls experience most rapid progression of their scoliotic curves prior to the onset of their first menses, at around 11 or 12 years of age, while boys face such progression slightly later, at around 13 or 14 years of age.

In fact, there is ample evidence to show that girls diagnosed with scoliosis in their adolescence, are likely to experience a progression rate of 10 to 15 degrees every year, especially if they are currently at the threshold of menarche.

In young girls, the curve progression is much higher if the curvature has been detected before the onset of menarche. In fact, girls at the pre-menarche stage are likely to experience rapid progression if they are diagnosed with a curve of more than 20 degrees.[1] On the other hand, those with mild curves, measured at less than 20 degrees, are not likely to experience such a quick progression, especially once skeletal maturity has been reached. You can refer to the sections above to know more about skeletal maturity.

As for the correlation of the menarche status of the adolescent with the scope of progression, it is noted that the curve pattern, Cobb angle at onset of puberty, and curve progression velocity are strong predictive factors of curve progression. For instance, juvenile scoliosis greater than 30 degrees increases rapidly and carries a 100% prognosis for surgery.[2]

The Tanner stage, a research based method used to assess the stage of sexual maturity, is a key tool used to predict curve progression. Basically, the curve will experience maximum progression during the Tanner stage 2 or 3.

The Tanner system is based on the growth of pubic hair in both sexes, the development of genitalia in boys, and the development of breasts in girls.

Other Factors

In addition to the above, there are other factors which have also been found to be of influence, such as genetic factors or even epigenetics. One research study shows how in the case of monozygotic twins, not only is the chance of developing scoliosis much higher, but the rate of progression of the curve is also almost similar, in spite of facing varied environmental influences.[3] Another factor that might be involved is the height of the individual. For instance, a 14-year old girl, with a curve of 25-35 degrees, who is shorter than other girls of her age, will be at a lesser risk of progression than a taller girl of the same age, with same degree of curvature. Also, in children born with congenital scoliosis, the condition is likely to worsen at a very rapid pace after birth and with age.

To summarize, the chart below tells you which factors govern the curve progression. It will also guide you in how much your current curve of scoliosis will progress and at what rate:

Summary – Factors that determine progression

GOVERNING FACTOR	CORRELATION
Age	The lesser the age, the more the scope of progression
Gender	Girls generally experience a higher rate of progression
Curve (degree/direction/extent)	Double curves will progress faster. The larger the curve at detection, the more rapidly will it progress.
Menarche/Sexual maturity	Curves diagnosed before the onset of menarche will progress more

* Available research reports might vary.

Key Risks of Progressive Curves

An untreated or rampant progression of a scoliotic curve can cause severe aesthetic as well as functional problems. Ongoing pain and postural imbalances often occur as the long-term impact of progressive curves, often in the back, shoulders, hips, legs and neck.

However, the most common and alarming risk of progressive curves is their possible impact on the pulmonary function.

As thoracic curves progress further, they can cause severe shortness of breath. There is a linear decrease in the total capacity of your lungs to fill-up with breathed air. Meanwhile, in curves as high as 100 degrees, the total reduction can be estimated to be as much as 20%. As an allied effect of the progressive curves, the chest cavity becomes deformed, which can eventually cause a restrictive lung disease.

You can refer to chapter 4 to read more about pulmonary function and shortness of breath.

Spondylosis, an arthritic condition of the spine, is another related risk factor of progressive curves. As the curve progresses, the joints of the spine become inflamed, the cartilage, which cushions the disk, will get thinner and eventually painful bone spurs might develop.

In some cases, especially in women, scoliosis might eventually become associated with osteopenia, a condition that includes loss of bone mass. If left untreated, osteopenia will eventually cause osteoporosis, a serious loss of bone density amongst postmenopausal women. Adolescents having scoliosis are also at an increased risk of developing osteoporosis in their late adulthood.

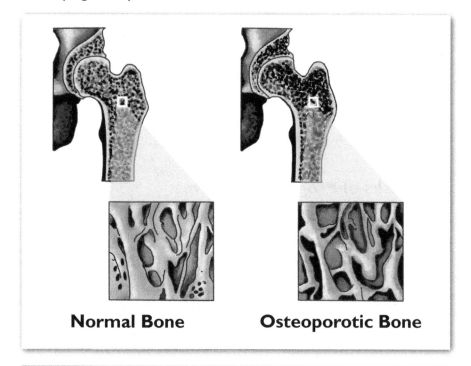

Normal Bone   **Osteoporotic Bone**

Another prominent risk of a progressive curve, especially in adults, is the impact it can have on the choice of treatment.[4] In fact, research strongly points out towards the fact that if a timely detection is made and the scope of progression is correctly measured, advanced surgical options can actually be avoided.[5]

In addition to these, patients with progressive scoliotic curves are likely to suffer a severe emotional impact that will arise from the physical disability, associated cosmetic issues and the consequent loss of productivity and quality of life.

Real Scoliosis Stories: The Pace of Progression!

Though the pace of progression of the curve is governed by a series of factors, yet a fast progression invariably has a similar psychological impact on the patient. Elena was in eighth grade and at age 13 when she was first diagnosed with scoliosis. The curve graduated from being a mere 30 degrees to a major 46 degrees in a few years. The doctors advised her surgery only if her curve went beyond 50 degrees.

In the meantime, her physical appearance began to worsen. The left side of her rib started sticking out and became unequal as compared to the other. Her hips were uneven and one side of her body started tilting towards a side, especially when standing. The hump on the right side of her rib cage made her look like a hunchback, especially when she bent down. This made her look and feel extremely self-conscious and uncomfortable. She started getting very wary of wearing a bathing suit in front of her peers. She could not dress up properly because the clothes did not fit her well. The impact finally boiled down to a point when her entire posture looked awkward and she became apprehensive of appearing in public. She was eventually listed for spinal fusion which she had when she was around 18 years of age.

CHAPTER 8
Your Treatment Options

I n this section, we will take you through the various options available for managing your scoliosis including the various non-invasive options. We will tell you in detail what each of the options entails, including an analysis of each one of them. We will also talk about when is the right time to decide on surgery as the last resort.

Introduction

Scoliosis is essentially a disease of your spine, literally the backbone of your body. To know that the very lifeline of your body is afflicted and that it might be diseased is intimidating and demoralizing. However, with the advent of scientific research and in-depth analysis of this spinal deformity, the patient with scoliosis has appropriate tools to manage and prevent the problem. Whether you just have a minimal degree of curvature or you are rapidly progressing towards a point where surgery will be the only option, each stage of scoliosis can be effectively handled, managed and treated.

In this chapter, we will explain the options of treatment available to you in accordance with the degree or stage of scoliosis you have been diagnosed with. Using these guidelines will give you a clearer direction on the line of treatment you should choose for management of your curvature.

1) Observation and Management

Largely considered to be a passive course of treatment, observation is usually the first step taken to manage scoliosis in patients of the following types:

→ Those with a curve less than 25 to 30 degrees, still growing who have not attained their skeletal maturity.

→ Those with curves less than 45 degrees who have attained full growth.

→ Those with curves that might be a result of conditions like inflammation, muscle spasms or unequal leg length.

→ Children with smaller curves, but having balanced patterns

Basically, curves that are at a low risk of progression are the ideal candidates for being kept under observation. For instance, a boy older than 17 years of age and a girl older than 15 years of age with a scoliotic curve in the range of 25 to 40 degrees will generally be kept under observation. In these cases, a physician will in such cases conduct regular physical screenings and x-rays to ensure that the curve is not progressing any further.

Illustrations - cases recommended for observation

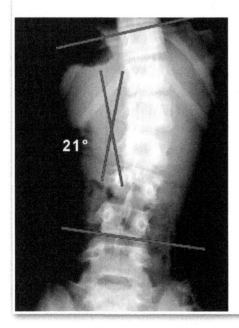

An x-ray of a 16-year old boy, diagnosed with right lumbar scoliosis was recommended to be kept under observation, since there was a low scope for progression.

21°

There are two main parts of this stage of treatment, observation and management. Before we go any further, first let's begin by understanding a bit about both of these.

Observation

The first and most important part of observation is to ensure that the existing curve does not pose any danger to the spine. By constant observation and monitoring of the spine and its curve through physical examinations and sequential x-rays, your doctor will record any possible growth and also attempt to predict the scope of progression. You can refer to Chapter 7 to know more about the possible factors that might contribute to the further progression of the curve of scoliosis.

Management

The second part of this mode of treatment is to manage the existing curve. Your doctor will try to halt the curve from progressing further by identifying the possible causes such as poor posture or suggesting non-medical interventions such as diet and exercise such as swimming / pilates / yoga or a tailored regime as found in my first book Your Plan for Natural Scoliosis Prevention and Treatment to help correct the curvature.

Tools for observation and management

Each of the above two objectives of observation and management of your curve at this stage is achieved by your doctor employing a series of tools, including one or more of the below:

– Posture control
– Physiotherapy, including exercises
– Occupational therapy
– Yoga / Pilates
– Nutritional therapy
– Electric stimulation
– Consulting chiropractic care
– Alternative remedies

What experts say

Whether observation for patients of scoliosis is the right and advisable approach is often a matter of debate. There is a particular group of experts who are staunch opponents of observation, expressing that if a curve can be controlled at a minor stage, there is no point in letting it aggravate before treating it. This particular group strongly advocates that as soon as the curve is detected, it is best to start conservative treatment to avoid surgery. This original, conservative approach preached throughout academics is perhaps the reason for this practice.

Meanwhile, the experts on the other side of the fence argue that it is best to wait and watch in cases where the curve is minimal or is not likely to progress much further to avoid any other possible treatment-related complications. In fact, as per this group of researchers, the triad of physiotherapy, scoliosis intensive in-patient rehabilitation (SIR) and bracing is often an effective, conservative form of treatment to manage scoliosis. In the sections that follow, we will explain the important aspects of each one of the above-listed methods that your doctor might use for observation and management of your condition.

Posture Control

Posture management is often considered the first step in the non-invasive treatment of scoliosis or the stage of observation and management. During the study of posture, the following aspects are usually considered:

→ Correlation of posture with scoliosis
→ Impact of scoliosis on postural balance
→ Altering the postural habits to control scoliosis

When you have scoliosis, there is a loss of arch height in the foot due to excessive pronation of foot, which in turn triggers of a series of postural faults and changes, which may include:

• Internal rotation of tibia and femur

- Pelvic drop, dropping of the pelvis to the pronated side during straight standing or walking
- Pelvic tilt, lowering the sacral base, which further triggers the imbalance
- A rib hump may develop,if the curvature progresses to the thoracic spine

An improper and imbalanced posture is perhaps the most prominent effect and at times an obvious impact of scoliosis, especially of idiopathic scoliosis. Patients with scoliosis have generally been found to have poor postural stability control with research clearly showing that idiopathic scoliosis alters balance control. In addition, the spinal curve has been known to change the very relation between body segments, which can drastically affect the posture of scoliotic children.

There is evidence that demonstrates the fact that the human brain actually has the ability to control posture, in turn altering its balance in scoliosis. In fact, in patients of scoliosis, several parts of the brain such as the vestibular cortex and the brainstem have demonstrated an imbalance.

Interestingly, patients of scoliosis depict different postural traits in accordance with the location of scoliosis they have .i.e. lumbar, thoracolumbar, thoracic or so on. Research conducted on static and dynamic postural control showed maximal postural impact in static conditions for patients with lumbar curves, while those with thoracic curves showed maximum impact in dynamic conditions.

So, what does this imply?

This particular analysis implies that if you have a curve towards the lower part of your spine (lumbar spine), you are likely to experience maximum postural instability in the sitting or static condition. On the other hand, if your curve is more prominent in the mid-spine (thoracic spine), you are likely to have maximum postural instability in dynamic or moving conditions.

Posture Retraining – 3 Key methods to use

Now, since we've demonstrated how wrong posture can contribute to scoliosis, we'll move on further to show how to modify your postural habits to manage mild scoliosis and discuss its efficacy.

a) Using devices

In recent years, people with scoliotic curves have largely benefitted from the use of devices and machines meant to stabilize postures to halt and correct the curves. An example of this is the Vertetrac and Dynamic Brace System (DBS) offered by Meditrac. This device offers a highly patient-friendly, dynamic lumbar ambulatory traction system for the treatment of the curve. To begin with, the brace system works by decompressing the spine and increasing the intervertebral space. However, with long-term use, it uses the pressure of force to eventually push your misaligned spinal segments back into their original balance in order to halt the progression of the curve.

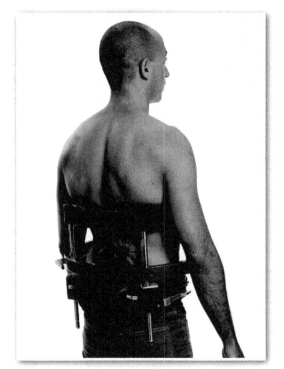

Vertetrac and Dynamic Brace System (DBS)

b) Voluntary observation and self correction

The second thing you can do is to observe your own postural habits and look for any abnormal, extended periods of improper posture. This is especially applicable if a curve has been detected and you still work long hours on the computer or in any other sphere where you might be straining your back or neck for too long.

Once identified, you can then work on rectifying these habits to attain better control over your posture. Such self-correction is seen as a major tool to attain spinal stabilization and hence resolving the postural deformities.

10 Important Tips of Posture

Here are 10 helpful tips you can follow to ensure that you regain your postural balance which you might have lost over the years because of slumping and slouching.

1. Practice standing straight. Put your back and head next to the wall and look forward. Hold position for a minute, relax and repeat.

2. Watch for any signs of slouching throughout your daily activities especially activities performed for prolonged periods of time..

3. Walk erect, especially outdoors.

4. Try to maintain ideal posture when performing all forms of exercise and physical activity.

5. Adjust your chair height so that your thighs are parallel with your floor and knees are level with your hips with feet flat on the ground.

6. Put a small pillow between the small of your back and the back of your chair, enabling yourself to sit with your spine straight. This is also important to consider when driving or riding in a car.

7. As far as possible, do not cross legs while sitting as it creates body misalignment.

8. Always sleep on a firm mattress.

9. Keep your muscles stretched with regular exercise.

10. When standing, keep both the feet flat. Leaning on one leg could cause or aggravate the curvature.

c) External stimulation

This tool involves the specific guidance of an expert who will give instructions for postural corrections, apart from pointing out the obvious postural irregularities. The patient is also taught how to make slight corrections or adjustments to his or her posture in different parts of the body by means of exteroceptive stimulation or by provoking a reaction of balance, basically by the use of external force or pressure.

2) Physiotherapy

Since scoliosis is all about the basic spinal structure being out of balance, physiotherapy can go a long way in strengthening your back as well as helping your body regain its original balance.

If you have scoliosis, you may be advised to go for physiotherapy in order to be prescribed exercises to achieve optimal symmetry, fulfilling the following objectives:

- To achieve postural corrections independently
- To strengthen the muscles of your trunk
- To improve overall back support

Physiotherapy and its various exercises, such as in those in the form of Pilates and the Alexander Technique are considered to be quite a gentle way of realigning your body's balance and improper posture. In fact, physiotherapy works much better if the basic cause of your scoliosis lies in muscular issues or postural defects.

Does physiotherapy work for scoliosis?

Research across communities has shown the effectiveness of physiotherapy exercises in managing scoliosis. Either taken up independently, or along with orthopedic assistance, these exercises have often helped in maintaining flexibility and function in scoliotic individuals. According to data obtained from the Schroth clinic in Bad Sobernheim, Germany, physiotherapy can effectively help in improving pulmonary function and reduce pain in patients of severe scoliosis.

> ## Important information
>
> Make sure you consult your physiotherapist before taking up any of these exercises. In fact, some types of physical exercises have often been known to worsen the curve by increasing the flexibility of the spine beyond permissible limits.

In other words, physiotherapy may work best for patients with scoliosis who do not have any other underlying causes, such as a neuromuscular disorder, congenital defect trauma, age-related degeneration and the like. However, even in these cases, physiotherapy can help to some extent in combination with other interventions.

Though physiotherapy cannot be seen as a focused cure for scoliosis, yet it is surely a way to facilitate the ultimate cure of scoliosis. It contributes to the success chart by strengthening your back and improving the natural balance of your spine to halt the progression of your curve.

Further in this section, we've listed some of the top physical exercises as well as yoga poses you can practice for the conservative treatment of scoliosis.

3) The Schroth Exercise Program

The Schroth Method is considered to be the key physiotherapeutic approach to spinal deformity. A three-dimensional approach to the treatment of scoliosis, this method views scoliosis primarily as a multiplicity of postural disorders and aims to help the patients of scoliosis in the following:

- Reduce pain
- Enhance vital capacity
- Halt progression of the curve
- Improve postural balance
- Avoid surgery

Developed in the 1920s by Katharina Schroth (1894-1985), the Schroth method became the standard non-surgical treatment for scoliosis in Germany by the 1960s. The Schroth Method of exercise is taught to physiotherapists and patients at the Katharina Schroth Spinal Deformities Centre, Sobernheim, Germany. Every year, close to 1,200 patients attend the intensive course of in-patient physiotherapy for a period of four to six weeks.

Though the range of possible curve patterns is quite diverse, the Schroth method considers only 3 basic curve patterns in order to address most of the typical findings in scoliosis. These include:

- Functional 4 curve pattern, and as a special form of the 4 curve pattern the Thoracolumbar curve pattern
- Functional 3 curve pattern with neutral pelvis
- Functional 3 curve pattern with decompensation

The 3 Key Underlying Logics of the Schroth Method

The Schroth Method of scoliosis works on the basis of 3 fundamental logics, including:

- Trunk as a composition of three different blocks
- Rotational breathing
- Postural corrections

We've explained each one of them in the following sections.

a) The 3 blocks of the trunk

In the Schroth Method of treatment, the trunk is divided into three rectangular superimposed blocks, including the pelvic girdle, rib cage and shoulder girdle. When you develop scoliosis, these three blocks of the trunk will deviate from the vertical axis, eventually resulting in the lateral shifting of the spine. The image below explains this well.

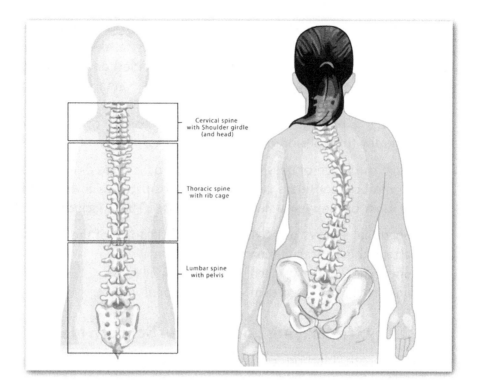

Cervical spine
with Shoulder girdle
(and head)

Thoracic spine
with rib cage

Lumbar spine
with pelvis

b) Rotational breathing

As per the readings and learning of this method, the ribs are connected by the articulations with the lateral processes of vertebrae. When the Schroth exercises are done, the said torsion of the trunk is reduced with the help of suitable respiration.

This concept of exercise works on the principle of a novel concept, referred to as the respiratory thoracic movement. As per this concept, the depressed side of the ribs is widened from the inside using respiratory exercises. Eventually, a wider space will be created, allowing the ribs to move back into the correct alignment.

c) Postural correction

This particular aspect of the Schroth Method of Exercise is in continuation of the above measure of rotational breathing. The widening of rib space discussed earlier is achieved through first correcting the postural disorder through postural correction.

What does it imply for the layman?

The Schroth method of exercise works on the basis of principles formed by its founder Katharina Schroth. She worked on the logic that scoliosis is primarily a disorder of postural irregularities which further has its impact on the spinal structure. Through her principles of breathing exercises and postural corrections, her method guides the patient to recognize these faulty patterns and also re-trains the body to develop the correct postural alignment through self-awareness and a set of systematically planned exercises.

4) Yoga and Exercise

Yoga, the ancient Indian practice for attaining relaxation and relief from illness, is considered to be an effective, conservative remedy for scoliosis as well.

Apart from achieving postural balance and correcting the irregularities, yoga is also believed to be a major tool for relieving stress, thereby improving your ability to relax, which is a very important factor in the treatment of any ailment. Regular practice of yoga has actually proved to regulate weight and alleviate stress levels, thereby expediting the treatment process for scoliosis.

6 ways in which yoga helps scoliosis

Before we go any further to explain more about some of the most important physical exercises and yoga exercises, let's understand a few highlights on how yoga helps scoliosis.

1. Iyengar Yoga, a form of Hatha Yoga which places emphasis on postural alignment, is especially helpful for patients with scoliosis, since postural irregularities are one of the defining features of scoliosis.

2. Yoga gives you an increased awareness of body imbalances and insight for improving your posture.

3. Yoga relieves the pain and tightness associated with a spinal deformity by helping to lengthen and strengthen the muscles.

4. Yoga poses involving standing postures strengthen the legs, which in turn helps the spine stretch more and relieve itself of the tightness associated with scoliosis.

5. Yoga poses that stretch hamstrings, quadriceps and hip flexors are extremely helpful in curing scoliosis since they are instrumental in improving posture.

6. Yoga poses that enhance breath awareness help improve the abnormal pulmonary function associated with scoliosis.

Point To Ponder

Like all other tools of observation and conservative management for scoliosis, yoga too will only be effective in reversing the curvature if it is done as per guidelines, on a long-term basis in a disciplined and a consistent manner.

Physical exercises and Yoga Poses

Read on for a step-by-step listing of some of the most common exercises you can do for scoliosis.

Thoracic curve correction

The aim of this particular exercise is to practice maintaining the correct position so as to be able to re-train your body on its kinesthetic sense. To do this exercise, follow the below steps:

1. Sit straight in a tall chair.
2. Hold the chair with your left hand.
3. Slowly stretch your right arm up and bend diagonally. Stretch to your full limit.
4. Repeat with the other arm in sets of 5.

Right thoracic, left lumbar scoliosis correction

This particular exercise aims to correct the thoracic rotation that is the underlying feature of the right thoracic curve. To do this exercise, follow these steps:

1. Lie down on an exercise mat, with your back aligned to the floor.
2. Place both the hands behind your head.
3. Lift your left knee up in a bent position.
4. Attempt to lift your head and touch your right elbow with the left knee, keeping your abdominal muscles relaxed.
5. Repeat with the other side to the count of 10.

Seated twist

Exercises involving spinal twisting have often been found to be helpful in reversing the curvature of scoliosis. Follow the below steps to do this exercise in the right manner.

1. Sit straight in a tall chair, your left side facing the back of the chair.
2. Keep your feet flat on the floor.
3. Push gently with your left hand and twist your torso to the left.
4. Squeeze your shoulder blades together behind you, keeping your spine lengthened.
5. Deepen your twist after each attempt.
6. Repeat with other side.

Hitch Exercise

This exercise works best for lumbar or thoracolumbar curves. With your pelvis lifted on the convex side you are able to use your muscles to assist with gaining proper spinal alignment. Follow the below steps to do the hitch exercise:

1. Stand straight on both your feet.
2. Your heel on the convex side of the curve, trying to keep your hip and knee straight.
3. Hold this hitched position for around 10 seconds.
4. Support yourself with the back of a chair, if required.

Trunk Strengthening Exercises

In addition to the above, you can also perform a series of trunk strengthening exercises. The most important amongst them include:

Abdominal Strengthening

1. Lie down straight on the mat.
2. With arms on your side, slowly, bring the right leg up to a 90-degree level and hold to the count of 10.
3. Bring it down gradually to first 60 and then 30 degrees from the floor and relax.
4. Now reverse the leg and repeat.

Bicycle

1. Lie down on the floor, with your legs elevated.
2. Now perform the action of cycling in the air with your legs.
3. Maintain your low back on the floor at all times.

Back stability

1. Lying on your stomach with your arms stretched ahead.
2. Raise your trunk and arms in a straight line with the alternate leg and hold for 5 sec.
3. Repeat on each side 10 times.

Angled Wall Stretch

This particular exercise is meant to lengthen your spine and open your shoulders to create balance amongst the muscles of your upper back. Follow the below steps for the angled wall stretch:

1. Stand a few feet from a wall.
2. Keep your feet at hip-distance from each other.
3. Lean forward and place your hands on the wall, shoulder distance apart.
4. The end result should be a right angle between your torso and legs, while your hands will be pressed against the wall, right at the level of your hips.
5. With feet firmly on the ground, push into the wall with your hands.
6. Repeat 5- 6 times per session

Hamstring stretch

Since tight hamstrings can contribute to poor posture, this exercise can prove quite useful. Follow the steps below.

1. Lie down on your back on an exercise mat.
2. Take a resistance band or towel and loop it around the band of your right foot, holding the ends of the strap in your hands.
3. Keep your left leg flat and gently extend your right leg upwards, over your head.
4. When you feel the tightness in your hamstring, pause for a second and then deepen the stretch a bit more.
5. Repeat with the other leg.

Lunges

Follow the below steps to do the lunges to help scoliosis:

1. Sit on the floor in a kneeling position.
2. Bring your right foot forward and the back knee down on the floor.
3. Gently, lunge forward so that your front knee is over the ankle bones, it is important for your knee not to go forward beyond your ankle.
4. Try to feel the stretch in the back thigh and groin.
5. Repeat.

Hip opener

To do this yoga pose, follow the below steps:

1. Come down on your all fours.
2. Bring your right foot and knee forward and place them on the floor.
3. Square your hips and try to slide your left leg straight back.
4. Slowly, try to come down with your hands in the front.
5. Repeat with the other side.

Three part pull

Follow the below steps for doing this yoga pose:

1. Stand straight, facing the kitchen sink, or any other platform with a railing.
2. Pull back from the railing of the sink.
3. Keep your feet in towards the sink and keep your legs straight, bending from the hips and stretching the buttocks.
4. Take steps forward in a manner that when you bend your knees, your legs should be at a right angle with thighs parallel to the floor and knees above the heels.
5. Now pull back a bit.
6. Take a few steps forward with the heels in touch with the ground.
7. Drop buttock to a squat and then pull back.

5) Occupational Therapy (OT)

Scoliosis is generally viewed as an umbrella disorder, which encompasses many aspects of the patient's life. As the postural and spinal deformity sets in, related dimensions of daily life begin to get affected. For instance, with the onset of scoliosis and a possible need for therapy or bracing, the patient's professional life might beget affected, related bodily functions such as breathing might also get compromised and, above all, the level of self esteem and confidence might take a blow. Refer to the image below which explains this better.

It is for such reasons that a disorder such as scoliosis crosses the mark of being a mere physical disorder and calls for a comprehensive, holistic approach for treatment.

The Multi-Dimensional Impact of scoliosis

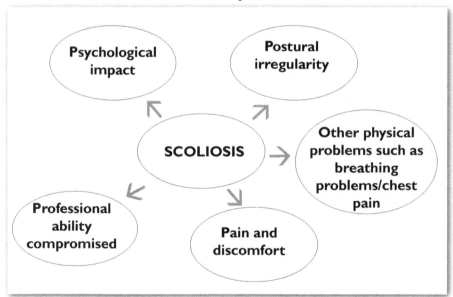

Towards this end, occupational therapy is considered to be an effective approach of treatment just after the patient has been diagnosed with scoliosis. Regarded as an integral part of the observational stage of scoliosis, the holistic approach of an occupational therapist is believed to be helpful in addressing the spinal deformity in a multitude of ways.

So, what does an occupational therapist do to help you? An occupational therapist assists in the overall management of the condition of scoliosis. He basically strives to restore your normal life functioning by developing a treatment approach that:

→ Reverses / halts your curve

→ Restores your optimum professional ability

→ Repairs any loss of self-esteem / self-confidence

The most important underlying feature of occupational therapy is the role played by the patient who is encouraged to actively contribute during the treatment process.

Occupation therapy for scoliosis - Key highlights

Though most patients with scoliosis will benefit from the services of an occupational therapist, the group of patients most likely to benefit are those who have developed scoliosis due to an illness or injury, because of causing a hindrance in performing their activities of daily living, ADLs.

An occupational therapist will basically assist you in becoming fully independent in your daily life through the following steps:

→ Assessment of your condition and its impact on different aspects of life

→ Planning a suitable strategy for intervention

→ Ongoing evaluation to assess performance for revision of strategy

Here, let us understand a few key highlights on how occupational therapy will help you with your spinal curvature.

→ Perform appropriate activity analysis and modification of ADLs and plan the intervention strategy accordingly.

→ Help you in understanding your symptoms better and guide you in the best ways to manage them.

→ Guide for postural retraining in positions including sleeping, sitting and standing.

→ Guide you in the best ways of performing self-care, which might have been affected due to your condition

→ Assess the efficiency and performance of your treatment modalities, especially those involving pain management tools and exercises

→ Guide you on the best ways to enhance your productivity and assess the need to use instruments such as the electrical wheelchair.

→ To take up proper work analysis and suggest ways to improve your overall output and productivity.

→ Guide you on the best ways to alter your lifestyle to suit your condition

→ Train you in the best use of adaptive equipment such as orthopedic devices, special garments and support items such as corsets, rolls, wedges and pillows.

6) Diet

The human body works on the premise of balance in its entirety, ranging from physical structure to nutritional quotient and psychological well being. The body and its systems operate well if this natural balance is maintained and followed in our everyday lives. However, abnormalities begin to surface when the body is pushed out of its natural balance due to factors such as disease or improper lifestyle.

When it comes to diet and nutrition, the food groups that pushed the body out of its natural balance can be identified and then a suitable dietary regimen may be established for the purpose of setting this balance right.

To study how diet can help as a tool in the first stage of treatment, it is first important to understand how dietary deficiencies can be an etiological factor in scoliosis. A relevant review of American and European articles from 1955 to 1990 reveals nutrition to be a major factor in the etiology of idiopathic scoliosis.[1] The fact that dietary modifications can alter the way our genes drive our taste preferences and dietary habits helps explain the crucial role of nutrition as a tool to treat scoliosis. In fact, there is ample evidence to show that such alterations in our epigenetic status can be directly modified by various environmental changes or even maternal dietary factors.[2]

Such research stands as an effective illustration for the twin facts that:

→ Diet can be a critical, probable cause of idiopathic scoliosis
→ Dietary modifications can be effective as one of the first steps in the treatment of scoliosis

Once the role of diet has been established, we will now move on to how to spot dietary irregularities and the essential guidelines for developing a good dietary routine.

Step 1 – Identifying faulty diet patterns

When you decide to use diet as a means of treatment for scoliosis, the first important step to take is to identify the areas where your diet might be causing problems.

Research shows an interesting correlation between the symptoms of scoliosis and wheat or gluten sensitivity. In this relevance, autoantibodies associated with wheat are often related to the development of scoliosis. Towards this end, you first need to ensure that you identify whether you have any such allergies or food sensitivities. This step will also help you analyze whether you are suffering from any nutritional deficiency that may be acting as one of the causes of your spinal curve. Melatonin, a hormone secreted by the pineal gland in the brain, is an example of one such deficiency.

Melatonin is associated with pubertal growth cycles. A deficiency of melatonin can trigger puberty earlier than normal, which will mean that the adolescent will gain pubertal maturity faster, eventually impacting the rate of growth of the curve. Besides, melatonin also binds to calmodulin, which in turn affects the intracellular calcium functions. Patients diagnosed with idiopathic scoliosis have often been found to have high levels of calmodulin, which occurs in correlation with lower levels of circulating melatonin.

Hence, you need to regularly assess your diet for any such food allergies, sensitivities and deficiencies if you have been diagnosed with scoliosis.

Step 2 – Developing a Healthy Diet

The most important dictates of a healthy diet apply in a nutritional approach to scoliosis. The correct diet for scoliosis will help you achieve the following objectives:

- Help you lose unnecessary weight
- Help you improve your metabolism
- Help you overcome any related nutritional deficiencies

The 4 essential nutrients

A proper diet for a patient with scoliosis is all about fulfilling the needs for balanced bone health and bone nutrition. If you have been diagnosed with scoliosis, make sure your diet has enough of the below discussed nutrients.

1) Calcium

Apart from helping in building bone mass, calcium also serves as an important mineral for nerves and muscles. It is important that you include a proper dosage of calcium and also ensure that your body is absorbing it in the right manner. Refer to the list below to learn more about which foods to have and to avoid if you have scoliosis.

2) Vitamin D

This nutrient helps your body to absorb calcium and phosphorus from your diet and nutritional supplements in a better manner and is also vital for good bone health.

3) Vitamin E

Vitamin E has strong anti-oxidant properties and also strengthens the immune system by fighting free radicals. This important nutrient is also known to be helpful in strengthening muscles and maintaining healthy muscle tissue.

4) Vitamin K

Vitamin K is supposed to a nutrient in rich bone building abilities. Owing to this attribute, it can even help in preventing bone-related problems like osteoporosis, especially in the elderly population.

Foods to have and avoid

The table below will give you a detailed listing of what foods you should consume and which ones to avoid in order to help your condition.

Foods to have	Foods to avoid
Fresh vegetables	Citrus fruits and juices
Fresh fruits	Soda and aerated drinks
Meat, eggs and poultry	Artificial sweeteners
Milk, cheese and dairy products	Fats and oils
Fermented foods	Corn syrup, fructose syrup
Nuts and seeds	Sweets
Healthy fats	Tea, coffee
	White flour
	Junk/Fried foods

Just a point...

At this point, it could actually be useful to refer to 'Your Plan for Natural Scoliosis Prevention and Treatment' (Dr. Kevin Lau) that explains in detail the essentials of a good diet for scoliotic patients. From food groups which help, to nutrients that are required and finally, the ideal diet plan you must follow based on your own individual metabolic type and scoliosis, this book has it all!

7) Electric Stimulation

There are cases of scoliosis which might not respond to physical therapy and nutritional modifications as expected. For such individuals, electric stimulation can be considered as an option to gain relief from pain and also, possibly, halt the curve.

As the name suggests, electric stimulation is a process which is used to strengthen the muscles by passing an electrical current into a muscle or group of muscles, causing them to contract. Electric stimulation is believed to be helpful for scoliosis by improving the blood circulation and increasing the range of motion. It is widely considered as the safest way to increase the muscle flexibility and adaptation.

Before we go any further, first let us understand more about electric stimulation therapy. There are three basic types of electric stimulation therapy, including general, muscular and Transcutaneous electric nerve stimulation (TENS), with each of them having specific uses as below:

→ General electric therapy – Used for relieving pain and healing wounds
→ Muscular electrical stimulation – Used to strengthen muscles by reducing muscle spasms
→ TENS – Used to treat chronic pain

How it works?

The aim of using electrical stimulation for scoliosis is to facilitate muscle contraction at the location of the skeletal curve.

To use electrical stimulation, the physical therapist trained in this mode of treatment will apply skin electrodes to the muscles of the trunk. The electrodes are placed in such a manner that they will allow for the maximum level of contraction at the point where the scoliotic curve is at its peak. Experts advise that most of such electric stimulation therapy for scoliosis should be carried out at night, when the patient is sleeping, especially in the case of children.

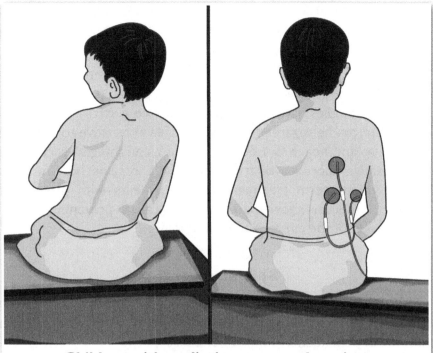

Children with scoliotic curves undergoing electric stimulation therapy

Important information

Experts point out that for a child to be eligible for electric stimulation therapy, the spinal curve should be less than 35 degrees and also, there should be at least two years of growth still left.

Does it work?

A controlled analysis done amongst a group of scoliosis patients treated with electrical neuromuscular stimulation showed an efficacy ratio of around 44%. According to this study, the amount of correction achieved increased at the same level as the length of the skeletal lever arms i.e. ribs and pelvis, interconnecting the stimulated musculature with the vertebrae of the spinal curve.

However controversy abounds, as in another study, electrical stimulation has been found to be effective in 40 patients being treated with this method, with the rate of failure going up to 50 percent. Yet other studies have reported that surface electrical stimulation treatment can be regarded as an acceptable alternative to the brace treatment and hence can be considered as an integral part of the conservative approach of treatment. On the same note, a study involving long term treatment of 107 patients with progressive idiopathic scoliosis showed a 93% success rate in preventing further progression of the curves below 30 degrees.

8) Chiropractor

Chiropractic care is seen as a holistic approach to scoliosis, with the emphasis being on spinal manipulation and lifestyle management instead of dependence on drugs or surgery.

Generally speaking, the chiropractic approach is expected to meet the following objectives:

- To improve steadiness and stability of the spine
- To halt progression of the curve
- To reduce the degree of the curve

Random reports show chiropractic care to be effective in almost 70 percent of cases, where it managed to alleviate pain and discomfort and, in some cases, even halt the progression of the curve. According to a latest study, chiropractic care has been seen to be quite effective in easing the pain and disability associated with adult scoliosis. As per these results, chiropractic adjustments were found to be helpful in easing the compression of nerves as well as facilitating proper spinal alignment.

How is it done?

On your first chiropractic visit for your scoliosis, you will learn that chiropractors follow a highly standardized procedure for the initial examination as well as a thorough assessment of your previous medical history. Most chiropractors will also prefer to go into detail about your lifestyle, family history and overall health status. Towards this end, your initial visit is most likely to include Adam's Forward Bending Test (FBT). Refer to chapter 5 to know more about this test. This test, along with a few range of motion studies, will primarily be done to ascertain whether chiropractic care is the right option for your treatment.

Your chiropractor will provide therapy through performing manual manipulation in an attempt to loosen the tendons and ligaments. Through this spinal stimulation, your chiropractor will also attempt to retrain your muscles to return to their original position.

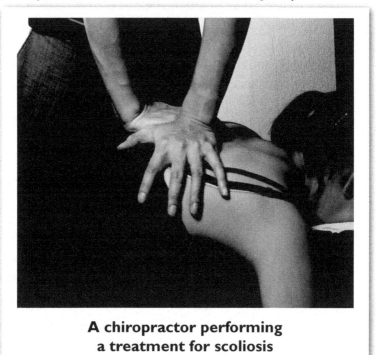

**A chiropractor performing
a treatment for scoliosis**

Depending on the severity of your curve and also the details of your medical history, your chiropractor will use one of the below-mentioned therapies for your treatment. If it is appropriate, your doctor might even decide to combine 2 or more of these chiropractic techniques.

→ Traction-massage: the purpose of this method is to relax the muscles around your spine, making spinal movement more effective and comfortable. For this method, you will be first asked to lie down on your back with a pillow under your knees. Now, a set of specifically designed rollers will move up and down your spine to massage and stretch the back muscles.

→ Physical exercises: As we have discussed above, physical exercises can go a long way in alleviating the pain and discomfort associated with scoliosis. As a part of your chiropractic treatment, you will be prescribed a specific set of exercises to strengthen the back, neck and extremities of the patients.

→ Manual massage: Done using the correct technique, massage can effectively reduce pain and also improve circulation, thereby helping your condition. For an added effect, it might be combined with other options such as electric stimulation, muscle stimulation, ultrasound or ice/heat therapy.

→ Lifestyle alteration: Lifestyle issues may have a larger impact on the cause of scoliosis than most people may know. A chiropractor will suggest suitable changes to your lifestyle for this purpose, which is likely to include steps such as reducing alcohol consumption, smoking cessation, having a healthy diet etc. In fact, some of the best chiropractors treating scoliosis also prescribe a detailed diet and exercise schedule for their patients to help their condition.

As a part of your chiropractic treatment, your doctor might also suggest supplementary treatments such as a shoe lifts, spinal manipulation, electric stimulation therapy or isotonic/active exercise techniques. Interestingly, there have been quite a few positive outcomes from the use of such devices in patients with scoliosis.

Integrating approaches

Scoliosis often responds to treatment very well when different approaches are integrated together for a holistic and natural treatment of the deformity. For instance, a combination of the right dietary modifications with appropriate exercises are often seen as an effective approach to manage scoliosis. You can refer to the vast set of similar resources and methods explained in the series of books and DVDs including Health in Your Hands, Scoliosis Exercises For Prevention And Correction DVD (International Edition) and the like. You can also schedule an exclusive appointment at the clinic to know more about such an integrated approach to treatment.

9) Alternative remedies

When it comes to human health, natural remedies often turn out to be an effective solution to restore the body's original state of balance and vitality. Experts do argue that scoliosis, being a major spinal deformity, might not respond as well to mild alternative or natural remedies. However, research has demonstrated that these natural, herbal and alternative remedies are effective in resorting the human body's physical balance as well as providing pain relief, both of which are essential requirements of scoliosis treatment.

That being said, it is important for the patient to first verify that the alternative remedy in question has been researched enough and has a scientifically proven role in the management of scoliosis.

In this section, we will talk about some of the common alternative remedies available for scoliosis.

a) Homeopathy

With the aim of curing the key symptoms involved, the following homeopathic remedies might be chosen for scoliosis:

- Calcaria carb
- Bryonia
- Calcaria flour
- Calcaria sulph
- Merc cor
- Silicea
- Phosphoric acid
- Numx vom
- Arsenic
- Belladonna

b) Essential oils and aromatherapy

Experts also talk of an effective technique, known as the Raindrop Technique which uses nine different essential oils along the back, neck and feet using a variation of pressure releases and moist heat.

c) Herbal remedies

To fulfill your body's need for essential nutrients, like the mineral silica which is vital for bone health; you can try the herbal horsetail remedy. In addition, you can even add the horsetail herb to your herbal tea. Alternatively, you can add around 10-15 drops of this tincture to water and have regularly. One tablespoon of herbal horsetail juice taken everyday can also serve as an effective remedy.

d) Biofeedback

This is another complementary medicine technique you can employ for scoliosis. Biofeedback basically teaches you to control your bodily functions, such as heart rate, with the help of your own mind. Connecting you to electrical sensors, you are taught to measure and receive information about your body. Eventually, you are then taught to make subtle changes to your body, the main result being muscle relaxation and pain relief.

Other remedies

A series of other remedies can be tried in case the patient is ascertained as an appropriate candidate for the same. These include the likes of:

- Bach flowers
- Emotional Freedom Technique (EFT)
- Cranial/Sacral therapy
- Bowen technique

The Thin Line Between Choices – Multimodal Approach

Making a choice between treatment methods used for observation may not be simple. There may be a thin line between the benefits of various methods, such as physical exercises, yoga, posture control and so on. The multi-modal approach, the concept of using a variety of treatment methods in conjunction with one another, often works the best since a combination of therapies is mostly effective. You have to learn to listen to your own body's responses and devise your own customized scoliosis management plan at this stage.

At this stage, the patient is also strongly advised against resorting to methods that have either been not research well enough or make unrealistic and false claims to offer quick results or treatment.

10) Bracing

What are braces?

A brace is a customized orthotic device meant to drive the body into its original alignment. The history of modern bracing is believed to date back to 1946, when Blount and Schmidt started using a brace for the purpose of post-operative immobilization or non-operative treatment, According to the National Scoliosis Foundation, 30,000 children are fitted every year to manage scoliosis.

A brace is typically devised with the aim of preventing the curve from progressing further and might not have much effect on the reversal of the curve or treatment of scoliosis.

When to go in for braces?

Clinically you will be advised to go in for a brace if your scoliotic curve falls into any of the below categories:

→ A moderate sized curve (25 to 40 degrees)
→ A progressive curve, having increased by more than 5 degrees over 1-2 years
→ A young stage of skeletal maturity, with majority of growth still pending (Risser grade = 0 to 2)

Types of braces

There are different types of braces that can be used to halt the progression of your scoliotic curve. Braces can be differentiated from each other on the basis of the materials they are made of, the areas of the body that they cover or the time of the day they will be worn.

Factors to consider

Your doctor and orthotist (a professional specializing in the manufacture of such devices) will generally take into consideration the below set of factors while deciding on the kind of brace you shall use.

- → Location of your curve
- → Flexibility of your curve
- → Number of curves
- → Position and rotation of the vertebrae of your spine
- → Your age, gender and professional occupation
- → Previous medical history

Below, we have given brief descriptions of each of the bracing options available.

a) Milwaukee brace – full torso brace

A full-torso brace, the Milwaukee brace is to be worn for 23 hours a day, only to be removed for brief periods of time during activities like exercise and bathing. This type of a brace consists of a wide, flat bar in the front and two small bars in the back. The bars at the back are then attached to a ring that goes around the neck. This ring has a chin rest and also a rest for the back of the head.

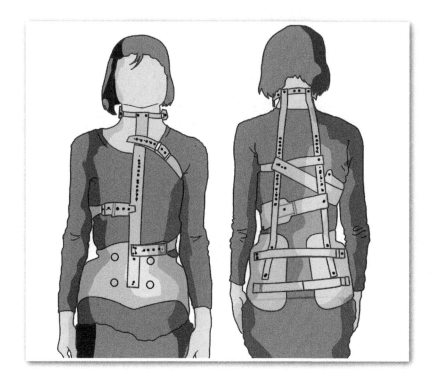

b) Charleston bending brace – nighttime brace

A popular nighttime brace, the Charleston Bending Brace is made of molded plastic, held securely in place by three straps to facilitate adjustment. The Charleston Bending Brace serves a useful purpose since it saves the patients from the discomfort of wearing it in the day time. Experts also believe that such nighttime braces make full use of the teenager's natural hormone growth production, which is at its peak between the hours of midnight to around 2 a.m.

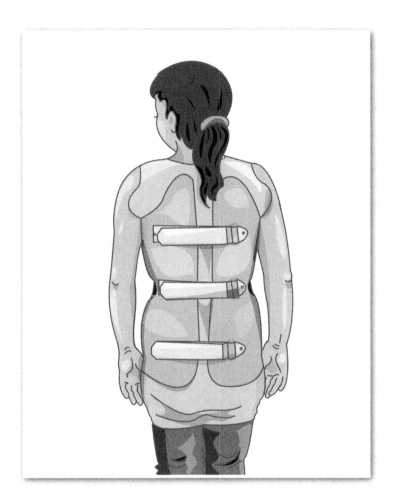

c) The boston brace – Thoracolumbar sacral orthosis (TSLO)

The Boston Brace is often said to be the most effective type of brace in treating the curves of the middle or low back. Also the first patented modular pre-fabricated bracing system in the world, it is basically a type of thoracolumbar sacral orthosis, which means that these are molded back braces than can be fitted very close to the skin.

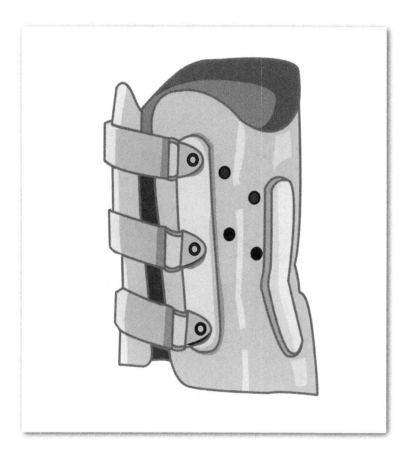

d) Providence nighttime scoliosis system

Another nighttime brace, the Providence nighttime brace promises to take away the awkwardness and discomfort of having to wear the brace throughout the day. It is made from measurements taken by having the patient lie down on an orthometry board, which predetermines corrective pad placement. This brace might also be used in conjunction with the Boston Brace.

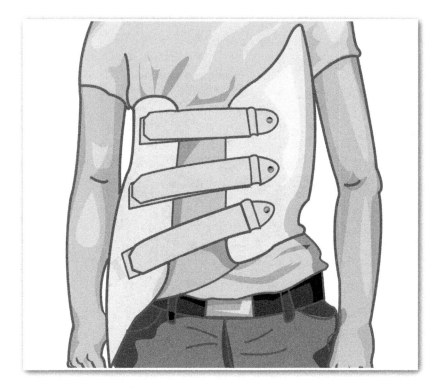

e) SpineCor Corrective scoliosis brace – Flexible brace

SpineCor is a well-known flexible brace, giving the patient the much-needed respite from the rigid and form-fitting metal and plastic braces. The SpineCor uses adjustable bands and is basically made of a cotton vest, thereby not restricting the movement.

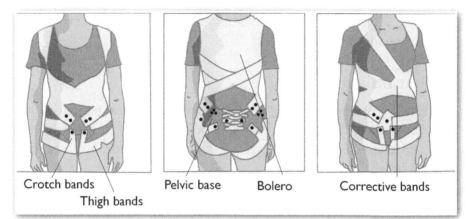

Crotch bands   Pelvic base   Bolero   Corrective bands
Thigh bands

Does bracing work?

Multiple theories exist regarding how useful or avoidable bracing is. Before we move on to explain what research has to say about the efficacy of braces, let us quickly examine some of the more obvious pros and cons of using them.

Pros: Factors that favor the use of braces

→ Can stop the progression of the curve
→ Can push the spine back into its correct alignment
→ Modern varieties can be conveniently worn under clothes
→ Can facilitate better day time functioning (Nighttime bracing)

Cons: Reasons to avoid braces

→ Rigid, non-flexible structures can restrict movement

→ Materials that make braces might cause further disease/ allergy

→ Curve might worsen if the brace is not worn properly

→ Most of the braces have to be worn all day, thereby causing discomfort

→ Curve might resume to worsen once the brace is discontinued

→ Serious cosmetic problems and confidence issues can occur, especially in teenagers

What do experts say?

Bracing has been a long time standing option for patients with scoliosis, due to which research is quite divided on whether or not it is effective for scoliosis treatment. Take for instance the observational study reported by Goldberg in 1993 in Dublin on patients who did not wear braces. Interestingly, she reported that her clinic had almost the same number of surgeries even when the patients had used braces previously[3].

We can also consider the set of studies indicated by the Cochrane Summaries which show that there is indeed very less evidence to prove that bracing is more effective in managing scoliosis than the observation management or even remedies like electrical stimulation[4]. Such studies pose a serious doubt on the validity and efficiency of the brace system today.

However, a similar research commissioned by the Scoliosis Research Society revealed that bracing did prevent the curves from getting larger as compared to the cases where no treatment was applied.[5] Though such studies do point out at the possible valid efficiency of braces, but the medical reports definitely stress on the decreasing utility of this treatment option.

In fact, varied opinions exist on the matter. For instance, there is evidence to show that the nighttime braces such as the Charleston nighttime brace are quite effective, primarily due to the fact that they can be used at night, when sleeping. In one such study, 77% of the 95 patients studied showed improvement with the Charleston nighttime brace, with a success rate of 80% noticed for patients having a curve ranging from 25 to 30 degrees and 76% for those with a larger curve in the range of 31 to 40 degrees.[6]

Yet another analysis carried out by the SRS Natural History and Prevalence Committee revealed that while patients treated with lateral electric stimulation showed a success rate of 39%, the curves could be halted by bracing in at least 92% cases.[7] Similar research also shows that the curves which are curtailed to 50 degrees or less at maturity with the use of bracing are unlikely to progress over time.

Summary - What does this imply?

For you, as a patient, we have summarized here the key points regarding the efficiency of bracing as a means to treat scoliosis:

→ Bracing definitely serves as an attempt to halt the progression of your curve.

→ It is more of a tool to manage your condition or to halt the progression of the curve than to cure the deformity.

→ Bracing will work much better if you combine it with a proactive approach of identifying the signs and dealing with the onset early enough, as explained in *Scoliosis Exercises For Prevention And Correction DVD, the book Health in Your Hands and other related works.*

→ Rigid bracing can often cause muscle atrophy.

→ Bracing is generally not a very favorable option for adolescents and teenagers due to cosmetic reasons.

→ Braces will not be effective for curves more than 45 degrees.

→ Braces will give the best results if the child is still young and wears the brace for the prescribed number of hours a day and for the prescribed number of years until skeletal maturity has been reached.

→ The prolonged durations for which these braces have to be worn (especially the Milwaukee and Boston Brace) may result in other allied physical damage and disease. It can also result in skin issues such as itching and rashes.

→ Rigid braces may restrict breathing and lung capacity.

→ As it might be with all the other non-invasive forms of treatment, bracing alone cannot ensure relief from scoliosis.

→ Results vary in boys and girls, as they do in patients of different age groups as well.

→ Results from clinical studies also vary on whether the improvements obtained with bracing continue to exist once the bracing has been discontinued.

→ Bracing cannot be a lifetime option due to the physical discomfort involved and the restrictions in   your range of motion.

11) Surgery

The Final Alternative

As per the estimates of the National Scoliosis Foundation, almost 38,000 patients go in for spinal fusion surgery every year. Another set of reports declares that almost 6% of scoliosis cases will require surgery, regardless of the method of treatment adopted.

When we talk about options of treatment for scoliosis, observation and management using the above explained tools is still the most widely preferred option. There is a general set of expected results when using interventions such as undertaking posture control, physiotherapy, electric stimulation, diet management and the like. The most important amongst these expectations are:

→ Halt of the progression of the curve
→ Relief from pain
→ Partial reversal of the curve
→ Increase in efficiency, earlier marred by the curvature

Varied combinations of these approaches are used by the specialists involved until an appropriate measure of relief is achieved. However, there are various situations in which conservative management does not gain the necessary results and surgical intervention will need to be considered. Here, we list the top 10 reasons where surgery may be indicated.

Top 10 reasons to consider surgery

1. If the spinal curve is more than 40 degrees and other conservative methods produce unsatisfactory results.

2. If the curve is lesser, but the result is not satisfactory for specific reasons such as cosmetic issues or the condition has a negative impact on professional or personal life .

3. If the extent of the curve makes it impossible for measures like exercise and electric stimulation to be effective.

4. If the curve, at whatever degree and whichever treatment it is being subjected to, is causing unbearable discomfort or inconvenience or is interfering with the normal life.

5. If the curve is likely to lead to serious issues like abnormal lung function or heart problems.

6. If the majority of medical advice points towards the possibility of a correction.

7. If the medical advice states the patient is at an appropriate stage of skeletal maturity and rate of curve progression. Both of these should be suitable for surgery.

8. If measures like exercise and bracing are not viable, considering the patient's health condition or lifestyle.

9. If the curve has progressed to its maximum extent and is not likely to progress further, but the complications continue to increase.

10. If the curve is having an overall impact on your quality of life.

Real Scoliosis Stories: A Personal Account on Bracing

An 11-year old, school going girl was diagnosed with scoliosis. An avid swimmer, she wasn't really worried as she thought she will overcome the deformity owing to her active lifestyle. She also knew that it was a genetic issue with her family, so the occurrence of the curve was quite expected.

Once she learnt of her curve, the doctors put her on the wait and watch approach for around 2 years. Unfortunately, another visit to her doctor after a span of 2 years revealed that her curve had progressed quite drastically. She was instructed to wear a brace for 2 years, 24 hours a day, 7 days a week. Already living a very active lifestyle, she found it very difficult to adjust with the hard brace which made her feel uncomfortable and sweaty.

Anyways, having managed to live with it for 2 years, she was expecting to be told that her curve has improved. However, it was a shock for her to know that her spine had developed two major curves, including a thoracic as well as a lumbar curve, both of which were increasing at an alarming rate. While her thoracic curve had increased up to 45 degrees, her lumbar curve went up to 55 degrees.

Inspite of trying bracing for quite some time, she could see no improvement in her curve. Hence, the only option left with her was that of a spinal fusion. It's my opinion through working with my patients that bracing alone often doesn't help. My first book, 'Your Plan for Natural Scoliosis Prevention and Treatment' explains the logic as to why bracing alone cannot effectively handle, reduce or halt your curve. At the end of the day, natural treatments including lifestyle modifications, regular exercise and active rehabilitation in combination with or without bracing usually turn out to be a much better and effective methods to strengthen the spine and stabilize the curve.

PART TWO

The Road to Surgery

CHAPTER 9

Decision Making For Surgery

This chapter is meant for the patients who have already gone through the entirety of non-invasive treatment or those who have been advised to consider surgery as their best course of action. Here, we will discuss various factors that will help you decide whether you are an ideal candidate for scoliosis surgery.

Surgery – The Option

The entire treatment process for scoliosis started with you and your healthcare provider pondering over the typical 'wait and watch' approach. Your curve would have been detected and measured to understand what state your condition was. If you were still a bit far from attaining skeletal maturity and were at 25 to 30 degrees, or had achieved full skeletal maturity with a curve around 45 degrees, chances are you would have been put through the rigors of posture and diet management, physical exercises, yoga, electric stimulation, physical and occupational therapy treatments, chiropractic adjustments and so on. If you were a person whose curve halted and the symptoms subsided, you could have easily continued with these management options in the near future as well.

However, research shows that there are cases of scoliosis that will either:

→ Respond only to surgery, failing which the curve can progress to a life-threatening situation

or

→ The curve is causing pain or discomfort and is causing major interference in the daily life of the patient

Surgery comes as a last resort in the entire treatment plan for scoliosis. However, by no means is surgery to be considered as just another form of treatment. A surgery for scoliosis is a life-time decision that needs careful analysis and thought. After all, scoliosis surgery is a heavily invasive procedure that also comes with the potential of complications, immediately post-surgery as well as later.

As we previously guided you through the entire phase of screening, diagnosis and measurement of your curves, we will now move on to guiding you through a challenging decision, that of having surgery. We will explain a set of 7 handy factors that you can use as a tool to help you decide whether or not you should undergo surgery for your scoliosis. The later chapters will also ensure that you have full knowledge about the procedure you are having, its after-effects and the influences it will have on your life.

Read on for a detailed explanation of each of these 7 decisive factors.

7 Questions to Ask Yourself

1. What is The status of your curve?

It is important to look at the status of your curve when deciding whether to consider surgery for correcting your scoliosis. You will need to look at a few key aspects regarding your curve, such as the degree of severity and its location. Here, we have explained each of these aspects of your curve:

Degree of severity: Generally, surgery will be suggested as an option for you if the Cobb angle of your curve is more than 45 to 50 degrees and is causing major discomfort. This is especially true for small children, adolescents and pre-adolescents.

Location of your curve: Depending on whether your scoliosis is located in your upper spine (thoracic), mid-spine (thoracolumbar) or lower (lumbar) spine, your doctor will decide whether surgery is the only probable option left.

2. How mature is your skeletal system?

Depending on how much spinal growth is still remaining, your doctor will make a decision accordingly. The key here is whether your spine is still growing or if it has reached its full growth potential. If you have a high degree of curvature and you are still far from attaining your spinal maturity, your doctor might want to delay the surgery. On the contrary, if your curve has reached somewhere around 45 degrees and you have attained full skeletal maturity or growth potential and the curve is causing major issues, surgery might be the right option for you. You can refer to chapter 7 to read more about skeletal maturity, the Risser sign and how it influences the rate of progression of your scoliotic curve.

The bottom line here is that, in most cases, surgery can wait if your curve is still likely to progress and you are yet to achieve your skeletal maturity.

3. What is the risk of progression of your curve?

Patients who are under a greater risk for progression of their curve are more likely to be advised to have surgery. You can refer to chapter 7 to read more about factors that help predict your risk of progression. For instance, if you have not yet attained skeletal maturity, the chances of curve progression are much higher. Likewise, adults who have a degree of curvature greater than 50 degrees are likely to have further progression of their curve and hence require surgery.

4. How effective have the conservative, non-invasive methods been?

In general, an individual patient's response to observation methods is studied for a period of approximately 6 to 12 months in order to analyze the effectiveness of measures like posture control, diet management, physiotherapy, yoga, electric stimulation, chiropractic adjustments and the like. Another important question to consider here is that how effective an option of bracing is for you. For instance, in some hospitals, surgery for children is avoided unless their curves go to the extent of 80 degrees or so. However, at the same time if there is a child with a curve of 50 degrees accompanied by rapid progression, then he/she would be an immediate candidate for scoliosis surgery.

I strongly believe that conservative management using non-invasive methods should always be the first option. Before you consider surgery, make sure you have exhausted all other options. Also, it is often advisable to consider a series of opinions of neurosurgeons or orthopedic surgeons in order to make an informed decision.

5. Are you healthy enough to endure surgery?

Apart from the above, you will also need to look at your health. How is your medical health? Do you follow a good, balanced routine for diet and exercise? In other words, do you follow a healthy lifestyle already? All these factors will help determine if you are healthy enough to endure the possible risks associated with surgery and the recovery. We will tell you more about the risks involved in surgery in the next chapter.

6. Do you have the appropriate Financial status?

A surgery for scoliosis can be one of the most expensive procedures you might have undergone in your entire life. Research shows that in the US, every year close to 20,000 Harrington rod implantation surgeries are carried out amongst patients of scoliosis, with an average cost of $120,000 being incurred, per operation. You need to know how much of the cost your insurance covers and the related modalities as well, such as the cost of doctors' visits, rehabilitation fees etc.? You will read more about such costs in Chapter 11. These factors also vary from country to country, hence researching and verifying the cost is extremely important.

7. Compare the scenario

What is more important: The cost and discomfort of living with scoliosis or bearing the cost of the surgery? This forms one of the most critical aspects of decision-making which will require you performing a comparative study of each of the three factors listed below.

Each of these factors compares the kind of life you are having now to how your life will be after the surgery. After studying each of these three factors, you will be able to decide if you are able to live with your deformity as opposed to having surgery done and facing the possible risks, consequences or side effects.

To begin with, analyze the impact of your scoliosis on the following three aspects of your life:

a) Your health

How much is your overall health suffering? Are you beginning to experience any further complications such as difficulty in breathing or an inability to perform everyday activities? Ask yourself, whether living with these symptoms is feasible enough or if having surgery done will be better?

You would also need to ascertain whether your curvature is beginning to impact any other aspect of your health. For instance, scoliosis surgery might be the right option for you if you are beginning to experience symptoms such as neurological complications, abnormal pulmonary function or tightness in the chest.

b) Your finances

How much cost are you incurring on the everyday treatments, therapy and medications you are currently using? Would you rather spend decently on the right diet, exercise and lifestyle to treat yourself, instead of spending on the surgery?

c) Your productivity

How much is your productivity suffering in your daily life? Do you think it will be more advisable to live with this loss of productivity or instead, do you want to attempt to improve your productivity by having an operation? A comparative analysis of such will help you decide if you are in favor of or against surgery.

Note: It helps to know that each of the above factors exists in correlation to one another. For instance, if your curve is more than 45 degrees, but you've already attained your full skeletal maturity and also believe that you can manage your condition with the non-invasive methods; then you might be able manage scoliosis well without surgery. However, you will still need to visit your specialist to look for any signs of the progression of the curve, at least once a year.

Summary

As a final round up, the chart below gives you a quick summary of some of the most critical questions you need to ask yourself as you decide whether or not scoliosis surgery is the right option for you.

Summary – Do you need scoliosis surgery?

☐ Do you have a Cobb angle measurement of around 40 degrees or more, which is progressing in repetitive measurements across a series of examinations?

If yes, you need to seriously consider surgery as an option.

☐ Are you at an age where you body, skeletal structure and spine are still growing?

If yes, you can consider waiting for some time to decide on scoliosis surgery.

☐ Do you suffer from any specific factors that make you more vulnerable to curve progression?

If yes, then consider surgery since your curve might not respond as well to non-invasive methods.

☐ Are you able to financially afford the expenses involved?

If you think that surgery is the only viable option, this is a crucial aspect since it is an expensive procedure that will also require appropriate insurance coverage.

☐ Are you healthy enough to endure surgery?

Ensure that you maintain a good diet, exercise regularly and have a healthy immune system before you have surgery.

☐ Have you tried a variety of combinations available in non-invasive methods?

Make sure you have exhausted all other options.

☐ Have you analyzed the cost of living with the pain and discomfort as opposed to the risks of surgery?

Make sure you have done a comparative analysis of all factors to the best of your ability.

Real Scoliosis Stories: A Difficult Choice to Make!

The extent of the curve is usually the single most important factor that helps in making a decision for or against surgery.

A 12-year old girl was diagnosed in her school screening with a 15-degree curve. Since the curve was mild, she was put on a wait and watch approach (something which I have never recommended).. However, another screening after 2 years revealed that the curve had already advanced to 30-35 degrees. At that stage, she was put on braces, hoping that the curve could be reined in using a non-invasive approach as this. Unfortunately, the teenager hit puberty quite late, because of which the brace had no effect on her curve. By the time she reached her sophomore year, her curve reached up to 45-50 degrees. However, the doctors put off the surgery for some time since she was having very less pain.

Unfortunately, in a few years time, her curve shot up to a shocking 70 degrees. This was just a few months after she delivered her first child. The doctors finally advised immediate surgery for spinal fusion which was eventually carried out 7 months after the baby was born. Watching and waiting is an out dated approach which tends to see the curve worsen. At the first sign of scoliosis the person should work on strengthening the spine and rebalance the surrounding muscles. Pregnancy is a crucial period where the mother to be needs to learn how to effectively take care of their baby and prevent there scoliosis from worsening. More information can be found in my book, 'An Essential Guide for Scoliosis and a Healthy Pregnancy'.

CHAPTER 10

Evaluating Risks of Scoliosis Surgery

Having assisted you in making the decision for surgery in the last chapter, here we go a step further by helping you in the decision-making process. Throughout this chapter, we list the possible risks and complications associated with scoliosis surgery.

In this chapter, we will discuss the various risks and complication that can occur during or after the scoliosis surgery. This information is meant to educate the patient regarding the risks he or she might face during or after the surgery. The patient, along with the surgeon, is then able to make a decision regarding whether the potential benefits of surgery outweigh the potential risks.

Overall, risks of surgery can surface in around 5% of all patients having undergone the procedure for curve correction. Meanwhile, a survey of fusion surgeries done for correcting curves of idiopathic scoliosis between 1993 and 2002 revealed that while the complication rates for children stood at 15%, the rate was as high as 25% in adults.

8 Medical Risks You Should Know

In this section, we have listed the top 8 serious medical risks that might occur with a surgical procedure for scoliosis correction.

1. Infection

Postoperative infections arising due to use of instrumentation, or other environmental factors are one of the most common complications of surgery done for scoliosis. Though occurring only in about 1 to 2% of cases, infections are more common in children who suffer from cerebral palsy due to their low levels of immunity.

One of the major reasons for infection is the fact that after the surgery, your immune system can be in a compromised or weakened state for as long as 3 weeks.

Wound infections are another common scenario in the intraoperative as well as postoperative stage. This risk is minimized to quite an extent by the use of antibiotics prior to the operation, continued upto a week or more after the surgery, given orally or intravenously. In rare cases, a minor operative procedure might be required to cleanse and disinfect the wound to ward off further illness.

2. Nerve damage

During the surgery that will be done for correction of your curve, extra force is placed on the spine. Paraplegia is the most common form of neurological damage a patient can suffer from in such Instances.

When this happens, the patient is then likely to experience partial or complete weakness or numbness in one or both the legs. If faced with such intraoperative nerve damage, you could experience bowel and bladder weakness later in life. It is for this reason that constant neuro-monitoring is done for the patient during the surgical procedure.

Both the sensory and motor tracts of the patient's spinal cord are monitored continuously during the surgery using a combination of tools and tests as explained below.

Grafts and Fusion - What Happens in the Surgery?

Though the further chapters will explain the actual surgical procedure in detail, here it is important to understand the basics of this surgery to better understand the risks involved.

Broadly speaking, your surgery will usually be done in two parts, as explained and shown in the image below.

Part 1: Your spine will be straightened using rigid, steel rods.

Part 2: The correct position obtained in part 1 is then fused in its correct position using bone grafts, which are basically pieces of bone obtained from other parts of your body, such as the pelvis or from a bone bank. This fusion will then prevent the spine from curving further.

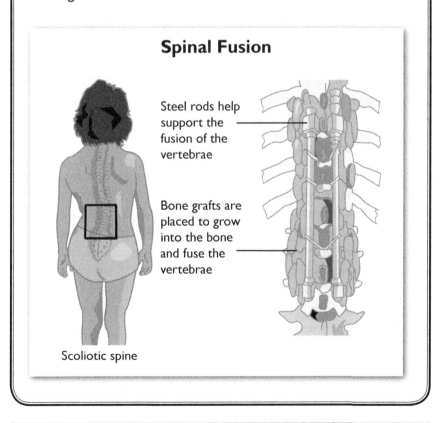

Spinal Fusion

Steel rods help support the fusion of the vertebrae

Bone grafts are placed to grow into the bone and fuse the vertebrae

Scoliotic spine

The Stagnara Wake-Up Test

A wake-up test is often performed during the surgery to evaluate the function of the motor pathways. In this test, a patient is briefly brought out of anesthesia during the procedure to be checked for the response of bodily sensations. Your anesthetist will wake you up, ask you to wiggle your toes, move your feet or do similar actions. If any abnormalities are noticed, your doctor will take suitable steps. Otherwise, the entire procedure of surgery will go on as planned.

Somatosensory Evoked Potentials (SSEPs)

This is another specific test involving small electrical impulses being given to the legs with the readings of these impulses taken from the brain. Any fall in such an electrical response will indicate damage to the spinal cord and the need for immediate corrective action. The Motor Evoked Potentials (MEPs) is another tool to assess any possible damage to the spinal cord during the intraoperative stage. In this process, responses are recorded from the muscles after direct stimulation of the motor cortex.

Apart from being able to identify any damage, these tools and tests will guide your surgeon about the extent of correction that is safe and possible during the scoliosis surgery.

3. Hardware and fusion system issues

In many cases, the instruments and devices such as hooks, rods and screws that were used for the fusion surgery might create a postoperative issue. The hooks or screws becoming dislodged is one the most commonly reported risks in this relevance. In a few cases, the hooks that were used to straighten the spine may actually move a bit away from their original position. Such displacement might take place in about 5% of the cases and will usually require an additional surgery to be rectified, especially if it is causing a lot of pain or indicating a further scope of curve progression.

In addition, rod displacement and discomfort are another potential complication. In some cases, the rod system does not have a proper fixation to the spine, which could lead to some loss in the correction obtained earlier. Rarely, the rods, which are usually made from titanium or stainless steel, might break indicating that the spine has not fused properly.

In yet other cases, the rod might begin to rub on sensitive parts of the body. Such discomfort can arise one to five years after surgery and is generally observed in about less than 10% of patients who have undergone surgery.

Most of the issues arising out of such hardware and instrumentation issues need a revision surgery to be fixed, mostly involving replacement of the hardware and reattachment and realignment of the hardware with the spine.

4. Pseudoarthrosis

This is a condition that is defined by a typical failure of the bones to fuse at any of the operated spinal levels. Occurring in about 1 to 5% of patients, pseudoarthrosis will usually surface many years after the surgery. More specifically, pseudoarthrosis is typically a painful condition in which a false joint will develop at the surgical site. In simpler terms, it is a case where the bone graft that has been used doesn't heal properly and causes further complications. To cure the condition, your surgeon will place more bone graft in the area that has not fused.

5. Reaction to medications and anesthesia

In some cases, the patient might develop an adverse reaction to the anesthesia or medication used for surgery. In case you are aware of any allergies or reactions you might have to anesthesia, meet with your anesthetist in advance and discuss your case to avoid any complications during the surgery.

6. Lung problems

In certain cases, patients are likely to develop mild to moderate lung disorders. Though it can develop in all sorts of patients, this complication is most likely to occur in children who have scoliosis due to neuromuscular disorders such as spina bifida, cerebral palsy or muscular dystrophy. Such breathing and other issues related to lung functions, generally appear after a week of the surgery and take around 3-4 months to resolve, if not too serious in nature.

7. Disk degeneration

Fusion surgeries carried out in the lower back can cause a lot of stress on the disk, which can eventually lead to disk degeneration. Owing to the age factor, patients in the elderly age group are most likely to suffer from disk degeneration following scoliosis surgery. Once the fusion has been done in some part of the spine, there would be segments above and below the fused portion which would have to work harder to sustain mobility. It is this strain that causes advanced degeneration and wear and tear.

8. Hemorrhage

Most surgeries bring with them the risk of hemorrhage or excessive bleeding and blood loss during the operation due to the large amount of muscle stripping and enormous exposed regions. For this purpose, experts advise the patients to donate their own blood (autologous blood donation) or arrange for blood beforehand to help if transfusion is required. You will read more about such preparation for surgery in Chapter 13.

One of the latest breakthroughs in this regard has been the use of preoperative erythropoietin (rhEPO), which is believed to increase the production of red blood cells in the bone marrow.

Other complications

Though rare, other complications can also occur and cause serious damage if not treated within a specific time frame. Some of these include:

- Gallstones
- Blood clots
- Pancreatitis
- Intestinal obstruction

What do I lose?

When evaluating risks and trying to decide whether they are worth taking, ask yourself a single, straight question:

Are you more comfortable living with your present condition than you are with considering the possibility of the above risks?

General Hazards and Risks

1. Long recovery period

Although this is a risk associated with most type of surgeries, a surgery done for curve correction is likely to take a very long time to recover.

For a child, the recovery period from scoliosis will be at least 6 months if no other health complications occur. Even for adults, the recovery time is expected to be as long, the pace of recovery being exceptionally slow. During the entire phase of recovery, your movement could be highly restricted, though the benefits obtained later could be worth it. In fact, how long you take to recover will depend on a number of factors such as your medical history, age, gender and severity of your present curve.

Ask your doctor to explain the recovery phase clearly and whether the risks outweigh the benefits expected.

2. Chronic pain

Once you have had surgery for scoliosis, you might have to live with chronic pain in your back, especially the lumbar area or the lower back region for quite some time. The key explanation of this lies in the fact that your spinal bones have been fused, which can further limit the movement of your spinal column, leading to moderate to severe pain upon exertion. In addition, the instrumentation such as rods and screws used for fusion are generally not removed. But, in some cases the pedicle screws used during surgery become loose and painful , which then need to be removed.

When you have a surgery for scoliosis, you can suffer from a loss of trunk mobility, balance and muscle strength, which could all contribute to chronic lower back pain. You are likely to have less flexibility in your back which can further cause some pain upon sudden jerks or movement. .

In rare cases, some patients continue having major pain-related issues with their back even after years of surgery.

3. Growth compromise

In many cases, especially where the surgery involves very young children, there is a major risk of an overall stunted bone growth owing to the fusion involved. Your surgeon will need to make a careful analysis between how much damage to the growth is expected versus the risk of the curve progressing rapidly with age, if the surgery is not performed. Though your child's height might not be majorly affected, an overall compromise in growth is more likely to be present.

Interesting to know!

Though experts warn of stunted growth, in adults, surgery for scoliosis might make you eventually look taller. Research shows that after such a surgery, an average adult might appear to be taller by 3/8th or even 3/4th inch taller than their preoperative height.

4. Development of arthritis

Though spinal and other forms of arthritis are a common end result of the usual age-related wear and tear, the risk is increased in patients who have undergone scoliosis surgery. This is due to the fact that the forces that are transmitted to the spine through bending and twisting actions are focused over a smaller area and are, hence, stronger and have the potential to cause greater damage.

5. Long term scars

The largest cosmetic fallout of a scoliosis surgery is your scar, which will be mostly as long as the part of your spine that has been fused. In case you had more than a single curve, your scar might actually start from the middle of your shoulder blades and go right down to your pelvis (see the image below).

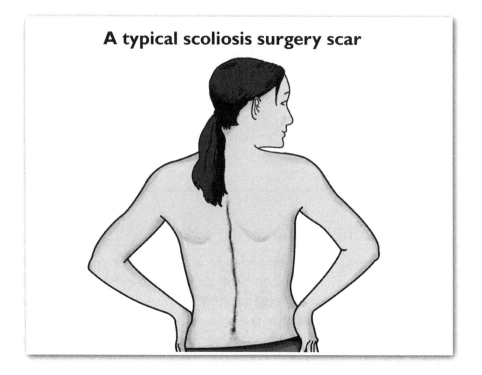

A typical scoliosis surgery scar

What Does Research Say?

Complications and risks of surgery done for correcting a scoliotic curve are a factor the medical community has always considered before advising a patient for this procedure. Both, the standard Harrington method as well as the relatively new Cotrel-Dubousset procedures have their own set of risks attached to them. Research also is able to identify certain segments of patients who are more vulnerable to develop complications from scoliosis surgery. For instance, a study published in a recent issue of *Spine* talk of children with neuromuscular scoliosis to be more vulnerable to the risks of surgery, especially if their curve stands at 60 degrees or more prior to the surgery[2].

Moreover, the rate of complication has also been observed to be higher if the patient undergoes osteotomies (a surgical operation whereby a bone is cut to shorten, lengthen, or change its alignment.), revision procedures or has been subjected to a combined posterior and anterior approach. You will read more about these approaches Chapter 15.

Meanwhile, the rate of complications has been observed to be higher in elderly patients, though the expected benefits are also likely to be higher in this population. A survey conducted to this effect showed that while complications were observed only in 17% of patients in the age group of 25 to 44 years, they were seen in 41% of patients in the age group 45 to 64 years and a whopping 71% in the age group 65 to 85 years. However, the elderly population also had a disproportionately higher rate of improvement in disability and pain associated with the surgery as compared to the younger age group.

Real Scoliosis Stories: The Story of Broken Rods!

A lady in her early 30s had a Harrington procedure done to correct her scoliosis in the mid 1980s. She was made to stay in her plaster cast for 6 months, followed by a plastic cast for another 6 months. By the time her cast came off, both her rods had broken. After a total of 5 years, she had another surgery to have the rods removed. However, when she was around 39 years of age, her spine began to worse rapidly. Within a few years, she was limited to a wheelchair and had a carer to help her dress and shower.

As per the doctors, the bottom of her spine had almost crumbled away. This was the only part of her spine that wasn't crumbled. She was told that her scoliosis has resurfaced. The patient also feared that her lung might begin to get compressed as it did when she was a teenager with scoliosis.

CHAPTER 11

Money Management – The Big Hole in Your Pocket

aving surgery for scoliosis, as with any major surgery, is a big decision. Whether it's for yourself or for any of your family members, the decision to undergo a scoliosis surgery should include prior planning and careful analysis of the various aspects involved. Once you have decided upon surgery, the first and most important aspect to consider is the financial implication of the surgery. In this chapter we will discuss the various financial issues involved in such a surgical procedure.

The Money Drain - Factors to Consider

Estimates show that in the United States, over 20,000 Harrington rod implantation surgeries are performed every year, at an average cost of around $120,000 per operation.

Planning your finances for a scoliosis surgery in the near future is surely a big procedure on its own. As you set out to understand the financial implications of your surgery, your first need is to specify the exact amount that might be involved. However, since all individuals and situations are different, the cost involved for the rectification of your scoliotic curve will also vary to a great extent.

When trying to determine at an estimate for the cost of your procedure, there are a number of factors you will first need to take into consideration. Here, we've listed some of the most important factors you need to look at to assist you with determining the cost.

1. Severity of your curve

The first and most important factor in determining the cost of your scoliosis surgery is your curve itself. How severe is your curve, what is its exact location and what all will be required to correct it will all be considered in the exact cost of your surgery. In fact, the severity of your curve will also determine most of the other related factors such as duration of your stay in the hospital, the type of instrumentation to be used and even the type of surgeon you will require.

2. Duration of hospital stay

You will need to have an idea of how long you are likely to be in the hospital. This will depend on your age, the exact type of surgery you are having and also on your state of health. The duration of your stay in the hospital will also be affected by any post surgical complications that may occur.

3. Your choice of hospital and surgeon

Each physician, medical institution and even country has its own set of financial policies. In fact, every country has a specific policy as regards the assistance they offer to the patients of scoliosis surgery. For instance, the Shriners Hospital in the US and Canada offer discounted rates to all patients for scoliosis below the age of 18. Meanwhile, some sources also claim that in countries like Germany, the prices for scoliosis surgery are usually 75% less than the cost of scoliosis treatment in US, though figures might vary.

You will need to carefully analyze your available budget as compared to the various options available. The specific hospital and surgeon you choose for your surgery will determine a large portion of the cost involved for your procedure. In chapter 12, you will read more about how to select the correct surgeon for your case.

4. Type of instrumentation involved

The cost of surgery will also depend on the kind of instrumentation involved for your procedure. Moreover, the cost can also depend on how new the procedure is. At times, new procedures that are under trial are cheaper than the others which have been in practice since long. It will be helpful to learn about the type and standard of hooks, rods and screws that will be used as they also may vary in price.

5. Your insurance coverage

You need to research what exact coverage your insurance company provides for the procedure you will be having. For instance, some insurance companies might not cover certain elements of the surgical costs, such as the instrumentation. Make sure you speak to your insurance provider and discuss all of the elements involved in your case. You will also need to discuss this with the hospital's billing department to ensure the financial issues are settled before the surgery.

The Estimates – Foreseen Expenses

As with any major medical treatment, scoliosis surgery is an expensive procedure. You need to plan properly and take all factors into account to ensure that you are adequately prepared to meet all the expenses, including budgeting for unforeseen expenses.

The cost of a scoliosis surgery will usually vary in accordance with the number of factors we've discussed above. Keeping all factors in view, a standard scoliosis surgery will usually cost in the range of $75,000 to $300,000 per operation.

Here, we've given a brief breakdown of the total cost of the foreseen expenses involved in scoliosis surgery.

i) Infrastructural costs

Infrastructural costs usually involve the charges for the hospital stay itself for the patient, as well as the attendants.

ii) Cost of surgery

This includes the cost of the actual procedure, which is basically your surgeon and the hospital's fee for the scoliosis surgery.

iii) Medication costs

This includes the cost of all the medications including antibiotics, pain medication and anesthesia used during your operation, as well as before and after the procedure.

iv) Instrumentation costs

Your surgeon will use a variety of screws, rods, wires, hooks and other instruments to correct your curvature. Depending on the exact type of instruments used, the cost can vary amongst different surgeries.

v) Therapy cost

Once out of the surgery, you will need a series of additional therapies for the purpose of rehabilitation. To return to your normal routine, you will need the help of a physiotherapist and other healthcare professionals which will further add to the total cost of surgery.

vi) Attendants' cost

Hospitals usually allow one or two attendants to stay with you in the hospital. There will be a cost incurred on their stay, meals and other requirements, which should ideally be included in the total estimates.

The below table gives you a chart you can use to plan the expenses and arrive at an approximate estimate for your surgery.

Table of cost estimates

Type of expenditure	estimated costs
Infrastructural costs	
Cost of surgery	
Medication costs	
Instrumentation costs	
Therapy costs	
Attendants' cost	
total	

Insurance Coverage

Owing to the large amount of costs involved in a scoliosis surgery, it is very important that you look for alternate means of meeting the expenses, apart from your own existing resources. When it comes to options, health insurance definitely comes up as the most natural choice to help cover the costs.

Inclusions and Exclusions

Though insurance coverage is usually available for a scoliosis surgery, there are some fine details which you should be informed of. In quite a few cases, your insurance provider is likely to point out that some aspects of your proposed surgical procedure may be unnecessary, experimental or extreme. Insurance coverage for such costs is usually denied in the first attempt. Your surgeon's staff will then take up the relevant reasoning with the insurance provider and work out basic modalities, as we've explained in the 'Pre-authorization' section below.

In this section, we've summarized a few important highlights related to the insurance coverage possible for your scoliosis surgery.

→ Bone grafting is an essential part of your surgery. However, certain insurance providers will view the Bone Morphogenetic Protein (BMP) technique for bone grafting as an experimental process and deny coverage.

→ Since titanium instrumentation is more expensive than the stainless steel rods, your insurance company might term it as an unnecessary expense.

→ The cost of certain surgical assistants and attendants in the operating room might be denied, even though they are an integral part of the doctor's surgical team.

→ At times, your PPO (Preferred Provider Organization) might cover 100% of the hospital costs. However, some of the specialists associated with your surgery, such as your anesthetist, pathologist or your physiotherapist might not be associated with your PPO, due to which your PPO will not pay, or may pay at a lower percentage, for their services. On the other hand, your PPO might pay for these services if your specialist is a part of that particular PPO network.

Preauthorization

Before you schedule a final date for your surgery, make sure you've obtained a preauthorization from your insurance provider. In most of the cases, your surgeon will have specialized staff for this purpose that will ensure preauthorization has been attained. As a part of this step, your surgeon's staff will also attempt to negotiate with your insurance provider to provide you with the best possible compensation for your surgery.

However, it is important for you to know that this procedure of preauthorization is likely to take weeks or even months. Hence, you must keep this margin of time in mind before planning for other aspects of your scoliosis surgery.

In addition to the above, it is also important to know that the insurance policies regarding scoliosis surgeries usually vary in different states and countries. For example, in the United States, your insurance company will typically cover at least half of the expenses involved. Meanwhile, in Canada, a scoliosis surgery is usually 100% covered by Canada's Health Care System. The underlying logic is that if your surgeon decides that surgery is necessary, and it isn't merely for cosmetic reasons, then it can simply be billed to the government.

Your 5 Step Plan to Money Management

1. Study your factors and gain knowledge

Go through each of the factors we've discussed above and gather as much relevant knowledge you can about your surgery. You need to make a careful analysis of all the factors involved to draw an accurate estimate of how much money will you actually need.

2. Draw an estimate

Once step 1 is done, you can then move on to draw a better estimate of the costs involved, putting down a relevant cost against each sub-part and arriving at an approximate figure.

3. Work out your insurance modalities

Refer to the details discussed above to determine the extent of coverage your PPO or insurance company will provide. There may be a situation where you might find your insurance coverage inadequate and would want to look for further alternate means. Such a situation will arise in either of these two cases:

- You do not have insurance
- Your insurance provider doesn't offer sufficient coverage

In such a situation, you can investigate taking on a second policy, or switching to another PPO or insurance company. ,However, most insurance providers will have fixed rules regarding coverage offered for pre-existing conditions.

4. Know the gap

In cases where you have made all possible efforts to finance your surgery and there still seems to be a gap, you can look at a few other options to cover your expenses. Here, we've listed some of the options you might have:

→ Some surgeons might offer you a discount if you are willing to be part of a research study

→ Go to one of the many Shriners Hospitals , which offer surgery for children up to 18 years of age at no charge. These hospitals operate in cities including Chicago, Illinois; Greenville, South Carolina;, Honolulu, Hawaii; Houston, Texas; Lexington, Kentucky; Los Angeles, California; Minneapolis, Minnesota and Philadelphia, Pennsylvania. Internationally, there are also Shriners Hospitals in Montreal and Mexico City.

→ Check if you can borrow money from your retirement account, including your 401(k) or IRA plans.

→ Speak to your hospital representative regarding payment plans, such as those involving monthly installments.

→ Seek a bank loan or get your house refinanced using a cash-out mortgage.

5. Have a back-up plan ready

Even after you've gone through the entire drill above, make sure to have a back-up plan ready. You might consider speaking to a relative or close friend to have options ready in case you have unforeseen expenses or any other issues with the financial aspect of your surgery.

Real Scoliosis Stories: The Insurance Obstacle!

Mathew's story was already an unusual one. After all, he was all of 6 months old when his physicians diagnosed him as having infantile idiopathic scoliosis. Such was his present state that the doctors feared that Mathew was at a risk of respiratory problems at a mere age of 6 months. The reason lay in the nature of his curve, which was progressive and was probably increasing at a very rapid rate.

To curb the curve, his doctors advised the use of bracing, which was in itself a very difficult thing to do for such a young child. However, even bracing didn't help as the curve continued to progress. It was then that the family decided in favor of a scoliosis surgery. Unfortunately, another road block hit them at his juncture. The family had a health insurance plan which did not allow out-of-state treatment. The scoliosis specialist was only available in San Diego, California which spanned to be out of the scope of the family's current health insurance plan. It was only after the intervention of their local specialist in Nevada and that of the specialists in San Deigo, that Mathew was allowed to begin his treatment from the referred scoliosis specialist in San Deigo.

CHAPTER 12

Choosing the Time, Place and Surgeon

In the sections that follow, we will guide you through the entire process of choosing your surgeon, along with the time and place of your surgery. You will also learn about the areas you will need to research in order to make an informed choice.

Why Does it Matter?

Medicine and surgery is perhaps one of the most widely opted professions across the globe today. Specializations abound, and so do the opportunities to obtain an expertise in this field. However, since surgery is such a highly specialized area of medicine, the services offered by each individual surgeon do not suit all types of patients. A surgeon who performed the spinal fusion for an acquaintance might be absolutely perfect in his profession, but may not be a good match for you or your condition.

It is this comfort zone with the hospital and surgeon that eventually matters, once you've ascertained all qualifications and expertise!

When you opt for something as complicated as a surgery for scoliosis, you've undoubtedly put a lot at stake, but can expect good results with careful analysis and pre-planning. In all probability, you've gone considered the possible risks and complications that may occur during and after surgery. Though a majority of such risks may occur after the best of precautions, it is advisable to plan and prepare to minimize any possible issues later. Choosing your surgeon, along with the time and place of surgery, is perhaps one of the most important choices you can voluntarily make to ensure maximum success with your surgery.

Set a Date

So, you've decided to opt for surgery to correct the curve in your spine? By now, you've probably already evaluated your risks and even planned your finances, as we've discussed in the earlier chapters. It's time now to discuss the logistics and make a concrete plan for the surgery. As might be obvious, there are three main things you will need to decide on, including:

- Date of surgery
- Place of surgery
- Your surgeon

In this section, we will first begin by guiding you through the process of choosing a date for your surgery in a few basic steps.

Step 1 – Rate your curve

You have to begin by understanding the state of your curve. In consultation with your surgeon, you have to ascertain the progression of your curve and the best time to operate. For instance, if your surgeon views any further delays as a risk for your health, then you have good reason to set an early date for surgery. Decide on how much of a waiting period you need and then you can set a date accordingly.

Step 2 – Analyze your medical condition

Again, together with your surgeon and spine care specialist, analyze any medical conditions that need to be addressed before you undergo surgery. For instance, you might be suffering from a skin rash or an episode of arthritis which needs to be treated properly before you go in for your procedure. Since a scoliosis surgery is almost never a medical emergency, it will be quite possible for you to wait until such conditions are clear.

Step 3 – Work out the logistics

Once you've gone through all of the above, you can then look at other factors that might determine the best date for your surgery. Here, we've listed a few common factors to consider, however, there may be other considerations as well in accordance with your specific circumstances. A few factors that could influence your decision could include:

→ Whether there is any major professional commitment you need to fulfill since you are likely to be out of work for quite some time.

→ Whether there is any major event coming up in your family, such as childbirth, wedding, graduation ceremony or the like.

→ If you are a woman, try to set the date that is different from the expected date of your periods.

→ If there is a time of year, weather wise, which may impact your rehabilitation.

→ Whether you have any immediate travel plans.

→ Whether you have a family member available who will be able to assist you post surgery.

Choose the Hospital

This step will perhaps occur in coordination with the other two. In researching the logistics of your surgery, you will now go on to look for the hospital where your surgery will be performed.

In this section, we will furnish a set of factors that will influence how you select the place and hospital for your surgery.

The Factors that matter

1. Location and proximity

It generally helps to have a hospital that is accessible to your home. In fact, this may be one of the trickiest decisions to make. You must find a balance between the quality of care and the accessibility of the location. At the outset, it might look unnecessary to choose a hospital that is close to your home. But, having a hospital at an accessible location makes your treatment and post surgery care more convenient.

2. Your insurance coverage

Some insurance providers will provide less coverage for a hospital that is outside their network. Check the relevant details with your insurance provider before you make a choice to ensure that you get the maximum possible benefit of your insurance coverage. A good way to do this is to look for a qualified orthopedic surgeon in your insurance carrier's medical specialists category.

3. The hospital's reputation and track record

There are various sources you can consult to learn more about a particular hospital's reputation and track record. Some of the most important sources include:

- Patients' and their families' feedback
- Your General Practitioner's reviews
- Hospital's report cards, which give you details such as a categorized inventory of surgeries which have been performed at the hospital over the last year

4. Infrastructure and facilities

Many hospitals have a special area for patients undergoing orthopedic treatments. It will help you to take a tour of the area and even have a look at the rooms. Look for details like the number of nurses or attendants on call and the ratio of patients to nurses.

It is also important that your hospital has the proper set of facilities and technology for the purpose of scoliosis surgeries, a few examples being:

- Professional air exchange systems to prevent the spread of germs
- Advanced monitoring systems
- Special arrangements for the disabled

5. The team

The choice of the surgeon is extremely important and you will read more about it in the following sections. However, an entire team of healthcare providers is involved in your surgical care. Try to find out more about these specialists such as the:

- Radiologists
- Anesthesiologists
- Physical therapists
- Nurses

Place or surgeon – what takes priority?

You might wonder why you need to choose both the place and the surgeon. After all, you may think that the choice of the surgeon is the most important decision and that the specific hospital is inconsequential. However, all hospitals will not offer you the same set of facilities for a scoliosis surgery. The best bet is to try and find a balance of both, a suitable surgeon placed at an accessible and well-equipped hospital.

Choose Your Surgeon – Look Beyond the Scenes

In your pursuit for the most ideal surgeon for your scoliosis surgery, it is natural for you to look at some of the obvious facts such as the surgeon's qualifications, experience, reviews and reputation. As much as these factors matter, it also helps to know a few things about your surgeon, which may not be obvious.

In the sections that follow, we give you a detailed guide on what to check for in your surgeon, what to look for in a surgeon's reputation and, most importantly, any warning signs to be beware of.

About Your Surgeon – 10 things you must know

1. Is he or she duly qualified, licensed and registered?

Do your research to determine the standard set of requirements for a spine surgeon. Make sure your surgeon fulfills these requirements and is duly qualified to conduct surgeries for scoliosis. He also has to be duly licensed and registered to perform surgeries of this nature.

As a general rule, it helps to choose a spine surgeon who has completed a fellowship program with at least a year of additional training, which is specific to spine surgery.

2. Is he or she a member of a professional organization?

It is important for you to ascertain whether your proposed surgeon is a member of any professional organization. Each stream of medicine and surgery has its own professional organization which offers memberships to the relevant practitioners.

For instance, in the US, memberships for such surgeons are offered by the American Academy of Orthopedic Surgeons and are usually mandatory.

Also, specifically for scoliosis, you can refer to the Scoliosis Research Society (SRS) which has stringent membership requirements for such specialists. In fact, SRS actually maintains a proper list of qualified and licensed orthopedic surgeons you can look for in your area.

3. Does he or she specialize in spine surgeries?

Even if you are talking to a qualified surgeon, they may not be duly qualified to perform surgeries for scoliosis. It is important to know whether your surgeon has expertise in performing specific spinal fusions required for scoliosis. Make sure your specialist has the required expertise and experience with such procedures.

4. How much experience does he or she have in performing scoliosis surgeries?

Find out how many scoliosis correction surgeries the surgeon has performed to date. A general rule of thumb is to look for a surgeon whose spinal surgeries form at least 50% of his total cases. A surgeon being listed with an association such as SRS usually indicates that at least 20% of the experience of the surgeon has been in treating spinal deformities. You indeed have a reason to reconsider your choice if your surgeon has performed a limited amount of scoliosis surgeries.

5. What is his or her success rate?

Once you have learned about your doctor's level of experience, it is then time to assess his success rate. Seek active feedback from the surgeon's previous patients who have had a similar procedure. Discuss the patient's comfort level with the surgeon both during and after the surgery and whether they have had any serious complications. You can then ask your surgeon to further clarify any questions you may have.

6. What does the surgeon's staff say about them?

It helps to gain information from the people who are associated with your doctor. In most cases, nurses, attendants and other medical providers have a good insight into the way the doctor works. For instance, you can get an impression from these individuals regarding the level of attention your surgeon gives to details, which is important when handling precise matters such as spinal surgery.

7. Are you comfortable with him or her?

This is as important as all the other issues we discussed above. You have to ensure that you have a full comfort level with the surgeon you are considering. A scoliosis surgery is a life-altering event and having comfort with the person performing the procedure is extremely important to the success of your surgery. To begin with, your surgeon should ideally be forthright in answering all your questions, should not discourage you from seeking second opinions and overall, should be patient with all your queries.

8. Does he or she actively engage in research activities?

It often helps to know whether the surgeon you are considering is involved in research in his field of expertise. This is an indication that your specialist is involved in making new innovations and discoveries and hence, advancements in their field of specialization. You can also find out whether they participate in global events related to the profession, which help such professionals to stay abreast of the latest developments in their profession.

9. Does he or she adopt new techniques and tools?

It helps to know whether your doctor believes in updating their techniques and tools with the latest developments in the profession. Ideally, a successful surgeon will always look for ways to improve their methods using the latest techniques and tools available.

10. Is your surgeon covered under your insurance?

Looking at the costs involved, it helps to know whether the services of your chosen surgeon will be covered by your insurance provider. Crosscheck with your provider in accordance with the place they are working and the rates quoted beforehand.

A point to remember...

Just remember, there will never be a perfect formula to judge your surgeon's experience. Parameters will vary according to the kind of surgery you are looking for and many such factors.

Getting Honest

Apart from the above academic and standardized questions, there are a few more difficult questions you should ideally ask when choosing your surgeon. Answers to these questions will probably give you a better indication on the suitability of your surgeon to your case.

Our tip: Your surgeon might not be totally forthright in answering these questions. Be smart and look for signs of body language, expressions and indirect answers to determine any flaws in their responses.

The 5 dreaded questions you must ask

Q1. Have you ever been barred from surgery or faced any legal action relevant to your profession?

Q2 . What is the worst complication you've experienced following any of your scoliosis or other surgeries?

Q3. When was the first time you did such a surgery and how many have you done since then?

Q4. Do children feel comfortable with you?

Q5. Do you mind if I seek a second opinion?

The Red Flags

Though any serious issues with your surgeon might be already known, there are facts about the specialist which might become evident during your interaction with him. Watch out for any such red flags, which will clearly indicate that you need to strictly stay away from that particular specialist.

A few such warning signs will include:

→ If your surgeon has ever been implicated in a legal offence

→ If your surgeon doesn't welcome second opinions

→ If your surgeon is impatient with your queries

→ If your surgeon tries to influence your decision as whether or not to have surgery

→ If your surgeon shows any disregard for the existing treatment options you are following

→ If there is any ambiguity presented on the aspect of costs and other logistics

→ If your search for feedback reveals any major complications post surgery

→ If your surgeon's staff or other doctors give you some negative feedback

→ If you've ever come across any negative reference about your surgeon in the media

CHAPTER 13
Preparing for Your Surgery

Having made all the crucial decisions already, it will now be time to begin your preparation for the surgery. You will now need to think and plan ahead to prepare for the final day. In this chapter, we will guide you on the crucial aspects of preparing for a scoliosis surgery. We will give you comprehensive guidelines on how to prepare yourself medically in terms of tests and medications. We will also give you a detailed checklist of what you will need to carry with you to the hospital to make yourself more comfortable before, as well as after, the surgery.

A surgery for scoliosis is indeed a colossal decision. It carries with it a series of speculations along with a staggering scope of complications and unforeseen circumstances. Medical emergencies always abound within and outside an operation theatre and are seldom within the voluntary control of the patient, and mostly even that of the experts. Hence, it is advisable to plan with the best possible vision of potential complications so that any scope of such damage is minimized and a successful outcome is witnessed.

I) Exercise, Fitness and Diet

Read on as we lead you in a step-wise approach on how to prepare for the much-awaited day of your surgery. The stronger and healthier you are before surgery, the more quickly you will recover.

Being in a good physical state will help you cope much better with the rigors of a scoliosis surgery. It is in your best interest to exercise regularly, as the healthier you are pre-surgery, the faster will you recover once the surgery is over. In fact, regular exercise before your surgery will have a two-fold benefit, which includes:

→ Keeping you fit and healthy
→ Providing you relief from anxiety and stress associated to the surgery

In all probability, your doctor will advise you to exercise to tolerance before your surgery, implying that you should exercise regularly, taking care not to exercise strenuously.

What your doctor might not tell you...

Not all surgeons prescribe specific exercises or a dietary regimen. Some specialists will generally advise you to exercise and follow a healthy diet. However, it helps to seek further help on the specific type of exercises you should do and particular foods you should have and avoid.

Forms of exercise

Your surgeon might advise you to take up specific exercises to attain certain important objectives such as flexibility and improvement in range of motion. As a general rule, it is best to combine the basic regimen of aerobic conditioning with that of muscle conditioning. Aerobic conditioning will basically include exercises that strengthen your heart and lungs, such as walking, swimming or bicycling. Meanwhile, muscle strengthening will include exercises that will help you build up strength in your legs and arms. This is crucial since you will need the strength of your legs and arms while transitioning from one position to another after surgery.

What you didn't know...

Unless you are obese, your surgeon might not want you to lose excess weight before surgery. Since you are already likely to shed a lot of weight post surgery, an extra cushioning in terms of a bit of excess weight might be actually beneficial!

Preparing for your surgery – exercises you can do

Here, we've discussed some of the most helpful forms of exercise you can follow to maintain and develop strength and ensure a speedy recovery for yourself.

a) *For range of motion (ROM)*

These exercises will give you the impact you are going to need the most after surgery since your muscles are going to be stiff. In most of the cases, the patient won't be even able to bend or turn properly.

The most helpful form of exercises for this purpose are those involving repetitive contracting and expanding of the large muscle groups in the body. By involving large movements, these exercises help improve your range of motion. The most common forms of exercises advised for this purpose include:

- Walking
- Bicycling
- Jogging
- Swimming

b) For blood clot prevention

You can follow the below steps to do an effective exercise that can help in prevention of blood clots related to your scoliosis surgery.

You can follow the steps for each of these three exercises to help ensure prevention of clots.

Exercise 1

- Slowly, point your toes forward, gently moving them towards the foot of the bed.
- Now, try to pull your toes toward your chin.
- Repeat 10 times.

Exercise 2

- Gently, bend one of your knees
- Now, slide your heel up the other leg, towards your hip
- Slowly, stretch your leg out again and relax

Exercise 3

This exercise can be done when you are lying down.

- Slowly, but firmly, move your feet in such a way as if you are drawing circles with your heels on the bed.

c) For prevention of lung complications

Lung and breathing complications are a very common problem associated with scoliosis surgery. To prevent the same, you can practice some breathing and coughing exercises beforehand to avoid lung complications to the maximum extent

Follow the steps below for one of the simplest and most effective breathing and coughing exercises towards this objective:

- Take a long, deep breath through your nose
- Hold your breath, counting up to 5
- Now, breathe out slowly, only through your mouth
- Repeat five times

- As you breathe out for the fifth time, try to cough hard from your abdomen

You can take further guidance from '*Your Plan for Natural Scoliosis Prevention and Treatment*', a rich source of useful information for natural treatment of scoliosis. Here, you will find details of all types of exercises that are beneficial for a scoliosis patient, such as those focusing on flexibility, rebalancing and strengthening, with a stress on core stability.

Diet Management

The key here is balance. When preparing for spinal surgery, you have to follow the best of dietary guidance. Your diet has to be nutritious and wholesome, giving you energy and vigor to help with a speedy recovery.

Read on for a few handy tips you can use:

→ Eliminate excessive calories and fat from your diet at least 6 weeks before your surgery.

→ Include loads of fruits and vegetables into your daily diet, especially just before the surgery. The fiber content therein will help in facilitating comfortable bowel movements, which can otherwise be quite painful after a surgery such as this.

→ Drink lots of water and fluids on a regular basis.

→ Make sure you have regular meals and take care not to disturb your digestive system by eating in excess or starving yourself.

→ Take iron supplements, if required.

→ You will be advised not to eat or drink for at least 8 hours prior to your surgery.

→ Make sure you do not consume salty foods and alcohol on the day before your scheduled surgery.

To equip yourself with the right diet plan, just refer to 'Your Plan for Natural Scoliosis Prevention and Treatment'. It is a comprehensive guide that offers you details on the food options and nutrients that aid recovery and are good for your spinal and bone health.

2) Blood Donation

It is very common for patients to lose some blood during a spinal surgery. In the absence of immediate replenishment, the patient can suffer from serious damage to the system. To safeguard against any possible damage owing to this blood loss and also to save on precious time, you will be informed of the various choices by which you can arrange blood beforehand. Read on as we list the two main options you will have so that you can make a well-planned and informed choice for your surgery.

a) Autologous blood donation

Your surgeon will encourage you to donate your own blood prior to the surgery. Under this practice, also known as autologous donations, you will be required to donate about 2-3 units of blood.

If you decide to donate your own blood, you might be advised to take a prescription of iron pills, such as ferrous sulfate. You can also add a regular dosage of vitamin C to it. If you are on these pills, just make sure you have enough of fruits, fluids and vegetables in your diet, since an iron supplement can actually cause constipation.

Will the autologous blood donation have any negative impact on my surgery?

Well, not really! If you are a healthy patient, your body will replace the blood content very soon and much before the time of surgery. In fact, autologous blood donation considerably reduces the risks associated with homologous blood donation. Just make sure you eat a nourishing meal around 3-4 hours prior to the blood donation.

Who cannot do autologous blood donation?

You will be advised against donating your own blood if you:

✓ Weigh less than 60 lbs.
✓ Have anemia
✓ Are medically unfit or weak

b) Blood Bank or Designated Donors

This option can be used if you are medically unfit for autologous blood donation or do not wish to do so for any other reason. In this case, you will need a volunteer who can donate for you. You can either decide on a family member or friend or seek assistance from a registered blood bank.

The blood units collected through the autologous donation as well as through volunteers will be subjected to a series of tests to declare them fit for transfusion.

c) Other methods

Apart from arranging blood beforehand, your surgeon might also take other measures to reduce blood loss during surgery. Some of the options they might opt for include:

- **Hypotensive anesthesia** – Considered as an effective method for minimizing blood loss during surgery, hypotensive anesthesia can be given using the regional or general anesthesia. In this technique hypotension is achieved through the use of deep inhalation anesthesia which further leads to the dilation of the arterial system. Studies report that if the arterial pressure is maintained at 50 mmHg during surgery, there can be a 2-4 fold reduction in the amount of intraoperative blood loss.
- **Cell saver technique** – This technology, though a bit costlier, enables a saving of up to 50% of red blood mass during surgery and is now becoming increasingly popular. In this technique, the patient's own blood is collected from surgical sites. This blood is then transfused back, as and when required during the surgery.
- **Normovolemic hemodilution** – This technique is also aimed at reducing the loss of red blood cells. Under this method, first blood is withdrawn until the level reaches at 9 g/dl or higher after hemodilution (a process in which the fluid content is increased in the blood). Once done, the volume is maintained using crystalloid replacement and the surgery is then performed at a normal blood pressure. Finally, the the excess fluid is separated after the surgery is over after which the blood that was withdrawn initially is transfused back into the patient.

- **Erythropoietin** – Used as a suitable alternative to autologous transfusion, erythropoietin (EPO) is basically a hormone administered to the patient just before the surgery. EPO works by raising the hemoglobin level to such a count where blood loss ceases to be a problem anymore.

3) Examinations and Tests

Prior to a scoliosis surgery, medical tests and examinations are performed with two key aims, which include:

→ To ensure that the patient is medically fit, and is eligible for surgery
→ To provide a guide for the surgical procedure

You will be required to go in for such pre-admission testing at least 1-2 weeks prior to your surgery. On this day, also known as the day for 'work-up', you might have to stay in the hospital for more than 5-6 hours, depending on the tests and examinations your surgeon advises you to have.

(a) Physical examination

Your medical tests are likely to start with a basic physical examination. This would include checking for aspects like fever, blood pressure and heart rate. This step is basically made to ensure that you don't suffer from any basic health problems which might need treatment before your surgery.

(b) Specific tests

Apart from a simple physical check-up, you might be required to go through a series of tests to be declared fit for surgery. Here, we've listed some of the most common tests you might be advised to have, along with their basic purposes.

1. **X-rays** – These are primarily done to help the surgeon plan his surgical approach. Your doctor will need to decide where he plans to place his screws, rods, hooks and the like.

2. **Pulmonary function tests (PFT)** – These tests will be advised if you have very severe curves. Alternatively, you might be also advised to go for these if you have been facing any difficulty in breathing or shortness of breath, which may or may not be related to your curve in the first place.

3. **Myelography and MRI** – These are done to rule out possibilities such as syringomyelia, diastematomyelia and tethered cord.

4. **Electrocardiogram (EKG)** – This is done to test the levels of your heart function.

5. **Electroencephalogram (EEG)** – This test is done to examine the state of nerve impulses which go through your spine.

6. **Blood tests** – These are more routine tests to ascertain details such as your blood type and hemoglobin levels.

7. **Urine tests** – These are also carried out as routine tests to check for any abnormalities.

8. **Clinical photos** – In most cases, your surgeon will want to take pictures of your curve before, as well as after, the surgery. The visit for pre-admissions testing will be a good occasion to do this.

4) Medications

When it comes to the use of medications as a preparatory step for your scoliosis surgery, there are two main things you need to learn about, which include:

→ Medications you need to discontinue
→ Medications that you might need to start before surgery for pain relief and other purposes.

To begin with, you need to start by informing your surgeon of all the over-the-counter and prescription medications you are taking. For instance, some of the most common pain relieving medications are contraindicated for spinal surgery and interfere with the effects of your anesthesia.

Here, we've listed a few important pointers in regards to the use of medications prior to your scoliosis surgery.

→ Stop all blood thinners at least 2 weeks prior to your surgery, such as aspirin and herbal supplements like Ginkgo Biloba, Vitamin E, St. John's Wort and Garlic pills.

→ Stop all forms of nonsteroidal anti-inflammatory medications (NSAIDs) and COX 2 inhibitors. Common examples will include:

- Motrin
- Advil
- Aleve
- Actron
- Oruvail

What you must know...

Research shows both NSAIDs and aspirin can increase the volume of blood loss during surgery ,as well as inhibit the process of bone fusion post surgery.

→ Discontinue all prescription pain medications and take your surgeon's advice on which pain medications you can safely use. You might need to discontinue the likes of:

- Lodine
- Indocin
- Celebrex
- Relafen
- Ultram
- Voltaren
- Cataflam

→ Make sure you stop all herbal supplements at least 1-2 weeks prior to the surgery.

→ For pain relief, Tylenol or acetaminophen is generally considered as a safe option to be used prior to the surgery.

→ Add a suitable multivitamin to your diet weeks before surgery. Your doctor should be able to prescribe you an appropriate supplement for the purpose.

→ In addition, your surgeon might also prescribe an anti-anxiety pill, such as Valium, that you can take prior to your surgery, if required.

Before You Leave Home

With all the modalities having been taken care of, you now need to look at the things you need to accomplish before you leave home for your surgery. From carrying some basic essentials with you to the hospital, making important changes to your lifestyle and making a few critical modifications around your home, there are a series of preparations you will need to make.

Read on as we furnish a detailed guideline on how to prepare yourself and your home for your surgery.

Lifestyle changes - Prepare your comfort zone

→ Sleep well for the nights before the surgery, exercise regularly and follow overall healthy habits.

→ Quit smoking as it interferes with the process of bone fusion, apart from enhancing the risk of anesthesia complications. Moreover, smoking slows down your body's healing process.

→ Avoid consuming alcohol for a few weeks before your surgery as it might impair your body's ability to heal itself.

→ Adjust the things in your house to make them more accessible as you are going to be unable to perform routine tasks post surgery. For instance, shift the items you use on a regular basis from the higher cabinets to the lower ones.

→ Prepare some meals in advance and freeze them for easy use.

→ Make sure that the switches you use more frequently, such as the bedside lamp are at a reachable distance.

→ Get helpful tools like a loofah and even a shaver with a long handle so that you can take a bath or shave your legs with ease. Speak to your occupational therapist who can suggest tools and ideas to assist you with daily activities like bathing, dressing, etc. Refer to the end of this chapter for a list of the twenty most important items you must carry.

→ Clear cluttered spaces in your house so that you can walk around with a cane easily. Also remove any slippery surfaces like rugs or carpets.

→ Get a neat haircut. It will be a while before you will be able to get a haircut again. In fact, post surgery you may require help with daily grooming.

→ Take care of your skin, especially the skin of your back. Take immediate medical attention if you are suffering from any injury or a rash on your back.

→ Pay all your bills in advance and if possible, set up automatic withdrawals for at least a couple of months after the surgery.

→ Go through all of your pre-set appointments well in advance. These might include visits to a dentist, gynecologist, your tax advisor, veterinarian and so on.

→ Get yourself ready emotionally. Learn to relax. As difficult as it might sound, you have to learn to consciously relax yourself to be able to take the brunt of surgery. Practice relaxation techniques using whatever method you can.

Knowledge is power

Equip yourself with as much information as you can. The more you are aware of what lies in store for you, the better will it be.

Seek Support

Identify your support group. Make sure you have someone who will be willing to stay with you post surgery, as you are going to need a lot of care and help.

- → Seek professional counseling if you feel overwhelmed by anxiety regarding your procedure.
- → If you are unmarried and live alone, try to identify help from your relatives, neighbors, colleagues and friends beforehand.
- → Always accept help if it is offered. Be very specific when expressing your needs to others.
- → Look for help from online scoliosis support groups and societies that are familiar with the condition and the impact of the surgery involved.
- → Let your close family and friends know that you might be emotionally a bit unstable post surgery. Hence, you might require the understanding and support of friends and family.

Point to ponder...

If this is going to be the first surgery you've ever had in your life, the emotional experience of it all can be especially daunting and perplexing. Prepare yourself mentally in advance for the months to come.

---

20 items you must carry*

1. Daily medications
2. Basic toiletries
3. Slip on shoes
4. Chapstick
5. Music (with earphones)
6. Cell phone
7. Back scratcher
8. Step stool
9. Knee length robe
10. Grabber
11. Cane

12. Bell

13. Phone list

14. Washcloths

15. Raised toilet seat

16. Dry shampoo

17. Handheld shower

18. Toilet tissue aid

19. Sanitary pads (for women)

20. Facial cleansing towels

* Since some of these items might also be provided by your hospital, it would be helpful to check in advance before packing your bags.

Real Scoliosis Stories: The tough part!

There are some patients, especially the younger ones, who really have a tough time preparing themselves mentally for their surgery.

Lara, a 5 feet 8 inch tall teenager and an avid swimmer was quote shocked when her scoliosis finally had to be treated with surgery. Though she was on a brace for two long years, yet a subsequent visit to the doctor revealed that she had 2 curves in her spine, including a thoracic (45 degrees) and a lumbar curve (55 degrees). She was advised the anterior-posterior spinal fusion, with the use of rods and screws.

However, what Lara found particularly intimidating was the row of tests, screening and the accompanying bouts of nervousness pre-surgery. She was subjected to a series of tests and also had to undergo blood donation to save up for the possible blood loss during the surgery. Other tests included an EKG to assess the pattern of the heart beat, general blood tests, a clotting test, chest x-rays and urine tests.

The most remarkable feature of Lara's preparation was the way her mother and she herself, geared to handle the critical hours. Her mother made sure she garnered up enough support for her daughter by spreading a message amongst her friends. She actually got customized t-shirts printed and sent them across to all her friends. It was an emotional and encouraging moment for Lara when she saw pictures of all her friends wearing the same t-shirts.

Lara also fondly remembers her last day at school before the surgery. She was given a very warm send-off by her friends and received gifts like flowers, balloons and cards. When in the hospital, Lara managed to counter her nervousness by continuously speaking to her friends all the time in the hospital. Being on the phone with her friends all the time kept her mind away from the forthcoming surgery and made the whole ordeal much more bearable.

CHAPTER 14

Use of Anesthesia

Medical research has progressed to the point of allowing for a vast range of surgical options. Meanwhile, there are now a multitude of facilities available for safe preoperative, intraoperative as well as postoperative surgical care. After having gone through the mechanics of preparations and key decisions in determining the relevance of your surgery, it's now time to know about the actual procedures. In this chapter, we will talk about the most crucial procedure that actually marks the beginning of your surgery. We will discuss each of the aspects of the anesthetic management of scoliosis surgery in detail, ranging from the types of anesthetic methods employed, proceeding to the important research highlights. Most important of all, we will also give you a thorough patient's guideline on the actual procedure, telling you in a step-wise manner, how exactly is it performed and other important details.

Key Terms

Knowledge is the key tool you can use to make your entire journey of a scoliosis surgery as comfortable as possible. Having an insight into the complex medical jargon can make you feel at ease about the whole process.

The medical world has now opened up a staggering range of options to patients with serious disorders, yet earlier unsuitable to surgery. Patients with various preoperative co-morbid conditions such as cardiovascular and respiratory issues were usually denied surgery for scoliosis for the fear of complications. However, the advent of the modern anesthetic techniques offers to assist in potential complications like:

- Airway management
- Excessive blood loss
- Prolonged influence of anesthesia
- Postoperative pain management

Before we take you any further into the perplexing world of anesthesia, the stages in which it is delivered and the agents or the ways and means your specialist will adopt to get you under the anesthetic impact, let's take a quick look at some of the most important terms you should know regarding this aspect of your surgery.

a) What is Anesthesia?

Anesthesia is basically defined as the process of administering medication to a patient which allows for surgical procedures to take place without pain. The patient may be in various levels of consciousness depending upon the type of anesthesia administered. The process of anesthesia is a specialized medical discipline and requires careful monitoring of the amount and type of anesthesia to be given to avoid any temporary or permanent complications to the patient.

Put in laymen terms, anesthesia will be the 'numbness', which a medical professional will induce in the patient before the commencement of a surgical procedure.

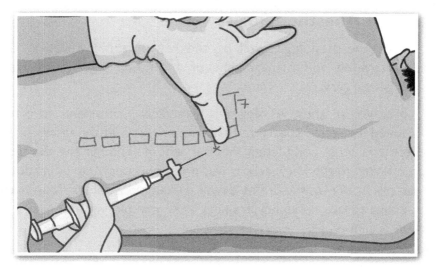

There are basically four types of anesthesia that a specialist considers for any type of surgery, including:

1. General anesthesia, marked by total lack of consciousness

2. Regional anesthesia, in which the region of the body likely to feel pain is numbed, while the patient retains overall consciousness and awareness.

3. Local anesthesia, also marked by full alertness, but lack of sensation in the specific location of surgery

4. Monitored Anesthesia Care (MAC), in which the level of consciousness of the patient is constantly being monitored and variations of how awake and aware the patient is at the time of the procedure are constantly being adjusted by the specialist administering medications which allows the patient not to experience any pain or discomfort during the procedure.

A scoliosis surgery will usually be done under general anesthesia, with the patient being in a totally unconscious state of being.

b) Your Anesthesiologist

Your anesthesiologist will be the key person involved in the administration and management of anesthesia throughout your scoliosis surgery.

Basically, an anesthesiologist is a medical professional who has attended a specific specialized training program in the discipline of anesthesia after completing medical school. Though the duration of training might vary across various countries and educational systems, in the United States a typical example would be four years of postgraduate residency training after completing four years of medical school.

Key objectives

There are three key objectives that an anesthesiologist serves to fulfill, which include:

- To enable enough sedation for the surgery to begin
- To enable enough alertness during the surgery to ensure intraoperative monitoring to detect any possible complications
- To facilitate easy intra and post operative analgesia, .i.e. facilitate pain relief during and after surgery

Scoliosis surgery - Role of an anesthesiologist

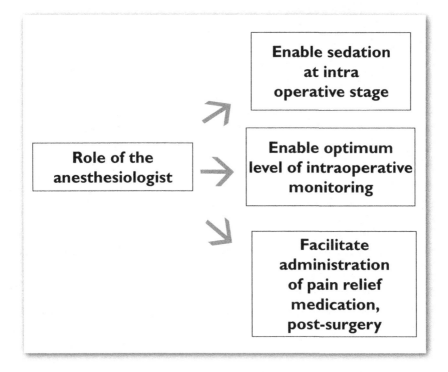

Role of the anesthesiologist

→↗ Enable sedation at intra operative stage

→ Enable optimum level of intraoperative monitoring

→↘ Facilitate administration of pain relief medication, post-surgery

Anesthetic Agents

An anesthetic agent is typically a drug that delivers the sedation and alters the level of consciousness of the patient. When you opt for a surgery, your anesthetist will use different types of anesthetic medications or agents at different stages of your surgery, such as before, during and after the operation to bring about the required stage of consciousness and pain relief. You will read more about such anesthetic agents in the below sections.

Preoperative assessment – The Parameters

Since the entire course of action for your scoliosis surgery will depend on and start with the anesthesia, it is important to foresee and prepare for any potential complications at this stage. Primarily, your specialist in anesthesia will need to calculate the possible rate of complications owing to the following reasons:

- Prolonged duration of the surgery
- Prone positioning of the patient
- Scope of blood loss, intraoperatively
- Regulation of body temperature
- Need to enable intraoperative spinal cord monitoring

It has also been observed that in some cases, the basic cause of scoliosis can influence the risks associated with anesthesia. For instance, if the scoliosis has occurred due to some neuromuscular disease, the risks associated with the use of anesthesia can substantially increase. Towards his objective, experts often advise carrying out appropriate preoperative assessment and choosing the right anesthetic technique for the purpose[1].

To be able to guard for any complications arising out of any of the above factors, your anesthesiologist will consider a few standardized assessment parameters, pre-operatively. In this section, we will explain each of these parameters, showing you the vital body functions that need to be looked into during the pre-operative assessment.

a) Airway assessment

Airway management is perhaps the most critical area your expert will need to evaluate, due to its crucial role in proper intubation and medicine administration. There are a few situations and factors that make some patients of scoliosis surgery more vulnerable to experiencing difficulties in their airway management, which will mainly include the following:

→ If you are getting operated on for your upper thoracic or cervical spine
→ If there is any previous history of having difficulty in intubation or restriction of neck movement
→ If there is any instability of your cervical spine
→ If any devices like halo traction are in use
→ If any disease such as the Duchenne muscular dystrophy exists which can further lead to a tongue hypertrophy

Investigations required: Cervical spine lateral x-rays with flexion and lateral views, CT scan, and/or MRI.

b) Respiratory issues

It is very common for patients of scoliosis or other spinal surgeries to have problems with their respiratory functions. Additional adjustments will need to be made in advance for patients with a high level of cervical or thoracic trauma, in order to avoid any respiratory system or breathing difficulties, mostly requiring artificial ventilation.

Overall, the condition of scoliosis itself causes a pulmonary deficit and a reduced total lung capacity (TLC). Put in laymen terms, this would imply that a patient suffering from scoliosis can be at major risk of experiencing respiratory complications, especially during surgery. Such potential hazards make evaluation of respiratory functions an important part of the pre-operative assessment.

Investigations required: Chest radiograph, arterial blood gas analysis, spirometry (FEV$_1$, FVC)

c) Cardiovascular issues

In patients of scoliosis, an abnormality of the cardiac system might occur due to any of the below listed two reasons. It is crucial to conduct a pre-operative assessment to look for any possibilities of an occurrence of such complications. The reasons could include:

- → Owing to specific underlying pathologies, for instance, if the patient has a muscular dystrophy
- → Occurring as secondary fallout of scoliosis, resulting in distortion of the mediastinum and pulmonary hypertension.

d) Neurological system

One of the most important investigations required pre-operatively, a comprehensive neurological assessment of the patient is important to avoid any irreversible damage during the surgery. More specifically, a detailed neurological assessment is vital owing to the following two major reasons:

→ Patients of cervical spine surgery are at a special risk of further neurological deterioration when performing processes like the tracheal intubation and positioning

→ Patients with muscular dystrophies might run an additional risk of postoperative aspiration due to the dysfunction of bulbar muscles

Key Anesthetic Agents

The entire process of administration of anesthesia during a scoliosis surgery follows the use of various types of agents at different stages. Varied medications and agents are used to bring about the desired effect at every stage of the surgery.

The Process

To begin with, we will explain the key steps in a scoliosis surgery, from the start of the surgery, along with the agents that are used to get the desired results.

Step 1 – First, anesthesia is induced intravenously. At times the use of anesthetic gas may be required due to certain risk factors of the patient.. However, typically the intravenous medications used include propofol and thiopental. The intravenous anesthetic is usually short acting, with a duration of around 5 minutes.

Step 2 – Now, a neuromuscular blocking agent will be administered to reduce the function of the muscles of breathing.

Step 3 – An endotracheal tube is placed into the trachea. Eyes are taped shut and eye pads put in place.

Step 4 – Throughout the entire surgery, the effect of anesthesia is maintained using a mixture of volatile anesthetic gas along with oxygen and nitrous oxide. Here, the anesthetic is being delivered from the anesthesia machine, through the endotracheal tube inserted earlier.

Important anesthetic agents

An anesthetist's role starts at the preoperative stage and continues to the point of post operative analgesia. The type of technique used for each of the objectives depends on a series of factors, such as the extent of your curve, mode of surgery adopted and most important of all, the level of intraoperative monitoring required. Let's understand this mechanism a bit more before we go any further. In consultation with other specialists, your anesthesiologist will first determine the level of monitoring required during the surgery. This is especially relevant in cases of complications where damage to the spinal cord or motor responses is quite possible during the surgery. Such monitoring is done through tests such as the Stagnara Wake Up test discussed earlier in Chapter 10.

Starting right from the pre-medication stage to the administration of pain relieving medication after the surgery, the technique for delivering the anesthesia has to be pre-formulated and ascertained. In this section, we will explain the options your anesthesiologist will consider when deciding on the various anesthetic agents and ways to deliver the medication at different stages, including:

1. Pre-medication
2. Induction
3. Intubation
4. Maintenance
5. Intra-operative monitoring
6. Post operative analgesia

Read on for detailed explanations for each one of the listed above.

1) Premedication

The most important golden rule of administering medication before the stage of anesthesia is to avoid the use of narcotics, especially in patients with a scope of pulmonary complication. However, other measures will be taken and medications administered by your anesthesiologist at this stage, a few of which have been highlighted below:

→ Your anesthesiologist might decide to use a bronchodilator to regulate your lung function.

→ In case the incision to be made in your spinal cord is expected to be long or if you are expected to be given a fiber-optic intubation, your specialist will consider giving you an anti-cholinergic agent such as glycopyrrolate or atropine.

→ You may be given a dose of a histamine-2 receptor antagonist like ranitidine if one or more of the below risk factors exist[2]:

- A risk related to your gastric function is foreseen, such as an aspiration or regurgitation of gastric contents like previously consumed opioids
- A recent spinal cord injury
- A recent accident or trauma of any other nature

→ An antisialagogue might be used if the surgery is likely to be in a prone position to prevent the tapes holding the endotracheal tubes from getting wet and coming loose.

2) Induction

Induction is a term the medical community gives to the process of administering the anesthetic drug to the patient. Your condition at the time of the surgery along with the expected difficulty required at the time of intubation are the two main factors that will help make a choice between the two major routes, .i.e. through inhalation or through an intravenous (i.v.) channel. However, in either of these two cases, preoxegenation will be important in all of the patients of surgery.

Recent research points towards strong evidence against the use of succinylcholine in patients of scoliosis surgery already suffering from muscular dystrophies or denervation, resulting in conditions like hyperkalemia[3]. Additionally, the use of this agent might also result in malignant hyperthermia in patients suffering from conditions like King-Denborough or the adenylate kinase deficiency[4].

If you had been diagnosed with any such conditions, your anesthesiologist may choose to use a nondepolarising neuromuscular blocking agent for intubation instead.

3) Intubation

The most critical decision your anesthesiologist will take during the preoperative assessment is whether to intubate you while awake or asleep. Put in laymen terms, intubation is a process in which a flexible, plastic tube is placed into your trachea or windpipe. This is done to maintain an open airway and serve as a passage so that drugs can be administered.

The options you have here will probably be discussed with you in advance. Generally, your anesthesiologist will prefer to intubate you while awake in case of the below situations:

→ If there is a possible risk for delay in emptying of the gastric contents

→ If your specialist wants to assess your neurological condition after the intubation is over, especially if you have an unstable cervical spine

→ If you are already supposed to use a neck stabilization device such as a halo traction

In situations where no such circumstances exist, the normal method followed for intubation will be to first induce the anesthesia and then use a non-depolarizing neuromuscular blocking drug.

4) Maintenance

Once the anesthesia has been induced and you have been duly intubated, the next key objective for your anesthesiologist will be to maintain an optimum and stable depth of anesthesia. This is important so that your doctor can monitor, detect and interpret any somato sensory evoked potentials (SSEPs) or the motor evoked potentials (MEPs).

Usually, to achieve this stable anesthetic state for the purpose of the critical intraoperative monitoring, an intravenous medication using propofol will be administered.

In addition, to enable such adequate SSEP monitoring, experts at times also might choose to employ a technique that includes the use of nitrous oxide 60% along with isoflorane, at less than 0.5 MAC[5].

However, it has to be kept in consideration that in nitrous oxide 60%, end-tidal isolurane concentrations which are any greater than 0.87% will actually render the MEP monitoring quite non-interpretable[6].

One of the major challenges that can crop up for the anesthesiologist at this stage will be the sudden decrease in the arterial pressure which will require an immediate change in the anesthetic depth. Another complication that might arise is an abrupt cardiovascular instability, which is likely to result from stimulation of the brain stem and spinal cord reflexes, or from blood loss. Finally, a change in technique might also be called for in case of the mediastinal distortion.

5) Intraoperative monitoring

To be able to spot any abnormalites and grave complications during the surgery, it is important that a basic, minimum level of monitoring be maintained. Appropriate anesthetic agents will be used to facilitate continuous monitoring through measures like NIBP, ECG, pulse oximetry, capnography and the use of an esophageal stethoscope.

Intraoperative monitoring has to be done to prevent any possible complications in the various vital parts of the body. Here, we've briefly listed the varied body functions that need to be monitored during the operation, when employing the use of anesthetic agents.

a) Cardiovascular monitoring, especially in cases where the patient has been unusually positioned or prominent hemodynamic effects of a thoracic surgery are expected.

b) Respiratory monitoring, primarily including the use of an end-tidal carbon dioxide concentration and peak airway pressure, to be able to monitor for any possible respiratory complications due to a prolonged exposure to anesthesia.

c) Temperature monitoring, especially since prolonged anesthesia can cause major heat loss, the basic body temperature needs to be monitored and duly regulated through the use of warm i.v. fluids as well as devices such warm air mattresses.

d) Positioning of the patient, which might have to be, altered intraoperatively depending upon the circumstances.

e) Spinal cord monitoring, especially in the critical zone of T4 to T9 where the vascular supply is minimal. Your anesthesiologist will apply a series of tests, as listed below, during the surgery to look for any possible complications:

> → Stagnara Wake-up test, in which the patient is a basic test of spinal motor function

> → Somatosensory evoked potentials (SSEPs), a type of sensory evoked response and enables monitoring of the sensory regions in a patient under anesthesia, undergoing a spinal surgery

> → Motor evoked potentials (MEP), a highly sophisticated indicator of motor function in which the motor cortex is stimulated by electrical or magnetic means to study responses.

> → Ankle clonus test, in which the foot is strongly dorsiflexed at the ankle joint either at the end of the surgery or during a wake-up test to look for any possible damage to the spinal cord. A complete absence of repeated movements at ankle joint will indicate towards a probable spinal injury.

6) Post operative analgesia

In order to facilitate optimum postoperative analgesia and pain relief, your anesthesiologist is likely to employ a series of anesthetic agents, as listed below:

> → Parenteral opioids, which includes opioids being delivered through various routes such as epidural, intrapleural and intrathecal.

> → Epidural analgesia, administered through the epidural catheter placed intraoperatively, either alone or in combination with opioids

> → Intrathecal analgesia, in which intrathecal medication can be injected during spinal surgical procedures before wound closure.

Real Scoliosis Stories: It happened in a flash!

For most of the patients, especially the younger ones, the effect of the anesthesia often happens in a flash, with the patient having no recollection of when they actually lost consciousness. Maria (name changed), a 12-year old due for a scoliosis surgery had a similar experience. Like all other children of her age, she was extremely nervous about the surgery and was quite anxious when she was being wheeled in. After signing the consent form, her anesthetist had briefed her about the agent they would be using. Though she could barely comprehend half of what he was saying, yet she felt thankful to the specialist for making the effort to familiarize her and make her feel at ease.

Soon after, she was wheeled in for the operation. It was then that the venflon was inserted and one of the nurses present there injected the medicine for anesthesia. Maria immediately started feeling dizzy and relaxed. That was the last thing she ever remembered. The next time she woke up, her surgery was over and she saw her parents standing on the either sides of her bed.

CHAPTER 15
Types of Surgery

B Y far, the surgical treatment for scoliosis is seen as the last resort for patients experiencing such a spinal curvature. In the previous chapters, we learned how the medical community advises us to go for a series of non-invasive options before considering surgery to correct the existing curve as well as to stop it from progressing any further.

However, once you've gone through the entire rigors of deciding on the benefits of surgery for your individual case, it becomes imperative that you attempt to understand the different available approaches of surgery. Though it is your surgeon who will mostly decide on the specific approach of surgery to be followed, it helps for you to understand the implications of each of the approaches, why it has been chosen for your type of curve and most important of all, what are the benefits and risks associated with each of the types of surgery.

Scoliosis Surgery – A Bird's-Eye View

Before we go any further, it is vital to understand the basic concept of a scoliosis surgery. This key concept has two major parts:

→ What exactly is done during a scoliosis surgery
→ What is the approach taken to perform the surgery

In other words, your surgeon follows a specific method to correct the curve in your spine. However, in accordance with type and severity of your curve along with any other specific medical history, this method can be performed in various ways. Your surgeon can reach your curve from the front of your body or the back of your body, or even both. The particular 'way' in which your surgeon approaches your spine will be determined by your surgeon to allow for optimum exposure and minimize risks associated with the surgery.

So, as we have learned, understanding the types of surgery first starts from learning what does the surgery include and then learning different ways to perform the surgery. Hence, in this section, we will learn about two key concepts:

→ Part 1: Surgery – What does it involve
→ Part 2: Different ways to perform this surgery

First, let's begin by understanding part 1 as described above.

Most of the modern approaches to scoliosis surgery will use a combination of different rods, hooks and screws to fix the curvature of your spine. Irrespective of the approach decided for the surgery, a conventional surgical procedure to correct a spinal curvature will generally follow the below sequence:

1. First, long rods are used to put the spine in its correct place
2. Various screws and hooks are then used to anchor or support these rods. You will learn more about all of these instruments in Chapter 16.
3.   These rods are then expected to hold the spine in its place; in the meantime, giving time for the new bone that is added to fuse together with the existing bone.
4. Once the bone has fused properly, it will then be capable of holding the spine in its place.
5. In most of the cases, the rods are left inside the body. They usually do not cause any problem. However, in some cases, these rods may begin to irritate the soft tissue surrounding

your spine; your surgeon might choose to remove them surgically.

The above explanation is merely a bird's eye view of the entire procedure of surgery, done primarily to enable you to understand the key concept of a scoliosis surgery. We will explain all about how the procedures of fusion and the placement of rods, screws and hooks are done further in Chapter 18.

Hereon, this chapter will focus solely on the different types of surgery, which curves are they more suitable to and most importantly, the specific benefits and risks associated with each of the approaches.

(A) The Anterior Approach – From the Front

The Definition

By its definition, when a surgeon uses the anterior approach for scoliosis surgery, it implies that he will access or reach your spinal column from the front of the spine. The term 'anterior' itself means 'nearer to the front', as per the dictionary, thereby explaining this approach to the surgery itself.

The anterior approach to surgery is usually preferred for the curves in the following category:

→ Curves in the middle or lower spine
→ Curves that are severe and rigid, especially in adults

The anterior or 'frontal' approach to surgery is usually done for curves that are located in the thoracolumbar region, .i.e. T12-L1. Broadly speaking, the surgery will be performed through the chest wall, in a procedure medically known as thoracotomy, following the below standardized steps:

1. Incision is made into the chest
2. A lung is deflated
3. A rib is removed
4. Spine is approach and fusion is performed

Let's understand this anterior approach to surgery in more detail by exploring each of the above steps.

Step 1 – Incision, lung deflation, rib removal

Your surgeon will first take into account the part of the spine that needs to be operated upon. As the first step, an incision will be made along your chest wall or on the lower end of the abdomen, depending upon the location of curve. Though the name might suggest otherwise, in the anterior approach your surgeon will actually make an incision along the side of the body to access the front of the spine.

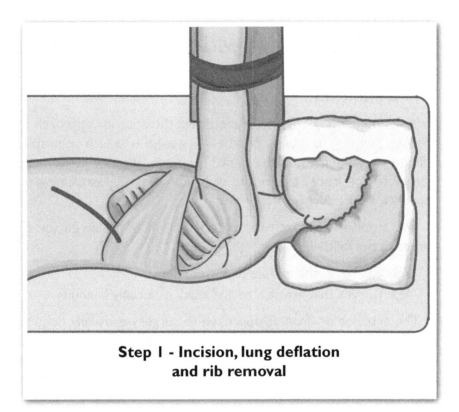

Step 1 - Incision, lung deflation and rib removal

Once the incision is made, your surgeon will then deflate the lung and remove a rib to expose your spine. In cases where the curve is prominent in the thoracolumbar region, your surgeon is also likely to detach your diaphragm to in order to expose your spinal column better.

Step 2 – Removal of disc

From your exposed spinal column, the surgeon will now slowly remove the disc material from between the vertebra in the region of the curve. This is an important step in the anterior approach to surgery as the removal of the disc offers a wider space for spinal fusion.

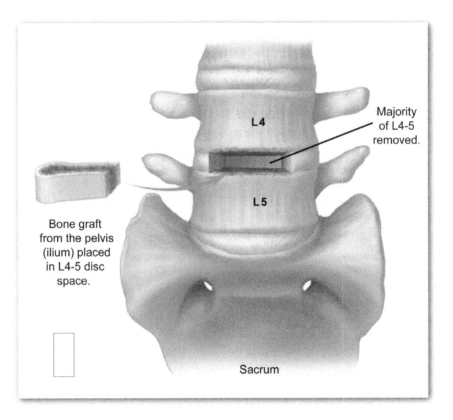

Bone graft
from the pelvis
(ilium) placed
in L4-5 disc
space.

L4

Majority
of L4-5
removed.

L5

Sacrum

Step 3 – Placement of instrumentation

In order to correct the spinal deformity, your surgeon will then place a series of instrumentation, including screws and rods in front of the spine. In the anterior approach, this will be done by putting a single vertebral body screw at each of the vertebral levels, which are a part of the curve. At each of the levels, these screws are then attached to a single or double rod. The compression caused by the rod along with the rotation of the rod will then eventually lead to the correction of this spinal deformity.

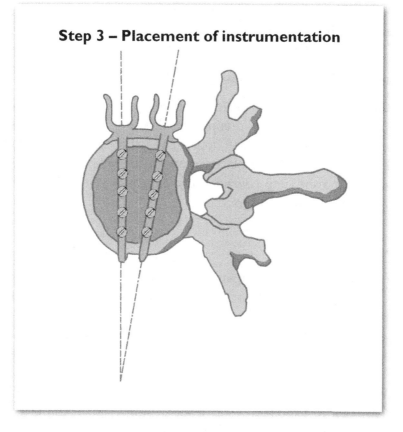

Step 3 – Placement of instrumentation

Step 4 – Fusion: The Process

Once the instrumentation has been put into correct position, the process of spinal fusion is then finally performed. This is done by roughening of the bony surface between the vertebral bodies and then packing the bone graft in the space in between the vertebral bodies. The material of this bone graft can be taken from a variety of sources, such as:

- Crest of the pelvis
- Removed rib
- Allograft bone
- Other bone substitutes

In most of the cases, the fusion generally happens in duration of 3 to 6 months, though it might take up to a year in some rare cases.

Step 5 – Incision to be closed

Once steps one through four are completed, your surgeon will then close the incision and apply the dressing. In the instance that your spinal column has been approached through the chest cavity, a chest tube will also be placed through the side of your chest to ensure that your lung remains duly expanded through the entire surgery and following surgery.

The Analysis

Experts have varied opinions on almost all types of surgery, whether it is anterior, posterior, a combined approach or the latest technique, which includes endoscopic surgery. Two major advantages are associated with the use of anterior approach for scoliosis surgery. These are lesser instance of back injuries and a lower rate of blood transfusions. In fact, research shows that though this approach was designed to enable better exposure of the spine, experts have also been using it to expose the entire aorta, along with both the kidneys and their blood supply. Exposure to the retroperitoneal area for excision of large tumors is also another possible application of this approach.

However, research is now pointing towards two major prospective fallouts of this approach, which include a higher risk of an impaired pulmonary function post-surgery as well as a higher incidence of hardware failure than expected in the posterior approach.

(B) Posterior Approach – From the Back

The Definition

When your surgeon states that he is considering a posterior approach, what he really means is that he is considering reaching your spinal column from the back of your body. More precisely, in the posterior approach, your surgeon will make a long, straight incision into your back and will gradually move your back muscles aside to expose your spine for curve correction. Once your spine is approached, the surgeon will attach a host of instruments like rods, screws, wires and hooks to your spine, reposition it and hold it giving time to the new bone graft to fuse properly and eventually correct the curve.

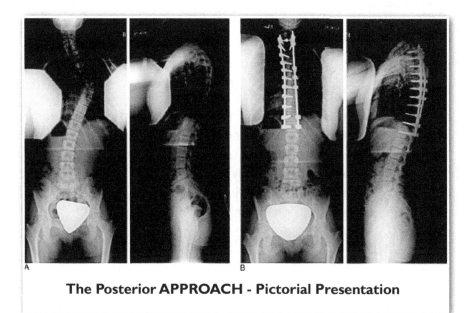

The Posterior APPROACH - Pictorial Presentation

Though it is the most common approach used in cases of Adolescent Idiopathic Scoliosis (AIS), the posterior approach can be used for almost all curve types. In fact, the posterior approach is also one of the most traditional as well as frequently used approaches for spinal surgeries.

The entire procedure for surgery for scoliosis using the posterior approach follows quite a similar sequence as outlined in the anterior approach above.

In the sections that follow, we will explain each of the parts of the procedure in a step-wise manner.

Step 1 – The Preparation

As in the case of most spinal surgeries, your surgeon will first start the whole procedure by having your anesthesiologist administer appropriate anesthesia. Once you are under sedation, a breathing tube as well as other catheters will be placed in appropriate veins to allow suitable monitoring of aspects like blood pressure and heart function during the surgery. One of the most important reasons these catheters are being placed is to continually monitor the depth of your anesthesia to ensure that you remain completely asleep during the full procedure.

Step 2 – Positioning

Once you are under sedation and all the appropriate monitoring devices are in place, you will then be brought into the correct position for the posterior approach to be used for your scoliosis surgery. For this purpose, you will be carefully placed on your stomach, in a flat position. Your arms and legs will also be properly padded to avoid any additional complications or injury.

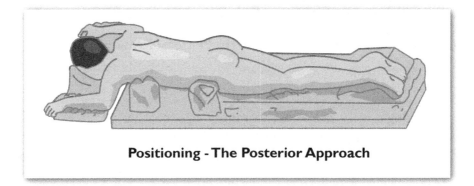

Positioning - The Posterior Approach

Step 3 – The Incision

Using a host of instruments, your surgeon will now make the all-important incision to reach your spine from the back of your body. To do this, an incision will be made in the middle of your back, going down in the direction of your spinal column.

The length of the incision depends on the exact location of your curve. In most cases, surgeons using the posterior approach prefer to keep the incision length a bit longer than the actual space required for the spinal fusion.

Step 4 – Placement of Instrumentation

The success of the scoliosis surgery depends on how well your surgeon manages to hold the spine together, in its original posture. When using the posterior approach, surgeons mostly prefer to use:

- Two metal (stainless steel or titanium) rods
- Hooks that attach to your lamina
- Pedicle screws that are inserted into your pedicle in the middle of the spine
- Wires to hold the instruments together and ensure proper positioning

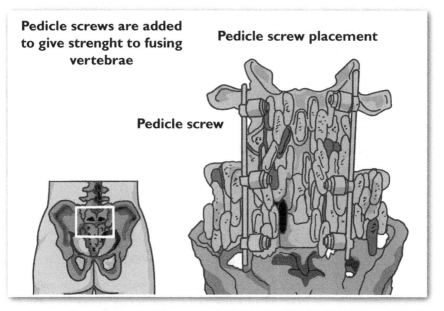

Pedicle screws are added to give strenght to fusing vertebrae

Pedicle screw placement

Pedicle screw

After all of the instruments are in their proper position, the rod that has been duly contoured to fit your spine is attached and the correction of the curve is performed.

Step 5 – Tightening

At this brief but important step, your surgeon will first ensure that all the implants are in the right spot and have been positioned properly. Once done, all of the implants will be properly tightened for the final time.

Step 6 – Closure of incision

Finally, the incision is stitched up and the dressing is applied. In some cases, surgeons might choose to add further protection to the incision by placing a drain into the wound after the surgery is over.

The Analysis

Posterior surgery is, by far, one of the most common approaches utilized in spinal corrective surgery for scoliosis. In fact, research shows that using the posterior approach for conditions such as scoliosis is an effective one-stage surgical treatment option that can help in avoiding the grave complications associated with the anterior approach.

However, though the posterior approach is a commonly practiced method, yet it is also plagued by a series of potential complications. A few common ones include possible tissue or nerve damage caused by improper positioning of implants, and a delayed or misplaced union and pressure on the skin arising from component parts in patients having insufficient tissue coverage over the implant.

(C) Posterior and Anterior – The Combined Approach

Surgery for scoliosis is perhaps the last resort for the patients with scoliosis. The technique used for surgery has great bearing on the success rate of the entire treatment process. Such facts make it important for the experts to keep evolving newer techniques for these spinal surgeries, the combined anterior and posterior approach being one of such developments.

Recent research has shown positive outcomes related to the use of this approach, though opinions still vary. For instance, it has often been found that using this approach for patients of a young age helps prevent the crankshaft phenomenon. Moreover, the combined approach is often useful for large and rigid curves, along with treating specific curves in the thoracic spine. However, research also shows that as compared to the combined approach, even the posterior approach on its own is just as effective for adult lumbar scoliosis, especially curvature between 40 and 70 degrees.

Crankshaft phenomenon

This is a phenomenon that usually occurs in younger children, especially with immature skeletal systems. In the crankshaft phenomenon, a type of curve progression is seen wherein the front portion of the fused spine will continue to grow even after the procedure. As the fused spine cannot grow any longer, it starts twisting and will then develop a curvature.

The Procedure – How is the combination approach taken?

By definition, the combined approach to scoliosis surgery uses both, the anterior as well as the posterior approach. Each of the approaches are used to achieve a different objective.

When following this approach, your surgeon will use the anterior as well posterior route. This will include using the anterior approach to access the spinal column and the posterior method to carry out the spinal fusion, In summary, utilizing the combined approach, your surgeon will use the:

→ Anterior approach to access your spinal column
→ Posterior approach to do the spinal fusion

Why the combined approach?

Both, the anterior as well as the posterior approach to scoliosis surgery have their own limitations. For instance, when your surgeon attempts to work on your spinal column using the posterior approach, the spinal nerves will always come in the way and attempt to block the procedure. This also makes it difficult to place implants between the vertebrae.

It is for such reasons that experts are beginning to look at the combined approach as perhaps the most effective one, especially in case of severe curves. In such cases, your surgeon will first make a separate incision in the abdomen and then use the posterior approach to perform the spinal fusion in two separate steps.

Let's try and take a closer look at how the combined posterior-anterior approach is implemented.

The Steps

The procedure will start with the anterior approach wherein your surgeon will first make an incision in your chest wall or abdomen, as the case might be, with you lying flat on your back. The disc material will be removed from in between the vertebrae to make your curve more flexible. As is the case in the anterior approach, a rib might also be removed to give the surgeon easier access to the affected area.

Once the spinal column has been approached from the front side, the necessary procedure as explained in the anterior approach is performed and the incision is closed. Following this, you are re-positioned on your back and an incision is made in your back to carry out the posterior portion of the surgery.

Types of surgeries – pictorial presentation

Anterior

Posterior

Combined Anterior
and Posterior Approach

(D) Endoscopic approach
– The Minimally Invasive Technique

The world of medicine and surgery are in a process of continuous evolution in order to achieve the highest rates of success and also to ensure minimum trauma for the patient involved. For instance, a minimally invasive technique, such as the endoscopic technique gives the patient an alternative to traditional form of open surgery wherein an incision, which is at least 3-5 inches long, is made and bone is harvested from the hip or rib area. Statistics actually show that as many as 27% of patients in such cases still experience pain in the hip up to two years after the open surgery, which explains why the minimally invasive techniques are being increasingly preferred.

The last few years have seen a major increase in the utilization of the minimally invasive techniques (MIS) to carry out surgeries of varied natures, including spinal fusion. A minimally invasive technique is basically the one that uses latest devices like fiber optic video cameras and other instruments and performs surgeries using smaller incisions. In fact, there has been a dramatic increase in the number of autologous bone graft procedures being carried out using the minimally invasive techniques for procedures such as spinal fusion.

Let's move on to further understand what is exactly involved in the endoscopic technique for scoliosis surgery.

The Definition

To begin, an endoscope is a very small instrument, which allows the surgeon to have a look inside the body, when placed on a short cable and inserted inside the body using a small incision. The endoscopic technique for scoliosis surgery makes use of an endoscope to allow the surgeon to clearly see the chest cavity along with the spinal column on the television monitor. This is to facilitate correction of the spinal curve using the process described below.

Before we go any further, let's take a look at the ideal criteria and which patients make the best candidates for the endoscopic approach to scoliosis surgery. You are an ideal candidate for the endoscopic technique, also known as the Video Assisted Thoracoscopic Technique (VATS), if:

- You have a thoracic curve (in the middle of the spine/chest area)
- You have already gone through a failed surgery for curve correction

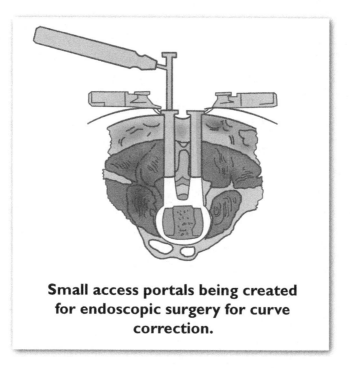

Small access portals being created for endoscopic surgery for curve correction.

The Steps

Experts usually follow the below set of steps to carry out an endoscopic surgery for treatment of your scoliosis surgery.

Your surgeon will first place an endoscope on a short cable and position it properly. The endoscope will then be inserted through a very small incision to magnify the area of operation. The whole area of your curve will be visible on a large TV monitor. A number of small incisions, each measuring up to 1 cm in length will be made, instead of a single big incision. Your surgeon will make a series of tunnel-like access portals or very narrow passages, through which the entire process of curve correction will be carried out. Through these tunnels, small surgical instruments will then be inserted to carry out the essential procedure of bone graft and fusion.

The Edge

The endoscopic technique for scoliosis surgery is being seen as a major alternative to the conventional open surgeries owing to a number of reasons. Research prominently shows how the endoscopic anterior short fusion for thoracic scoliosis offers major curve correction with minimal scarring taking place.

Let's have a quick look at why this form of minimally invasive surgery is being seen as a good option for scoliosis treatment:

→ It preserves the whole lot of healthy muscle.
→ It drastically reduces the pain and recovery time, post surgery.
→ It causes minimal damage to the surrounding tissue.
→ It reduces scarring associated with conventional surgeries, owing to the lesser duration and intensity of prolonged muscle retraction. A smaller size of the incision also means that there is a lesser amount of scarring.
→ It causes overall lesser discomfort and trauma to the patient.
→ It reduces the scope of respiratory problems during and after surgery.

However, there are a few fallouts or potential complications associated with the use of the endoscopic technique, though the eventual impact might vary. For instance studies report that rod breakages are possible following such endoscopic surgeries for scoliosis. However, this breakage might not be associated with any significant loss of curve correction.

(E) Thoracoplasty

Thoracic Scoliosis

When a patient suffers from thoracic scoliosis, the curve occurs in the thoracic vertebra, which is positioned right behind the chest and hence the occurrence of the hump. We know how the spine of a patient with scoliosis takes on a 'S' shaped curve, deforming his entire appearance. However, when this curve is in the thoracic (upper) spine, it takes the form of an outward deformity, more commonly known as the hump, giving you a hunchback look.

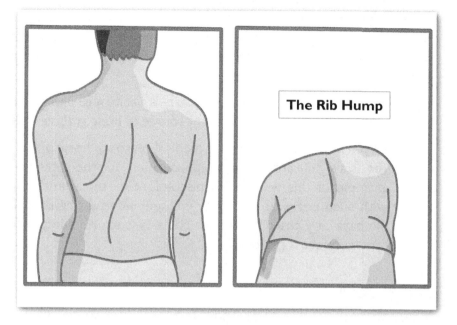

The Rib Hump

In such cases, what is required is to remove or reduce this hump by shortening or removing a few selected ribs. Thoracoplasty is a common procedure with patients of thoracic scoliotic curves, since it can work well to reduce the outward deformity. As the name suggests, the procedure of thoracoplasty is mainly relevant for patients suffering from thoracic scoliosis, or prominence of ribs in the chest or upper back area.

Thoracoplasty and Scoliosis

By its definition, thoracoplasty is a procedure that will shorten or remove a few selected ribs in order to reduce the typical rib hump. Let's read on to find out more about this surgical procedure and its relevance to scoliosis.

In most cases, thoracoplasty will be carried out only after the standard curve correction has been performed using the anterior/ posterior or an of the other approaches previously mentioned.

The Benefits

Performed for conditions like Adolescent Idiopathic Scoliosis (AIS), especially with pedicle screw instrumentation, thoracoplasty has often been seen to offer better rib hump correction without major pulmonary compromise or other related complications. In fact, it has also been reported that the purpose of curve correction is achieved much better if the procedure of thoracoplasty is combined with spinal fusion than by the fusion alone

In addition, in cases where thoracoplasty is performed along with spinal fusion, it can serve as an excellent source of bone graft as well.

Apart from reducing the hump for medical reasons, thoracoplasty also serves as a significant cosmetic improvement for the patient. A typical example of this will be the discomfort or the pain that a patient with such outward deformity will feel when trying to lean against the back of a chair. With thoracoplasty, such rib humps are reduced and comfort is restored.

The Procedure

The amount of ribs to be shortened or removed will depend entirely on the extent and severity of your curve and also on the size of your rib hump. However, experts are of the opinion that if a considerable difference to the hump is to be made, at least 5 ribs will need to be worked upon, though the figure might vary.

As mentioned above, in most cases, thoracoplasty will be done after a surgery for spinal fusion has already been carried out but a rib hump still remains.

During the surgery, your surgeon will gain access to the selected ribs by splitting open the periosteum, which is an outer bone-forming layer on the ribs, acting like a bark on a tree. Once done, the selected or earmarked ribs will be removed. The open ends will then be pressed downwards and finally joined by wires, afffixed through drill holes. The shortened rib, once fully healed will then be as strong as the original one.

(F) Latest Developments

Fusion - The Key Premise

Surgical treatment for scoliosis has previously been quite invasive as well as extensive in nature. Surgical procedures have traditionally involved accessing the spine either through a comprehensive exposure or through endoscopy and carrying out spinal fusion to correct the curve.

However, owing to the serious potential of complications and risks involved, medical research continually evolves newer, safer and above all, much less invasive techniques to carry out the curve correction. While some of these techniques have proven efficacy and have been adopted fully by the medical community, others are still being debated and are being adopted with certain modifications, or only for a few specific patients. Take the case of the modern Luqué trolley, which is a self-growing rod technique. Experts are of the view that this technique might be useful for managing early onset scoliosis (EOS) in young patients, but in a modified form, since it suffers from risks like the effect of wear debris and also the risk of spontaneous fusions.

Fusionless Surgery

Spinal fusion has always been the key premise of surgery to correct scoliotic curves. Fusion, traditionally performed through open surgeries has been the most common method used. However, recent research shows a high rate of success associated with a fusion less spinal surgery. Fusionless surgery is minimally invasive and especially helpful in addressing progressive scoliosis in growing children. Invasive surgical procedures like spinal fusion are likely to create complications in children with early onset scoliosis (EOS) or even those who are headed towards adolescence, with major growth spurts still pending. Even treatments like braces, which might be non-invasive, do not offer curve correction and just halt the progression of the curve and delay surgery for some time.

It is for such reasons that the fusions less treatment options are being seen as a major alternative to traditional spinal fusions, especially in growing children.

Read on as we list out some of the latest developments in the field of scoliosis surgery and attempt to understand the concepts and efficacy of each.

a) Vertebral Body Stapling

In this procedure, staples are placed along the vertebral growth plate to modulate the asymmetrical growth of the spine. The aim is to lower the rate of the growth of the anterior side of the spine, so that the lateral side can catch up. In fact, controlled studies show improvement in up to 80% of patients on whom vertebral body stapling has been tried as a way of fusion less surgery for scoliosis.

Experts suggest that the best candidates for this type of surgery are patients in the age group of 8 to 11 years, with a curve between 25 and 35 degrees.

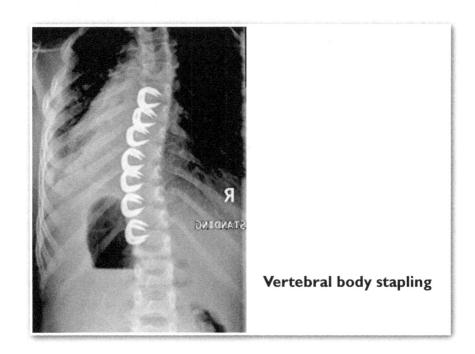

Vertebral body stapling

b) Vertical expandable prosthetic titanium rib (VEPTR)

The VEPTR is one of the latest techniques being analyzed by medical experts, especially in the case of congenital scoliosis. In this technique, an instrument is implanted through surgery into the child's spinal column, which can later be adjusted as the child grows. THE VEPTR works by expanding the thoracic column, allowing for thoracic spine and lung growth. This happens as the child ages and eventually corrects the curvature.

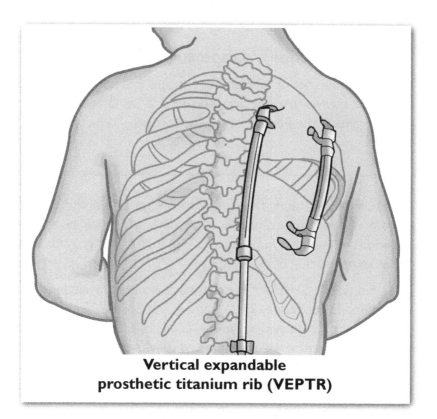

Vertical expandable prosthetic titanium rib (VEPTR)

c) The Medtronic's SHILLA™ Growth Guidance System

Aimed at treating young children with Early Onset Scoliosis (EOS), the SHILLA™ is Medtronic's first growth-guided instrumentation to help growing children with scoliosis. The instrument is commercially available in Europe as a treatment option for very young children with EOS. It is claimed to be helpful by allowing natural growth and simultaneously reducing the deformity of the spine without surgical intervention.

When the SHILLA™ concept is used, the apex of the curve is first corrected, fused and then fixed to a set of dual rods. The SHILLA™ system will then guide growth at the both ends of the dual rods through a preset, programmed procedure. This growth is made possible by pedicle screws that are implanted extraperiosteally.

What does extraperiosteally mean?

Being connected or implanted extraperiosteally will mean that the screws are not attached to the periosteum or the membrane of the fibrous connective tissue.

The screws slide along the rods at the either side of the structure. Research shows that eventually, the spine will grow at a normal place with the implants in place, allowing for regular growth in such children experiencing EOS.

This innovative SHILLA™ system has also been awarded the CE (Conformité Européenne) Mark during the Spine Week Congress in Amsterdam for providing young children suffering from a life-threatening curvature of the spine with a suitable alternative to debilitating and limiting surgeries.

The Author's Word

Minimally invasive and fusion less surgeries definitely appear to be the better option against the traditional, open surgeries for correcting scoliotic curves. There are a few distinct advantages associated with almost all types of minimally invasive surgical procedures for scoliosis such as minimal scarring, less recovery time, less blood loss and less pain. However, quite a few of these surgeries are aimed at children with curved spines and in a growing age population, a stage when permanent fusions can cause additional complications. On the other hand, traditional open surgeries are more time-tested and universally followed.

It is always beneficial to analyze each of the options available with your surgeon, in specific relevance of your age, type and intensity of your curve and most important, status of your health before you decide on a specific type of surgery you should have for scoliosis treatment.

Real Scoliosis Stories: The difference technology makes

Mrs. Richard (name changed) was around 49 years of age when she was diagnosed with scoliosis. At the peak of her active life, the idea of her efficiency getting hampered due to the deformity harrowed her to no end. It didn't help that all she knew about a scoliosis surgery was that it is painful and involves a series of instruments being inserted into your body.

However, when she was around 51, which was 2 years later, she eventually came across a surgeon who offered to carry out a minimally invasive surgery to correct her curve. The new technique actually involved approaching the spine with a lateral incision from the patient's side below the ribs. As per experts, both the amount of blood loss and complications as well as the overall recovery time is lesser with such techniques. The patient was reported to be back at work 3 weeks later and was also said to have resumed a fairly independent lifestyle.

CHAPTER 16

Your Surgeon's Armaments and Instruments

Y ou have now learned all about the preparations for your surgery, risks involved, and options available for the specific surgery. Moving forward, it's now time to know about the procedure itself, starting from the tools used to what happens in the operation theater and how the spinal fusion is actually performed. In this chapter, you'll read about all the major instrumentation systems and tools in detail, how and where are they used and so on.

The Surgeon's Tools

Ever since Jules Rene Guerin, the French surgeon, thought of applying surgery to correct scoliosis and Dr. Russel Hibbs invented spinal fusion surgery at the New Orthopedic Hospital in 1914, the instrumentation and tools used in scoliosis surgery have indeed been your surgeon's best friends.

After this, came the era of the famous breakthrough by Paul Harrington in the 1950s. The procedure basically had a single inflexible steel rod being used to straighten the spine. This rod, named after its inventor as the Harrington Rod, was one of the first pieces of instrumentation to be used in scoliosis surgery.

The instruments and armaments used by the surgeons in the operation theatre form the cornerstone of the success or, for that matter, the failure of a scoliosis surgery. After all, there is concrete research to show how important is it for spine surgeons and radiologists to be fully familiar with various types of instrumentation in the treatment of scoliosis and to be able to spot any possible hardware failure in such cases. Though there might also be evidence that instrumentation might not be totally responsible for accurate correction of your curve , such evidence is scanty and calls for further debate.

Hence, this makes it important for anyone undergoing scoliosis surgery to have comprehensive knowledge about each of these tools, what are they used for and so on.

Tools You Should Know

The most important tools and armaments to be used by your surgeon can usually be divided into two major categories, which are:

1. Bone gripping elements – Hooks, screws, wires and sublaminar wires

2. Longitudinal linking elements – Rods, plates

Read on as we give you a clear set of details on the lot of these armaments.

1. Rods

a) Harrington rods

As we mentioned earlier, the Harrington procedure is one of the oldest concepts of spinal procedures, though technology continues to evolve and newer procedures continue to make their mark in the field of spinal surgery.

The Harrington procedure basically achieves correction of spine by strengthening or distracting it. When spinal fusions were performed before Dr. Harrington's invention, the procedure was done in a rudimentary manner. The surgery was performed without using any metal implants and a cast was applied after the surgery, along with traction, to keep the curve straight until fusion could take place. However, since the rate of fusion failure or pseudarthrosis that came along with such a procedure was very high, Paul Harrington's path-breaking invention came as a much preferred option for the medical community.

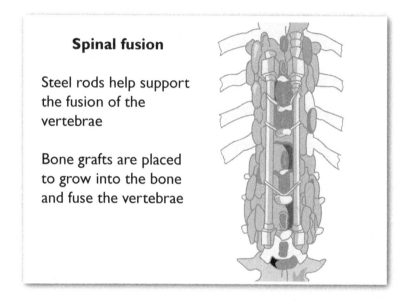

Spinal fusion

Steel rods help support the fusion of the vertebrae

Bone grafts are placed to grow into the bone and fuse the vertebrae

So, what is the Harrington procedure all about?

Dr. Harrington introduced a metal spinal system of instrumentation that helped in keeping the spine straight until the actual fusion took place. Though obsolete and no longer in use, the original Harrington system used a ratchet system. It was attached by hooks to the spine at the top as well as the bottom of the curvature, helping to distract or straighten the curve.

In the modern version of the Harrington procedure, a steel rod is used that runs from the bottom of the curve to the top. Post surgery, you will be required to wear a cast and take prescribed bed rest for a few months. Though variations might exist, the Harrington procedure follows a set of standard steps, listed as below:

- First, a steel rod will be used, starting from the bottom of the curve, going up to the top of the curve. Your surgeon might also choose to use two rods on either side of the spinal vertebrae.
- The rod is then attached by hooks, supported by pegs which have been inserted into the bone.
- The steel rod is then jacked up, quite similar to a situation when a car tire is being changed. It is then locked into its right place in order to secure the spine.
- The stage is now set for fusion of the vertebrae to occur.
- As mentioned earlier, a bed rest of 3 to 6 months is usually prescribed, along with a cast which the patient has to wear, at least for this duration.
- The steel rod usually stays inside unless it starts giving any problems.

Rod breakages in the case of Harrington instrumentation are usually uncommon, with research showing that even in the case of solid fusion, barely 10 to 15% of rods fracture. However, two possible complications are usually associated with the use of the Harrington procedure.

Here, we've explained each one of them briefly.

i) Crankshaft Phenomenon

This phenomenon usually occurs in younger children, especially with immature skeletal systems. It is basically a type of curve progression wherein the front portion of the fused spine will continue to grow even after the procedure. Since the fused spine cannot grow any longer, it starts twisting and then develops a curvature.

ii) The Flat Back Syndrome

This complication occurs when your lower back loses its normal inward curve, also known as lordosis. After a few years, the disks might also collapse below the point of fusion, which will make it difficult for the patient to stand erect and will also lead to a lot of pain.

b)Cotrel-Dubousset (CD) System

"The main goal remains optimal 3D balance of the spine and not the percentage of improvement of the Cobb angle!"
Jean Dubousset

This is one of the types of segmental systems used in which two parallel rods are cross-linked using multiple hooks in order to facilitate greater stability for the fused vertebrae. Suitable instruments are placed in each part of the spine that need straightening. The two key functions offered by the Cotrel-Dubousset Procedure are:

→ Correction of the existing curve
→ Correction of the existing rotation

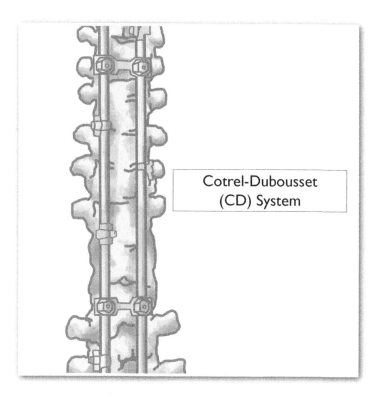

Cotrel-Dubousset
(CD) System

One of the controlled studies conducted to assess the efficiency of this system, rated the correction rate to be around 66%. Interestingly, while only 86% of patients who had undergone the Harrington procedure reported to be satisfied, the rate was as high as 95% in cases using the CD System. However, the operation time as well as blood loss are reported to be more when using the CD system as compared to the Harrington procedure. On the other hand, this system doesn't cause the flat back syndrome usually caused by the Harrington concept.

c) The Texas Scottish-Rite (TSRH) Instrumentation

Another type of segmental system, the TSRH system, is quite similar to the Cotrel-Dubousset procedure, especially in the aspect that it uses parallel rods to control curvature as well as reverse the existing rotation. However, this procedure goes a step further and uses smoother rods and hooks. The main advantage this feature offers is that it makes it easier to remove or adjust the instruments if any complications arise later.

Other Sets

a) Luque instrumentation – By now, we know that the Harrington rod system carries a major risk of the Flat Back Syndrome. The Luque instrumentation was originally developed to maintain the normal lordosis (the natural curve) of the low back in this context. Though additional complications like loss of correction after surgery loom large, this set of instrumentation is mostly used for patients with neuromuscular scoliosis and also for children with disorders such as cerebral palsy.

b) WSSI – Known as the Wisconsin segmental spine instrumentation, it is usually considered safe, like the Harrington rod system and the Luque instrumentation. In this method, the base of the spinous process is used for segmental fixation, along with an appropriate implant.

c) DDS – Termed the Dorsal Dynamic Spondylodesis (DDS) system, this concept is still at the testing stage in Germany. A semi rigid system, this basically offers greater flexibility to the spine as compared to the other conventional systems.

2. Hooks

Traditionally, hooks have been the tools most commonly used to secure the rods to the spine. Once the rods are placed around the curved spine, the hooks are then used to secure the rods in their correct place. Pedicle screws are the other option for securing rods and will be explained in the next section.

Here, let's take a closer look at the purpose of this tool, how and when is it used and various other aspects.

Usage and implementation

Used very commonly as a part of instrumentation sets like the Cotrel-Dubousset (CD) instrumentation, segmental hook constructs have been seen as a standard part of the surgical treatment of scoliosis since the 1980s. The key reason for the immense popularity of the hooks was because it provided the surgeon the ability to place a number of hooks along the same rod in either the compression or distraction modes.

Key Types of Hooks

A series of hooks of varying shapes and sizes are used by surgeons based upon the patient's age and the type, as well as extent, of curvature. In this section, we've discussed each of these types of hooks, along with details about their specific application and usage.

1. Pedicle Hooks

As the name suggests, this type is attached to the pedicles of your vertebrae. More specifically, pedicle hooks can be applied in thoracic (mid-spine) vertebrae, T1 to T10. (Please refer to chapter 1 for more details on thoracic vertebrae). With the hook blade always placed in the up-going direction, the pedicle screws are inserted using a hook holder, captive hook pusher or a mallet. Alternatively, a combination of any of these instruments can also be used.

2. Supralaminar hooks

Being always placed in the down-going position, the supralaminar hook is used in the superior portion of the lamina. As explained in

Chapter 1, the lamina covers the spinal canal, going right from the body of the vertebra and further forming a ring to enclose the spinal cord for the purpose of protection. In order to place the hook, an edge of the lamina is likely to be removed. Once done, the hook will be inserted using a suitable implant holder.

3. Infralaminar hooks

Generally used at the level of T11 or below, these hooks are always placed in the up-going direction. To insert this type of the hook, your surgeon will separate the ligamentum flavum from the inferior surface of the lamina, which will also keep your bone intact.

4. Transverse process hooks

A wide blade hook, this type of hook is usually used in a typical claw construct used in CD systems. Used as both the up-going and down-going hook, these hooks are implanted after the the transverse process is cleared of any soft tissues

5. Reduction hooks

A reduction hook, available in all of the above four styles, is typically placed at the tip of a thoracic curve on the side at which the curve is being corrected. The main purpose of reduction hooks is to facilitate the placement of rods, especially in larger curves or in cases where curves are also accompanied by a considerable amount of lordosis (curve of your low back).

3. Pedicle screws

Pedicle screw instrumentation is one of the latest tools which adds value to the various approaches of spinal surgeries, such as the posterior and anterior forms. Comprised of special screws for the pedicle portion of your vertebrae, this type of instrumentation is now being associated with factors such as a higher surgical success rate and a lower amount of complications.

Before we go any further, let's briefly look at some of the important terms you need to know here.

Terms you should know

(a) Pedicles

A pedicle or a vertebral pedicle is a small, dense, stem-like structure which projects out from the posterior portion or back of your vertebra. Each vertebra has two different pedicles attached to it, as shown in the image below.

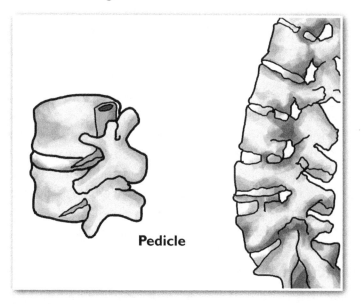

Pedicle

(b) Polyaxial pedicle screws

The polyaxial pedicle screw is the latest and most commonly used type of pedicle screw. Made of titanium, the polyaxial screw is threaded, with the head being mobile. Tolerant to even high levels of fatigue and corrosion, the polyaxial pedicle screws are MRI compatible and come in many sizes. Due to its head being mobile, the screw can swivel, which helps to defray any vertebral stress. Your surgeon will choose from various sizes ranging from 30mm to 60 mm and the diameter ranging from 5.0 mm to 8.5 mm.

Method and Purpose

Pedicle screws are used to correct the spinal deformity. In the specific case of scoliosis, the pedicle screws are used as a part of other instrumentation sets such as the Harrington procedure, with two specific purposes:

→ To fix rods and plates to the spine
→ To immobilize a specific part of the spine to help in spinal fusion

Though the exact procedure might vary with the exact surgical location in the spine (thoracic, lumbar or sacral), there is a generalized way in which the pedicle screws are implanted. Read on for a brief description of these steps below:

- Using a normal x-ray or fluoroscopy, the surgeon will first determine the depth at which the screw has to be inserted.
- Once the depth has been ascertained, the angle at which the screw has to be inserted is estimated and finalized.
- Then, a receiving channel will be drilled through the pedicle using appropriate instruments.
- Finally, the screw is inserted at this specific point.

Efficiency and Popularity

Pedicle screws typically attach to the pedicles, which are the sides of the vertebrae. These hold the rods in place by entering into the bone.

There is plenty of research to show the efficacy of the pedicle screw instrumentation for curve correction. For instance, a study from the Center for Spine Surgery and Scoliosis Center in Germany shows that the segmental pedicle screw instrumentation can be used for the surgical correction of frontal as well as sagittal plane deformity in thoracolumbar and lumbar scoliosis of less than 60 degrees. The results also show that pedicle screw fixation is accompanied by a shorter fusion length as compared to anterior fusion. In addition, pedicle screw instrumentation also offers better curve correction with an improved pulmonary function and minimal neurologic problems.

Another such study also reported that as compared to hook or hybrid constructs, the patients with whom the pedicle screw instrumentation has been used showed improved correction of the major curve and required less follow-up treatment. However, as relevant research shows, the only pre-requisite for the pedicle screw instrumentation to offer results like rigid fixation and improved deformity correction is to follow the proper technique that can be determined by adequate pre-operative analysis and judgments.

Research has also begun to show that pedicle screw instrumentation might offer better curve correction without the accompanying neurologic problems noted with the use of segmental hook instrumentation.

Polyaxial pedicle screws

Segmental Hooks vs. Pedicle Screws

The debate continues on whether the screws or the hooks do a better job in a scoliosis surgery! Originally, the pedicle screws replaced the segmental hooks, which were traditionally being used in the Harrington procedure, one of the first surgical techniques being used to treat scoliosis.

Academically, there are two main reasons surgeons see screws as a better option than the hooks, though complications and risk factors exist in both cases. The two factors which give pedicle screws an advantage over hooks are:

• The ability of screws to resist force of tension (strain) on the spine in a better way than the hooks
• The position of placement of the screws is believed to be giving them an advantage over hooks

In fact, it is also believed that when using screws, a shorter part of the spine needs to be fused and the patient also experiences a smaller amount of blood loss. However, a section of the medical community also believes that hooks offer a lesser scope of neurological complications than the pedicle screws.

Reference: Liljenqvist, et al. Comparative Analysis of Pedicle Screw and Hook Instrumentation in Posterior Correction and Fusion of Idiopathic Thoracic Scoliosis. In European Spine Journal. August 2002. Vol. 11. No. 4. Pp. 336-343.cv

4. Wires

Modern surgical procedures for scoliosis use a combination of tools and instruments that can provide the best possible results for spinal fusions.

Wires, typically used as connectors in a scoliosis surgery, are considered to be part of the second generation systems (1960s-1970s) for the surgical correction of scoliosis. These systems are believed to have come up one step ahead of the Harrington rods procedure, attempting to overcome the complications associated with the latter.

An example of how wires came to be used for scoliotic curve correction is in conjunction with the Luque instrumentation, a common part of the second generation systems. In this particular technique, two rods were placed on either side of the spine and attached using wires.

Sublaminar wiring – Present day

After this, came the era of sublaminar wiring techniques, which are still in use, although not very common. The sublaminar wiring is mostly used for patients in two categories:

→ Those whose bones are too fragile to hold hooks or screws
→ Those whose curves have occurred due to problems with their nerves and muscles

Of late, the typical stainless wires have now been replaced by titanium cables. However, experts express concern over the fact that when a patient has a rigid curve, such sublaminar wires can easily pull out or even break.

Wires are also used to fix curves in the instrumentation for the Wisconsin method and in the case of Dorsal Column Stimulation, a surgical procedure done in order to treat back pain.

What does research say?

Many different types of wires are used in accordance with the type of surgery being performed, with each having different results. For instance, the cobalt chromium alloy wire offers greater advantages over the steel wire, especially in terms of tensile strength and titanium compatibility. In fact, cobalt chromium alloy solid wires are also used as sublaminar implants with titanium spinal instrumentation, often producing remarkable results . However, results in the case of Luque instrumentation using wires show the correction rates to be quite low. Even the rate of damage to the spinal canal through which the wires were passed was considerably high. Generally, wires are considered hazardous, as even the process of removal of damaged or broken wires after such surgeries can prove dangerous, causing complications like neurological injuries.

On the contrary, there are yet other studies that report sublaminar wire placement to be a safe and useful adjunct for surgical treatment of idiopathic scoliosis.

5. Clamps

In the world of spinal surgery, a surgical clamp is a small metallic instrument that acts as an interface between the parts of your spine and the metal rods, holding the entire instrumentation system together. The clamp fixation system attaches the rod to the spinal structure using the pedicle-sparing band passage technique.

When an implant is placed in your spinal structure for reducing the curve of scoliosis, it usually causes a massive amount of friction, or what is medically known as contact stress. Clamps reduce the amount of contact stress by allowing compression, distraction, de-rotation and translation of the spine..Most of the well-known clamps, such as the Universal Clamps, can work well along with other tools such as hooks, screws and wires to give the surgeon greater flexibility in the spinal procedure. The clamp is usually put in place with the help of a woven polyester band and a locking screw.

A relevant research study analyses the usefulness of the Universal Clamp, a relatively new osteosynthesis implant, as an instrumentation device for treating AIS. The clamp, mainly comprising of a sublaminar band and titanium clamp, was seen as an effective device, reducing the risk of laminar fractures and helping in reducing the curve progression. Research also shows that the Universal Clamp distributes stress over a larger area of the laminar cortex than sublaminar wires, thus reducing the risk of severe laminar fracture.

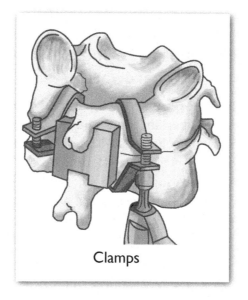

Clamps

The Combination

The type of curve you have will determine which category of tools will your surgeon use, especially from amongst hooks and screws. In fact, in quite a few cases, a suitable combination of hooks, wires and screws will be used to keep the curvature in control.

Real Scoliosis Stories: The experience with hardware!

Jane, all of 16 years when she had her first surgery, had quite a traumatic experience with the use of all hardware and armaments. She got scoliosis as a part of her genetic structure since her mother was also diagnosed with the curvature 20 years back. After wearing a brace for almost 24 hours a day for quite some time, the curve could not be halted. She had her first surgery in the year 1987. Unfortunately, she had to undergo a second operation to remove the rod in 1995.

Inspite of both the surgeries, Jane used to feel uncomfortable and in pain after the procedures. She also suffered from serious infections and fluid leakages after the operations.

Even after years of her operation, Jane finds it difficult to lie down flat on her back or even sit straight with her back against a chair. Jane generally assumes that hardware used for her operation continues to cause her the said discomfort and pain.

CHAPTER 17

In the Operation Theatre

Psychological mindsets have always played a major role in the world of medicine. Getting the patient and even the support staff into the right frame of mind has always been critical to the success of any medical procedure, especially the more sophisticated ones like spinal fusion for scoliosis curve correction. For you as a patient, it is important to know what is in store as you approach the operation theatre for the final moment. In this chapter, we will give you a complete view of what will happen from once you are wheeled into the operation theatre, right to the point when the surgery actually begins.

Knowledge is power!

Indeed, rightly said! To be informed is truly to be empowered. When it comes to personal health, and more importantly, personal safety, you are probably never able to trust anyone but yourself. Going in for a surgery as massive as the one for scoliotic curve correction requires you to be aware, informed and duly educated about what you are headed for.

In the previous chapters, you read all about the various risks involved with your surgery, the different surgical methods used, details of financial preparations and so on. In the sections that follow, we will explain all about what exactly happens when you reach the operation theatre, going up to the point when your surgery actually starts. Here, we will explain the entire scenario in three different steps, which include:

1. Pre-operative routines
2. Get wheeled in — Your trip to the Operation Theatre (OT) after all the initial formalities and checks have been carried out.
3. Get settled, monitored and sedated — The way you will be physically placed on the operating table depends on the surgical approach that will be used. Various devices and monitoring tools will be attached in order to spot any potential risks. Eventually, you will be sedated for the purpose of surgery.

Read on for a detailed explanation of each one of these steps.

1. Pre-operative routines

Foremost, as we discussed in the earlier chapters, by now you would have already gone through the major pre-operative assessments and examinations. These are done in order to ensure that you are medically fit for such a surgery. These checks will usually include the following:

- X-rays, to help plan the surgical approach
- An Electrocardiograph (ECG), to ensure that your heart is working in a normal manner
- Lung function tests to ensure normal breathing patterns
- Medical photography, for record purposes, so that pictures of before and after the surgery can be maintained
- Blood tests to rule out any infections or other complications

Each of these procedures/tests will be usually performed a few days prior to your surgery as a part of the formal pre-operative assessment. Once done, you will then be assigned a specific date for your operation. While some hospitals will require you to be admitted on the same day, some of them would want you to get admitted a night before to ensure proper screening and preparation.

Once you are admitted and all the routine formalities are over, you will be handed over a set of instructions for the next few hours.

Briefly before you are wheeled into the OT, the medical staff will undertake the following steps:

- Take details of your weight and height
- Take your body temperature, heart rate, breathing rate and blood pressure
- Ask about the last food and beverages consumed
- Give you an identity band which you are likely to wear around your wrist
- Fill out a few important forms, like the consent form
- Take some blood for autologous blood donation, if decided earlier (refer to chapter 13 for details)

Just before you are taken in, you will be given a set of clothes to wear which will usually be a gown, knickers and a cap. You will then be wheeled into the operation theatre for the next procedure to start.

2. Get wheeled in

Once into the operating theatre, you will face a different scenario altogether. You will suddenly witness an army of complicated machinery, wires and tools all over with men and women garbed in green. It often serves best to keep yourself focused and try staying calm, even if it means practicing a few relaxation techniques. Some of the professionals preparing for the procedure in the OT will include:

- Chief surgeon
- Anesthetists
- Nursing staff
- Technicians
- Other specialists

The Anesthetist

At this stage, you will also have an important conversation with the chief anesthetist. He is the professional who will be responsible for getting you under sedation for the surgery and ensuring that you stay as sedated as is required to ensure intra-operative monitoring, like spinal cord monitoring. This is important to ensure that no damage is taking place to the spinal cord or other functions of the body during the surgery. Refer to Chapter 10 on risks and complications to know more about such tests.

Your anesthetist will ask you some important questions regarding your previous medical history and whether there are any allergies you suffer from. This is in order to ensure that your body complies with the important drugs which he is going to use for the purpose of sedation.

Keeping your wits in control...

There are quite a few surgeons who advise their patients to take a professional's help in case they are too stressed out about their operation. After all, your psychological state plays a very crucial role in the success of our surgery. All the paraphernalia of wires and instruments in the OT can be intimidating even for the calmest patient. It helps to consciously keep your composure and try not to get fidgety as you approach the final stage of the procedure.

---

3. Get settled, monitored and sedated

At this stage, once you are in the OT, your doctor will start preparing to place you suitably on the operating table. The position and precautions that will be taken depend on the method or approach of the surgery decided, such as posterior, anterior, combined approach or even the VATS approach. You can read more about these methods in chapter 15 on 'Types of Surgery'.

Padding and Positioning

Accordingly, you will be placed on the operating table and adequate padding and positioning would be done. For instance, if you've been set up for spinal fusion through the posterior approach (from the back), you will be then placed in padded frame, with your stomach hanging free. This will help in minimizing bleeding and will also facilitate smooth progression of the surgery.

As another important aspect to ensure overall bodily protection, suitable positioning will done to protect your nerves and joints with additional cushioning. In addition, all the sensitive portions on your skin and face, including your eyes will adequately padded for protection purposes.

Along with padding and positioning, all the important catheters and arterial lines will be affixed, which can actually take more than an hour to finish from the time you enter the OT until your operation actually starts.

In the section that follows, we've given a brief outline of the various intravenous and arterial lines as well as the catheter that will be used.

IV Lines and Monitors

You will also be hooked on to a series of tubes, intravenous (IV) lines, monitors and devices which are meant to deliver medication, nutrition, transfuse blood and so on. In addition, you will also be put on certain monitoring devices to ensure that your vital bodily functions are working fine.

In this section, we've explained each of these tools and devices that you will be hooked on to, for the purpose of your scoliosis surgery.

(A) IV line, tubes and catheters

→ The Foley catheter, which is a small, soft tube meant to help you empty your bladder so that you don't have to get up to go to the washroom. It is usually removed in around 4-5 days. This will be inserted during your surgery into the same opening from where you urinate.

→ PCA (Patient Controlled Analgesia) - An intravenous line that delivers the necessary antibiotics and painkillers.

→ An arterial line, that goes into your artery to monitor your blood pressure levels (see box).

Did you know?

An arterial line is different from an intravenous (IV) line. While an IV line goes into the vein, the arterial line goes into your artery. Moreover, the IV line is mostly used to deliver medication and nutrition, while an arterial line usually works as a monitoring device and is used to check your blood pressure. It can also be used to draw blood samples for the repetitive lab work and tests which might be required later.

→ An endotracheal tube (ET tube), which is placed into your mouth and throat to help you breathe easily. Owing to this, your throat might hurt and your voice might become scratchy. Like the Foley catheter, this is also placed during the surgery.

(B) Monitors and devices

→ A series of electrodes, which will be placed on your chest. These will be like small, soft stickers with wires that are hooked onto a cardiac monitor right above the head of your bed. These electrodes and wires are meant to show your heart rate and breathing rate, which will be displayed in forms of lines and numbers on the monitor.

→ An oxygen mask, to help you breathe easily, since your lungs might not have still recovered, especially if you've had an anterior (from the side/front) incision.

→ A pulse oximeter machine, which will check your oxygen level and is connected to your finger by a bandage.

→ A set of pressure stockings and pneumatic compression boots, which will prevent the formation of any blood clots in the veins due to long hours of inactivity.

For monitoring purposes

At this stage, you will also be set up for regular neurophysiology examination during the surgery. For this purpose, a medical specialist known as a neurophysiologist will attach a few special wires on your head to ensure intra-operative monitoring. Other important monitors and intravenous/IV lines will also be duly placed to ensure proper monitoring and drug administration during the surgery.

Getting sedated

This is where your anesthetist will come in. There are different ways in which the dose can be administered, including the one through the IV line or through a mask. Your anesthetist will usually ask your choice and also see which option is most suitable for you. Interestingly, this step is often the most perplexing for the patient. The reason for this being that this is actually the first physical procedure which will be done on the patient apart from the tests and assessment after reaching the OT. Just take a quick look at the quote below:

"I thought it was going to be way scarier. I didn't know what the operating room was going to look like. I thought it would be like it was on TV. Like the big room with one little bed and everyone staring at you. But it wasn't like that at all. It was freezing cold though. They gave me my teddy bear and I had it in my arms when I fell asleep. When I woke up, it was still in my arms. It was really good!"

Once you've been administered the said drug, you will slowly drift into a sound sleep and the actual procedure will begin.

Real Scoliosis Stories: A daunting experience even for the brave

Angelina was quite a confident and cheerful girl and even took the prospect of surgery in her stride. She was upright about her condition of scoliosis and along with her mother gained complete information on what all could be done to make the entire procedure of surgery more result-oriented and comfortable. However, even for such a strong-willed teenager, the experience of being in an operation theatre and the entire schedule of activities before the surgery was daunting enough.

She was diagnosed with scoliosis at 13 years of age. After a series of diagnosis and varying approaches of treatment, she was finally advised surgery by the time she was 16, confirmed as having a double major curve. She was pretty happy and satisfied with the way the nurses and the doctors explained the entire procedure to her. However, the moment she was wheeled into the operation theatre, she saw the huge spread of tools, which began to unnerve her. Her most traumatic experience was when the doctor wanted to take photographs of her spine so that the same could be compared with the post-surgical spine. In fact, Angelina described those few moments of getting herself clicked, just in her underwear as one of the most uncomfortable and 'humiliating' ones!

CHAPTER 18
Surgery – The Actual Procedure

O nce you are in the operation theatre, it's finally the time for actual surgery. In this chapter, we will take you on a literal tour of the entire surgery, the complete process as it happens.

About Spinal Fusion

That spinal fusion is the most common surgery performed to correct and control the scoliosis curve is something we know as a definite fact by now. However, spinal fusion remains a widely carried out surgery, even beyond scoliosis and is done to achieve a number of objectives. Here, let's begin by first understanding what is spinal fusion and why is it required in the field of pain, deformity and disease management.

Well, as the name suggests, spinal fusion is a surgery that joins or 'fuses' a part of your spine in order to treat any deformity or reduce pain.

As you read in the initial chapters, your spine is comprised of a number of inter-connected vertebrae, starting right from the skull to your tail bone. Each of these vertebrae are connected and inter-linked with each other like a chain and sit stacked on top of each other. Now, the vertebrae are linked in such a manner that they move in coordination and allow the spine to be flexible and move as required. To avoid friction, each of these vertebrae is also cushioned with soft intervertebral discs lying between them. These intervertebral discs, along with the facet joints, allow the spine its visible flexibility as well as adequate protection.

Here, owing to a number of conditions and ailments, these spinal vertebrae go beyond the routine of normal movement and become affected due to disease, trauma or age. When this happens, the normal movement between the 2 or more affected vertebrae becomes painful and leads to pain and instability.

It is this painful movement of the affected vertebrae that the process of spinal fusion aims to eliminate. This is done by fusing together the affected vertebrae through the use of bone grafts and instrumentation.

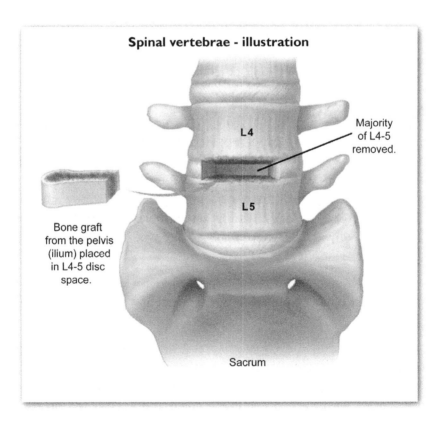

Spinal vertebrae - illustration

L4

Majority of L4-5 removed.

L5

Bone graft from the pelvis (ilium) placed in L4-5 disc space.

Sacrum

The Conditions

For further clarity, as a surgical procedure, spinal fusion is adopted in the case of one or more of the following spinal conditions:

- Trauma or accident resulting in conditions like a fractured vertebra
- Excessive motion between particular vertebrae resulting in spinal instability and pain
- Spinal disorders like spondylolysis, spondylolisthesis and osteoarthritis
- Spinal deformities like scoliosis and kyphosis
- Bulging or herniated disc

PUT SIMPLY...

As a process, spinal fusion tries to do instantly and artificially what Mother Nature would do gradually by mimicking the original procedure of bone growth. Through this bone growth, it permanently fuses the two vertebrae and eliminates all painful movement between them.

The Objectives

The above being said, spinal fusion will be carried out in patients with scoliosis to achieve the following specific purposes:

- To correct/straighten the curve and get the spine into its normal position, as far as possible
- To attempt to reduce pain and spinal instability, though the results might vary from expectations
- To halt any possible progression of the curve
- To prevent any possible damage to the nervous system or other organs

Having understood the key basics of spinal fusion and knowing the objectives it achieves, let's move on further to understand what exactly happens in the surgery and how is it performed.

The Process in Detail

A) Incision

The first step of the surgery will be the incision through which your surgeon will approach the spine. The type and location of the incision will depend on the single most important factor, which is the location of your curve. Through prior x-rays, consultations and other diagnostic measures, your surgeon would have already planned and decided on the approach to be used, which could be either posterior, anterior or a combined approach. You can refer to Chapter 15 to read more on each of these.

With the approach set clear, your surgeon will then move on to make the all-important incision. Depending on the exact location of your curve, your surgeon might proceed to make the incision in the following ways:

→ For the lumbar (lower) spine - With you lying on your stomach, your spine will be approached through the posterior location, .i.e. from the back. Your surgeon will make a direct incision over the spine.

→ For the cervical (upper) spine – To reach a curve and affected vertebrae in the cervical portion of your spine, you will be lying on your back, while your surgeon makes an incision from the front of your neck for the anterior approach and from the back for the posterior approach.

→ For the thoracic (middle) curve – In this case, your surgeon will make an incision in accordance with your typical situation. In fact, in quite few cases where the thoracic spine is concerned, the combined posterior and anterior approach is followed.

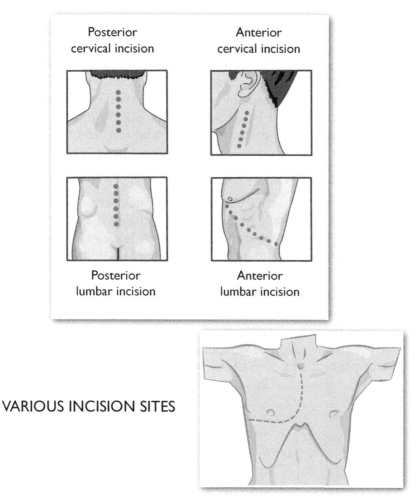

Posterior
cervical incision

Anterior
cervical incision

Posterior
lumbar incision

Anterior
lumbar incision

VARIOUS INCISION SITES

Using the decided approach, your surgeon will first reach the spinous processes, which are small bony projections at the back of the vertebrae. With fine surgical tools, he will then move aside the muscles along the spine to reach the lamina (the protective bone over the back surface of the spinal cord).

At this point, your surgeon will also check if the nearby nerves are under any sort of pressure. In a process known as decompression, he will carefully remove all such pressure and tension from the surrounding nerves either by removing a part of the lamina or even by scraping any nearby bone spurs.

With the incision having been made, your spinal segment that needs to be fused lies exposed. It is now that the next step of bone grafting will begin.

B) Extraction of the bony outgrowths

At this junction, your surgeon will be able to see the point where the affected vertebrae are forcing the spine to bend out of its normal position, placing pressure on the spinal nerves and resulting in the curve of scoliosis. In a process known as decompression or laminectomy, these bony outgrowths will be extracted or taken out, making way for the bone grafts to be inserted.

C) Bone grafts

A bone graft basically comprises of a set of slices of bone material that will be eventually placed between the two affected vertebrae. Various factors are used to decide which bone graft option is to be used for surgery including the type of spinal fusion, number of levels involved, location of fusion, risk factors for non-fusion (i.e. obesity, smoking, poor bone quality, advanced age), surgeon experience, and preference.

Over time and with support of instrumentation, the bone graft will eventually help the vertebrate to join or get 'fused' together. It is this process of fusion of the vertebra using the bone grafts which makes for the actual base of the entire surgery of spinal fusion.

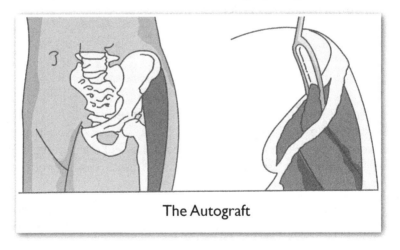

The Autograft

Refer to the box on the next page to know more about the various types of bone grafts that can be used.

Bone grafts

For the purpose of spinal fusion, the bone graft might be obtained from three different sources, including:

1. Autograft bone

As the name suggests, an autograft is a bone graft obtained from the patient's own body, most commonly from the iliac crest of the hip. If your surgeon uses this type of bone graft, an additional incision will be made at the top part of your hip during step A above. The bone material will be extracted from your hip at this stage, if an autograft is to be used.

2. Allograft bone

This is basically a cadaver bone and your surgeon would have already obtained the bone graft from an external bone bank prior to the surgery. An allograft will usually save the patient from the pain and risk associated with an additional incision for an autograft at the time of the surgery. However, your surgeon will be in the best position to decide on the type of graft to be used.

3. Synthetic bone graft materials

Owing to the massive developments and innovations in the field of surgery and medicine, patients can now also opt for artificial bone graft materials for the purpose of spinal fusion. A few examples of such commercially available artificial bone graft materials include:

- Demineralized bone matrix (DBMs) – Obtained by removing calcium from cadaver bones, DBMs have a gel-like consistency and are believed to be carrying proteins that aid and expedite bone healing.

- Ceramics – Quite similar in shape and consistency to the autograft bone, these are made from synthetic calcium or phosphate materials and are considered as an effective option to autograft.
- Bone morphogenetic proteins (BMPs) – Approved by the US Food and Drug Administration (FDA), BMPs are extremely powerful synthetic bone-forming proteins which will promote a solid fusion, totally eliminating the need for an autograft.

DBMs are made by processing allograft bone and demineralized to extract the proteins the stimulate formation of bone. Often they are used with autografts as alone they may not stimulate adequate fusion. BMP is only approved for anterior lumbar interbody fusion surgery and is expensive.

Placement of bone grafts

With the bone graft material ready to use, it will now be time to place them appropriately in the exposed portion of the vertebrae that lie along the curve. Carefully, using specific surgical instruments, your surgeon will now lay small, match-stick sized bone grafts vertically across the exposed portion. Here, it is worth noting that each of the grafts or slices will be placed in such a manner that they should touch each of the adjoining vertebrae. Only then will it be possible for the fusion to take place, which is the very purpose of the surgery.

D) Immobilization and instrumentation

At the time of the fusion surgery, metal instrumentation is used to provide stability and immobilization for the first few initial months with solid fusion of bone gradually providing long-term stability.

Here, your surgeon has actually started off a process that mimics the natural procedure of bone growth. The two vertebrate will now start getting cemented with the bone grafts on the either side and will eventually fuse together to make a single structure.

Until the time this fusion actually happens, your surgeon will need to hold all the material together, including your vertebrae and the bone grafts. This is where instrumentation will come in. In most of the cases, rods will be used to keep the spine in place, while pedicle screws, segmental hooks and metal plates will be inserted to keep the bone graft in place, allowing it some time before it all actually fuses into a single bone.

Refer to the image below for a detailed pictorial representation of the entire process of surgery.

E) Closure of the incision

Once the instrumentation has been inserted and suitably fixed to keep the bone grafts in place, your surgeon will carefully fold the skin flaps back into place and perform the necessary surgical closure. In addition to this, your surgeon might also place one or more drains beneath the skin which are likely to stay there for a few days.

Eventually the entire procedure will allow the grafts to regenerate, grow into the specific bone and finally, fuse the two affected vertebrae together.

Correcting the three dimensions of scoliosis

Tools To Untwist the Spine

Traditionally, scoliosis has been regarded as a two-dimensional deformity of the spine – for example, an "s" curve that a surgeon would try to straighten by "stretching out" the curve with rods. However, most patients, including Nicholas Sheridan, suffer a kind of twisting of the vertebrae that results in a three-dimensional malformation. Dr. Maric Barry, Nicholas's pediatric orthopedic surgeon, has developed a technique that corrects all three dimensions.

X-rays used during surgery aid the surgeon when placing the screws into the pedicles of the spine at a correct angle. If the screws are placed incorrectly, the spinal cord could be damaged, resulting in paralysis or worse. It took Dr. Barry a full hour to anchor the 19 screws that hold the two rods that were placed along Nicholas Sheridan's spine.

Straightening the spine

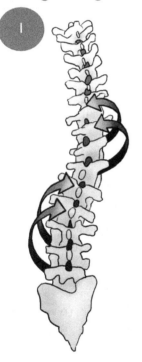

1

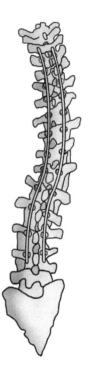

2

Scoliosis is a deformity which can cause the spine to rotate like a corkscrew resulting in constant pain, a compromised lung and heart function and the limitation of activity. The diagram above shows how scoliosis twists the spine in different directions.

Special screws are inserted into the pedicles of the spine and titanium rods of ¼ inch in diameter are threaded through the heads of these screws. A plug is slipped through the end of the screw to hold the rod in place.

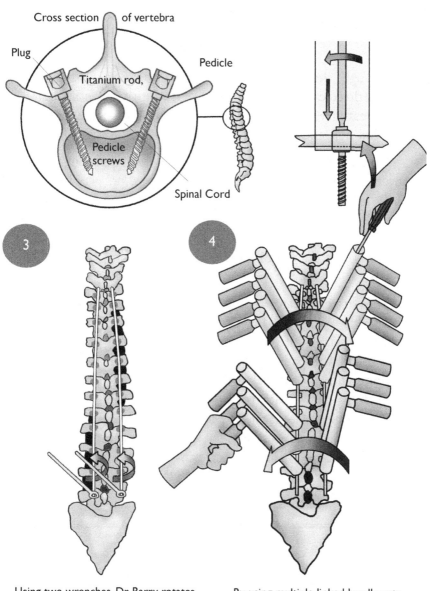

Cross section of vertebra

Plug

Pedicle

Titanium rod,

Pedicle screws

Spinal Cord

3

4

Using two wrenches, Dr. Barry rotates the rods until the spine looks straight from a posterior view, or from the perspective achieved by looking down on the spine. Two dimensions of scoliosis are corrected throughout this procedure, but the rotated vertebrae (shown in red) must still be treated by Dr. Barry's surgical team.

By using multiple linked handle sets that Dr. Barry himself designed, the surgeon and his staff rotate the twisted vertebrae into alignment. The actual process takes about a minute. A screwdriver-like tool is used to lock the screws in place. Donor bone graft is then sprinkled along the rods.

Real Scoliosis Stories: The Surgeon's Expertise

Though the procedure for spinal fusion is usually a standardized one, yet in some cases, the entire process is quite complicated. Here, it is only the surgeon's sound expertise that can help the patient gain respite from scoliosis.

It happened with Harry, a 14 year old, suffering from severe scoliosis. According to the doctors, he was bent at a 90-degree angle and his vital organs were almost getting crushed by the curvature. The experts carried out a surgery to correct the curve, which eventually saw him grow from 4'10 to a whopping 5'3", apart from reducing his curve to 20 degrees.

The surgery was a complicated one. In fact, Harry lost almost his entire's body's worth of blood and his brain was shut down. This left the surgeons almost fearing that he was brain dead and panic grew. However, gradually he began to respond and started inching back to normalcy. Such was the state of his curve prior to the surgery that the doctors had warned of possible paralysis post-surgery. However, an eight hour operation to put titanium rods on the either side of his spine actually helped straighten the curve and give the teenager the much-required lease to a new life.

CHAPTER 19

Possible Complications - What Could Go Wrong?

W ell, there is always a huge gap between what should have been and what actually happens in life! Yet, in situations like medicine and surgery, things that deviate even an inch from the intended plan of action can create havoc, at times even proving to be fatal. As you move ahead with your plans of surgery to treat scoliosis, here we give you a clear insight into the darker side of the procedure. This chapter talks about what all could go wrong with your surgery, what complications can arise immediately and which ones can appear even after a long period of time.

What to expect

Just for a quick reference, here's what you will ideally expect after you have recovered from your surgery:

- A straighter back, with your hump gone or reduced
- Drastic reduction in pain
- A greater amount of comfort in your daily routine activities
- Better cosmetic appearance

The process of fusion takes around 3 months to solidify, while it might continue to mature for a period of 2 years. Hence, your pain and numbness will take at least 3 months to resolve, after which you can expect your normal nerve function to return gradually.

However, all might not actually happen this way and some unprecedented complications might occur, as explained in the following sections.

If all doesn't go well...

It is quite obvious that a procedure as complicated as scoliosis surgery carries with it a huge risk of possible complications, though experts point out that a proper process of diagnosis and the right surgery technique can reduce these complications.

From neurological damage to excessive bleeding, pain, recurrence of the curvature and even paralysis; a scoliosis surgery brings with it a series of complications, ranging from mild to serious, though quite a few of them are often rare in nature.

In the case where external instrumentation is involved and the surgeon is dealing with such a sensitive body part like your spinal cord, the possibility of such complications just cannot be ignored. For instance, there is concrete research that shows an overall complication rate is not influenced by the type of your curve, but definitely increases if your surgeon is using a combined anterior/ posterior approach or if you've gone through additional procedures such as an osteotomy, a surgical procedure done to shorten, lengthen or change the alignment of a bone.

What is FBSS?

The Failed Back Surgery Syndrome (FBSS) is an umbrella term given to a series of post-surgery problems that present themselves through symptoms and complications such as the above.

Here, let's quickly look at some of the factors due to which the probability of such complications becomes quite high:

- Use of metal and other instruments, which are basically foreign bodies and might not be accepted by the body easily
- Existing weak state of the body due to additional complications arising out of scoliosis, such as back pain
- Unexpected discoveries in the deformity after the incision has been made
- Complexity of the curve, especially in the case of rigid and severe curves
- Pre-existing diseases such as Prader-Willi Syndrome (PWS) which increase the scope of complications

Owing to such factors detailed as above and many more which we'll discuss in this chapter, there could be a number of situations in which all will not happen as planned and the surgery might go wrong on quite a few accounts. Now, as apprehensible as this might sound, it is always advisable for the patient in question and even for the surgeons to be informed about and prepared for any such complications that might arise during or after the surgery.

The Redress

While each patient is different and every complication will have its own cure and treatment, it helps to know some of the common treatment options experts use to handle such complications of the surgery.

Usually, your surgeon will decide on one or more of the below listed approaches to address the complications, whether they are immediate or long-term, mild or serious:

- Pain relieving medications
- Infection-fighting antibiotics
- Other medications to control conditions like excessive bleeding
- Revision surgeries and repeat instrumentation/placement of bone graft

Types of Complications

Research shows that close to 40% of the patients experience minor complications while at least 20% suffer from major complications after a scoliosis surgery

Well, to begin with, it is important to know that there are two categories of complications that can occur, namely:

→ The ones that occur during the surgery, .i.e. Intra-operative risks

→ The ones that appear as after-effects of the surgery over a longer span of time

In this section, we will discuss each of these two types of complications associated with surgery, demonstrating what exactly happens to your body when these occur.

Immediate intra-operative complications

1. Excessive bleeding

Also known as hemorrhaging, this is perhaps one of the most common, immediate complications that arise from a scoliosis surgery. In fact, research often shows that excessive bleeding is one of the most serious complications that can occur, both during the surgery as well as at the post-operative stage.

Though the risk of excessive bleeding is associated with most types of surgery, it is paramount in spinal fusion due to the long incision involved. Conditions ranging from a difficult to access curve to complex, fatty tissue and even improper use of instrumentation can lead to excessive blood loss. Interestingly, factors like our bone marrow density (BMD) also influence the scope and amount of bleeding. Research shows that patients with a poorer BMD are at a nine-time higher risk of experiencing excessive blood loss during a scoliosis surgery

Experts explain that it is not only the volume of blood loss that is a problem. Additional complications can occur when blood replacement is carried out, the most common being diseases like

AIDS and hepatitis. Moreover, since such intraoperative (during the surgery) blood replacement takes time, it will create further complications by increasing the overall timespan of the surgery.

It is for such reasons that an autologous (self) blood donation is often encouraged by experts beforehand so that you are equipt in case blood transfusion is required. You can read more about blood donation in Chapter 13.

Your surgeon will take some important steps to minimize intraoperative blood loss. These steps may include:

→ Using appropriate devices such as the Relton-Hall frame to position the patient in such a way that the abdomen hangs free, which will reduce the intra abdominal pressure and hence the scope of bleeding

→ Using topical hemostatic agents like bone wax, or Ostene (the newly FDA approved water soluble material, prone to lesser complications) to control the bleeding from the bone

→ Placing thrombin-soaked gel foam into the excised facet joints for a brief duration

2. Infection

Infections are one of the commonly expected fallout of a surgery owing to the use of tools, instruments, external bone grafts and also from blood transfusion. An infection can occur due to a variety of reasons, such as listed below:

→ When the body doesn't accept the instrumentation in the right manner

→ Through blood transfusions which might carry infection-causing agents

→ Through the use of surgical tools

→ Through a bone graft obtained from a donor that could also carry disease causing agents

→ As a reaction to medications and drugs

→ A few pre-existing conditions such as cerebral palsy (CP) in children can increase the risk of infections, post surgery

Though antibiotics are administered on an ongoing basis before as well as after the surgery, yet infections can commonly occur. Some of the most common warning signs of such infections could be:

- Excessive tenderness, redness or swelling around the wound
- Drainage of fluid from the wound
- Acute pain
- Chills
- High temperature (more than 100°F)

3. Respiratory and cardiac problems

Pulmonary complications are quite a common problem related to spinal fusion surgery. As it is, the abnormal curvature of the spine often presses against the rib cage and can cause discomfort as well as impede respiratory and cardiac function. During the surgery, the patient might experience symptoms like shortness of breath, chest pain or other related cardiac complications. Some other respiratory disorders can also occur up to 1 week after the surgery is over. Such issues can arise due to a number of factors, such as:

- Stress related with surgery
- Physical pressure on rib cage
- Sudden alterations in blood pressure levels
- Previous history of impaired pulmonary function
- Adverse effects of medications

Research demonstrates that such lung and respiratory disorders are more common in children whose scoliosis is due to neuromuscular problems like spina bifida, cerebral palsy or muscular dystrophy.

To guard against such issues, your surgeon will ensure regular monitoring and intraoperative assessments to avoid any serious implications.

Long-term complications

Here, the first thing you need to keep in mind is that spinal fusion, which is the most common surgical procedure to correct scoliosis, permanently fuses a part of your spine. This implies that after the surgery, your back and spinal cord attain an all-new shape and structure. For most of the patients of scoliosis, this could mean regaining the original normal posture and getting rid of the deformity. However, in a few cases, the surgery doesn't go as planned and the results don't come as expected. In such cases, the complications that were caused by the surgery are usually visible after a few months or even years and can result in issues even more serious and debilitating than the curve itself.

Often in such cases, there is a need to later take up repeat surgeries. One such multi-center study amongst 306 patients of surgery reveals an overall complication rate to be as high as 39%. While 44% of patients were found at risk of a revision surgery, 26% of patients were actually re-operated for mechanical and neurological complications related to scoliosis surgery. In fact, there would be various factors that could influence whether such complications arise, such as the surgical technique, age, health, type of curve and the like.

Let's understand each of these long-term implications in detail.

1. Chronic back pain

It is quite natural for the patient to feel some soreness and pain at the site of the graft. However, this turns into a matter of concern when the site of your surgery continues to hurt long after the surgery is over, which can be even after 4 to 5 years.

It is possible that you might continue to feel the pain for a few months after the surgery.. However, in some cases the patient might also suddenly start having pain at the bone graft site after few years.

Perhaps one of the most common long-term complications of spinal fusion, chronic pain is a result of a series of factors related to your scoliosis surgery. Below, we've listed just a few reasons which might cause chronic pain for a number of years after surgery:

- Limited range of movement owing to fusion of vertebrae
- Permanent change to the shape and structure of your spine
- Discomfort caused due to rods, screws or other metal implants
- Infection or injury to the bones, nerves or tissue surrounding the site of fusion

- Inflammation of the surrounding tissue
- Disk degeneration

Apart from the above, you might also continue to feel general pain and discomfort long after your surgery without any specific, plausible reason. If this happens, make sure you consult your surgeon to look for any other causes that need to be suitably addressed.

Managing chronic pain...

In most of the cases, such long-term pain emanating from a scoliosis surgery is first managed by conservative treatment options such as over-the-counter (OTC) pain medication and even alternate therapies. It is only when the pain goes beyond a certain point that prescribed narcotic pain medications are used. If the pain is being caused by screws or other metal implants, your surgeon might decide to remove these surgically.

2. Hardware failure

Hardware failure or problems with the instrumentation used often reflects itself a few weeks, months or even years after the surgery. There are two main categories of problems that can occur due to hardware failure:

→ Failure of the body to accept the metal implants
→ Additional problems created by the instrumentation such as breakage, improper positioning, being ill fitted, etc.

Read on for a few specific situations that demonstrate more about such hardware/instrumentation failure:

→ Pedicle screws might get displaced or loose, disrupting the normal process of fusion. One such study conducted to analyze the complications of pedicle screw fixation in scoliosis surgery shows 11% of the total patients analyzed to have experienced misplaced or malpositioned screws after a scoliosis surgery.

→ Around 5% of patients are expected to experience rod displacement where hooks might move from their original position

→ In some patients, the rod that was initially placed to keep the spine straight might begin to rub on the sensitive parts of your body. This can happen anywhere from 1 to 5 years of the surgery and will usually require a revision surgery.

Since such instances of hardware failure and instrumentation displacement can prove quite risky, experts strongly stress on the need of the spine surgeons and radiologists to be fully familiar with the different types of instrumentation to be used. Such clinical experts also need to be suitably equipped to recognize the clinical and radiographic signs of hardware failure to enable early and effective management of the related complications.

3. Problems during the fusion process

Spinal fusion is a highly complex and intricate work of surgery. There is a scope of complications arising at many steps of the surgery and even later. Even if all has gone well during your surgery, there are chances that fusion might not have taken place as required. Watch out for the below common signs which indicate that the fusion has not taken place properly:

→ Ongoing, chronic pain in the back or neck

→ Dull or acute pain in the back or neck

→ Numbness and tingling in the back/neck that radiates through your extremities; i.e. shoulders, hands, arms, legs, thighs or feet

So, why does a spinal fusion failure occur?

In other words, what are the reasons due to which your vertebrae will not fuse properly in spite of the bone graft and all other procedures? Let's look at a few reasons:

• Rejection of the bone graft by the body
• Breakage or malfunction of metal implants and other hardware

- Emergence of problems with surrounding discs and vertebrae due to the increased stress on these areas
- Severe infections, post-surgery, which hamper the fusion process
- Formation of excessive scar tissue
- Excessive bleeding or blood clotting which will also disrupt the fusion process

4. Pain at the graft site

This will be relevant only if you've had an autograft bone fusion, which means that the bone graft material was surgically taken from the iliac crest of your hip area. Since this procedure is a minor surgery in itself, you could be experiencing pain at this point due to the following reasons:

- Infection due to the surgery
- Injury caused in the process of extraction
- Soreness or swelling
- General physical discomfort
- Slow scar formation

Rare Complications

Apart from the above, there are a few other long-term complications that are quite rare. However, since they do occur in a small percentage of patients, it is important to understand the meaning and implication of each one of them. Here, we've explained some of the most crucial long-term but rare complications associated with scoliosis surgery.

5. Nerve damage

In some cases, the nerves or blood vessels can get injured during a scoliosis surgery. As we read earlier, a scoliosis surgery involves exposing the layers of muscle and nerves to access the spine from either the front, back or combined approaches. During this procedure, there is often a possibility of injury to the surrounding nerves and tissue. Nerve damage can also occur due to stretching or bruising of the nerve, which might resolve itself over a period of time.

Moreover, when instrumentation and bone grafts are placed to fuse the vertebrae, the surgeon can accidentally apply additional force or pressure on the spine which can occur later in the form of various symptoms such as the ones listed below:

- Weakness in the bladder and or bowel function
- Partial or complete weakness, numbness, tingling in one or both the legs
- Foot Drop
- Erectile dysfunction

To prevent and detect such disorders at an early stage, your surgeon will use a series of intraoperative tests such as the Stagnara wake-up test to ensure that your nerves are functioning optimally.

6. Blood clotting

As an allied effect of surgery, you might develop blood clots in your legs. In quite a few cases the blood clot can get loose from the spine. In fact, these clots can prove highly dangerous if they break loose and travel towards the lungs. If you've had a surgery for scoliosis, you can watch out for the following warning signs which indicate the presence of a blood clot:

- Swelling in the ankle, calf or foot
- Excessive redness or tenderness going up to or beyond the knee
- Strong pain in the calf

In order to protect your body from such clotting, your surgeon might place you on blood thinners or use special devices like compression stockings.

7. Pseudarthrosis

Medically, pseudarthrosis is defined as a condition where the bones do not fuse together properly owing to a number of reasons. Once the bone grafts have been placed, instrumentation is added to maintain the alignment of the spine while the fusion is taking place.. However, in the case of pseudarthrosis, there is a disruption in this normal process.

Occurring in around 5% to 10% of the cases and very commonly in smokers, pseudarthrosis can eventually lead to discomfort and even partial loss of correction. In most of the cases, pseudarthrosis requires an additional surgery where more graft material is placed in the specific area where fusion has failed to take place.

8. Growth inhibition

We know how a scoliosis surgery will fuse two or more of the vertebrae together and alter the the original structure of your spine. While it might not make much of a difference in an adult or even an adolescent, yet such a process of fusion is likely to hamper a child's natural growth pattern in quite a few cases. Growth occurs in all areas of a child's body and appropriate spinal growth is extremely important and has the ability to affect change in much of a child's skeletal structure as well as organ function.

Hence, stunted growth remains a major long-term complication of scoliosis surgery in children.

9. Increased deformity

Though the surgery of scoliosis aims to reduce deformity of your back, yet in some cases, the result might just be the opposite. There are two types of deformities that could occur:

- Increased torso deformity, where rib hump will worsen due to the force applied to straighten the spine through the surgical procedure. Since the normal function of the rib cage can get permanently affected, your physical appearance can drastically change
- Flat back, sagittal deformity can worsen due to reduction in the lateral curve of the mid back, leading to the loss of your back's natural curve. This is a postural disorder which may result from surgery and cause a number of postural abnormalities, the most obvious of which is loss of lumbar lordosis.

10. Others

A few other long-term, rare complications include:

- Urinary Tract Infections
- Gallstones
- Intestinal obstruction
- Pancreatitis

Real Scoliosis Stories: Scoliosis, Ballet and Screws

Scoliosis often has the potential to catch the patient off guard and disrupt all the current goals and plans.

For someone who always aspired and practiced hard to become a ballet dancer, being diagnosed with scoliosis came as quite a hard blow. Samantha (name changed) was barely a teenager when she learnt she had a curved spine and was immediately put onto a brace, which she continued to wear for the next two years. However, this had no effect and the curve had progressed to around 52 degrees at the top and 45 degrees in the bottom by the time she was in her sophomore year. It was then that she had her first spinal fusion from T4 to L3.

Unfortunately, a check-up done just after a few months of her surgery revealed that the hooks in the top of her spine had become dislodged. She had her second spinal fusion just shortly thereafter. Merely two weeks after the surgery, it was discovered that the upper level hooks had dislodged again, which was then followed by a third surgery. In the last one, the instrumentation in the upper spine was removed while the lower hooks were left as it is. However, none of this helped and her condition continued to deteriorate through the next few years.

Luckily enough, Samantha came across a surgeon who carried out a fourth surgery using the posterior approach and pedicle screw fixation to successfully treat her curve.

CHAPTER 20

Surgery – Your 50 Most Important FAQs

Through the entire journey of the part of this book, we've introduced you to all the important aspects of a scoliosis surgery. Right from deciding to go for a surgery to explaining the actual procedure, this section of the book dealt with each of the aspects. As we round up the second part, it's now time to answer all the queries you could've ever had regarding scoliosis surgery.

For your convenience, we've divided all of these questions into 3 easy-to-understand categories so that you know where to look for answers to your specific questions. For instance, to know about the specific lifestyle changes that will be required, simply go to part 3 which answers the most common FAQs, post surgery.

Read on as we answer all your key concerns about the scoliosis surgery through a set of 50 well-laid out and detailed answers and explanations. Though the range of queries and doubts is indeed endless, yet we've attempted to cover all possible queries any potential patients of surgery could have.

A) Your concerns before making a decision

If you are at a stage where your doctor has even remotely suggested scoliosis surgery for yourself or your child, then this section is for you. Look for answers to your most crucial questions as you decide on the benefits and risks. The following set of questions will act as a guide, helping you through the decision making process.

Q1. Is the surgery really required?

This is perhaps the first and most common query a patient of scoliosis will have. Being highly invasive and also carrying a potential of complications later, scoliosis surgery usually comes across as a very intimidating concept. Hence, a patient would ideally want to explore all possible options before opting for surgery.

Though each patient will have a different medical history and concerns regarding their curve, there are a few factors that indicate the need for surgery. A surgical correction of scoliosis will usually be required if you experience any of the below:

→ If your curve is more than 45 or 50 degrees using the Cobb method (see box below) and you've attained skeletal maturity, .i.e. no major skeletal growth is pending.. This is especially valid for children, adolescents and teenagers. In case the skeletal growth is still pending, you should ideally wait for the surgery.

→ If there is a major scope of progression of your curve (according to your age, severity and location of curve), then you should go for the surgery.

→ If you are facing strong disabilities and limitations in your daily routine activities

→ If you are having a severe cosmetic problem, with the curve giving you a hunch back look

What is the cobb method?

The Cobb Method is a universally followed, standardized procedure for measuring the degree of the scoliotic curve. It is identified on an x-ray image of the curve. The end vertebrae of the curved portion are spotted and a set of straight, perpendicular lines are drawn to form an angle of measurement.

You can refer to Chapter 6 to know more about the Cobb method.

Furthermore, to have a better understanding of your situation and whether surgery is the right option for you, simply ask yourself the 7 important questions we discussed in Chapter 9, which are:

→ The status of your curve
→ Your skeletal maturity
→ The risk of progression of the curve
→ Results of non-invasive measures used earlier
→ Your current health status
→ Limitations being caused by your curve
→ Your current financial status

Q2. Will the surgery be very painful?

You will be under the effect of anesthesia during the surgery, so there is no way you would feel the pain in the operating theatre. Once the surgery is over, you are likely to be in acute pain, which will gradually subside. In some patients, a general discomfort will be felt along with some numbness and tingling, while others might also feel strong pain at the bone graft site. In addition, it might be less painful if you are younger and have had an uncomplicated surgery.

However, you do have to be mentally prepared for the pain associated with the earlier intravenous injections and tests. Overall, the magnitude of the pain will be kept in control and managed by your anesthetist and the pain management specialists, both before as well as after the surgery.

Q3. How much will a scoliosis surgery cost?

The total cost of your scoliosis surgery will depend on a number of factors, including:

→ The severity of your curve and the technique being used

→ The type of instruments being used in your surgery

→ Your geographical location, since cost estimates vary in different countries and within regions

→ The span of your insurance provider's coverage for the procedure

→ The amount of complications or additional hospital stay you might need post surgery

→ Your choice of the surgeon as well as the hospital

Though the actual costs might vary, scoliosis surgery is by and large considered to be an expensive procedure, costing anything from $75,000 to $300,000 per operation.

Q4. Will my curve totally disappear?

Well, this depends on the current state of your spine and how flexible is it pre-surgery. How much your spine will straighten after the surgery depends on a lot of factors like your age, severity of your curve, overall health status and so on. For instance, research shows that for teenagers and adolescents, as much as 50% of the curve can be straightened, which might not be possible in the older set of patients. In other words, how much of the curve will go away will vary and is best predicted by your surgeon.

Q5. Will I or my child suffer from any permanent handicaps later?

Clinically, the rate of severe complications after the surgery is not very high. However, if you are considering surgery for your child, there is a slight chance that it could hamper her normal growth pattern, also known as growth inhibition. In some adults, the fused vertebrae might make the normal bending or twisting activities of the spine a bit difficult or even impossible. No other major handicaps are usually reported after surgery unless some serious, unforeseen complications occur during the procedure, as discussed in Chapter 19.

Q6. Will a scoliosis surgery affect my chances of a healthy pregnancy?

There is a definite connection of scoliosis with pregnancy and child-rearing, since pregnancy and child-rearing both increase stress on the spine and therefore may influence the development or progression of a spinal curvature.

If you have a major curve and are thinking of going in for a surgery and also considering giving birth, it is best not to time these together. Though women who've had a scoliosis surgery usually have had successful pregnancies as well, it is important to take your expert's guidance on the timing of the surgery as well as conception and pregnancy.

MUST READ!

If you've been diagnosed with scoliosis and are pregnant or planning to conceive, it will surely be worth it to pick up a copy of 'An Essential Guide for Scoliosis and a Healthy Pregnancy' by Dr. Kevin Lau. The book acts as a month-by-month guide of all you want to know about caring for your spine and the baby!

Q7. When should I decide for my child's surgery? Will the curve go away on its own?

Well, it all depends on your child's age and the severity of the curve. If your child is still young (4-11 years) and is likely to attain a lot of physical growth, it is best to wait for the surgery, since his growth might get affected and the chances that his curve might recur would be higher. You can read more about this phenomenon in Chapter 7 (The Risser-Ferguson Grade).

However, one should never expect the curve to go away on its own. Detection and management of even the smallest curve at an early age can make all the difference as to how scoliosis will later affect the child's life.

Q8. Are there any new, minimally-invasive techniques I can consider?

By its original design, a scoliosis surgery is heavily invasive and carries a high risk of complications. It is natural for the patient to get intimidated and look for less-invasive options. You can discuss the following techniques with your surgeon if you want to explore the minimally invasive options:

→ Vertebral body stapling
→ Vertical expandable prosthetic titanium rib (VEPTR)
→ Video assisted thoracoscopic surgery VATS).
→ The endoscopic approach
→ Thoracoplasty

You can read more about each of these techniques and how they are less invasive in nature in Chapter 15. Overall, surgical correction, either done though spinal fusion, conventional surgery or the above minimally invasive methods, is largely seen as the only way for long-term curve correction.

However, before you opt for surgery, it is also advisable to use non-invasive therapies such as diet and exercise, for the purpose of curve correction. Refer to 'Your Plan for Natural Scoliosis Prevention *and Treatment'* by Dr. Kevin Lau where you can find all you want to know about treating scoliosis in a non-invasive manner.

Q9. How can I prepare myself/my child mentally?

The first step is to gain maximum information. Educate yourself or your child on all the aspects of the surgery. Tell her about the tests which will take place. If she is old enough to understand, you can also explain the procedure briefly. However, the post surgery aspect is the most important one and hence needs to be explained carefully. Tell your child about the major differences that will come along after the surgery. This should include information on how the surgery will change her looks, her lifestyle and affect her daily routine activities, at least for a few months.

Q10. Will a scoliosis surgery be covered by insurance?

Yes, in most of the cases. Since scoliosis surgery is a fairly common procedure, it is mostly covered by the insurance provider in the US and will come under the aegis of the NHS in the UK. Overall, the exact amount and extent of coverage in the US will be determined by your particular insurance policy.

Q11. Will I be required to go in for a lot of tests?

Pre-surgery tests and examinations are aimed to help your surgeon decide on whether you are medically fit enough for a surgery. These tests are also important to detect any major disorder or disease the patient might be suffering from. Refer to chapter 13 to know more about these tests and examinations. It is always in your best interest to fully cooperate with the medical team and go through all the required diagnostic measures properly. Some of the most important tests include:

→ Physical screening
→ X-rays
→ Pulmonary function tests (PFT)
→ MRI and Myelography

→ Electrocardiogram (EKG)
→ Electroencephalogram (EEG)
→ Blood tests
→ Urine tests

Q12. How to select the right surgeon and hospital?

Your choice of the surgeon and the hospital can make all the difference to the success of your surgery. There are many factors you can consider while deciding on both, as we explained in Chapter 12. Here we've explained just a few of them.

For the hospital

→ Physical proximity or distance from your house
→ Infrastructure and other facilities available
→ General reputation
→ Coverage by your insurance policy

For the surgeon

→ Academic/Professional qualifications
→ Certifications and licenses
→ Past experience, specifically in your type of cases
→ Success/failure rates
→ References of previous patients
→ Coverage by your insurance policy

Some patients get into a problem as the surgeon they prefer doesn't work at a hospital nearby. In such cases, you can discuss the issue with your surgeon and the hospital and try to work out a viable option.

B) During the procedure

Q13. Doctors talk a lot about spinal fusion. What is it?

Spinal fusion is basically a process in which two or more of your vertebrae along the curve are permanently joined or 'fused' together to straighten your spine. In this process, a bone graft will placed between the vertebrae. Instruments such as rods screws and plates will be used to keep the graft material in place until it fuses to the bone.

Q14. What are the 'instruments' used in a surgery?

'Instruments' is basically an umbrella term given to the hardware being used in your surgery. All the rods, screws, hooks and plates that will be used to straighten the spine and keep the bone graft in place are known as the instruments or instrumentation.

Q15. Are endoscopic and open surgery one and the same thing?

No, they are not. An open surgery will include only a single or a couple of big incisions. On the other hand, an endoscopic surgery will include a number of small incisions. Guided by an endoscope (which is a device consisting of a long, thin tube which contains a light and video camera and allows a surgeon to view the surgical area through a small incision),small surgical instruments are inserted and the process of fusion is then carried out.

Q16. How long will the surgery take?

The total time taken for your surgery can vary depending upon the severity of your curve and the approach your surgeon has taken. On an average, a typical scoliosis surgery can take anywhere from 3 to 8 hours.

Q17. Tell me about the different types of scoliosis surgery techniques available.

Broadly speaking, there are 4 main types of scoliosis techniques you and your surgeon can choose from. These include:

→ The posterior approach, in which your spine will be accessed from the back

→ The anterior approach, in which your spine will be accessed from the front,.i.e. chest wall

→ The combined approach, which will use both of the above approaches. While the spine will be accessed from the front, the fusion will be carried through the posterior route

→ Minimally invasive techniques such as the endoscopic approach (involving several smaller incisions), thoracoplasty, vertebral body stapling and the like.

Q18. Which procedure is better?

A skilled surgeon and a proper medical analysis make each of the above discussed techniques equally effective. Each procedure has its own benefits and risks involved. Moreover, there are specific types of curves that respond better to a particular technique. For instance, the anterior approach is usually considered for curves which are located in the thoracolumbar region (T12-L1). You surgeon will be in the best position to decide an appropriate technique for your surgery.

Q19. Will I be conscious during the surgery?

You will be under the influence of anesthesia once you reach the operation theatre. You will regain consciousness after the entire procedure is over and will not be awake to see any of the happenings throughout the surgery.

Q20. How long will be the incision?

The length of the incision will depend on two things, including the type of technique being used and also the number of the vertebrae to be fused. For instance, on an average, a typical posterior approach will include an incision of 6 to 12 inches, starting from the center of your back.

Q21. What are drains and why/when are they placed?

A drain is basically a tube placed into the wound after the surgery is over and the incision is closed. It is done in order to drain fluid from the surgical area in order to protect the incision from any damage or infection.

Q22. Can things go seriously wrong during the surgery?

Yes they can. Though rare, there is a possibility of serious complications happening during the surgery, which include:

→ Severe breathing/respiratory issues
→ Cardiac problems
→ Excessive blood loss
→ Nerve damage
→ Infection
→ Chronic pain
→ Clots
→ Death

Q23. Can I see the instruments being used?

If you are interested to, your surgeon can show and familiarize you with the instruments which are going to be fitted in your body, prior to your operation. If you are adequately informed, you can even request your surgeon to show you these instruments in one of your pre-surgery meetings.

Q24. How will you take the bone graft? Will it hurt at that point for long?

There are three options through which your surgeon will take the bone graft. These include:

→ Autograft, in which a bone graft will be obtained from the iliac crest of your hip area during the surgery

→ Allograft, in which your surgeon would obtain the bone graft material from a bone bank prior to the surgery

→ A synthetic bone graft, which includes the use of several synthetic artificial bone graft materials available commercially

If your surgeon has chosen to take a bone graft from the iliac crest, it will usually not result in any major complications or excessive pain later.

Q25. Will I lose a lot of blood?

Some blood loss is natural during the surgery owing to the heavily invasive nature of the procedure. It is quite common for the patient to need some amount of blood transfusion owing to this blood loss. However, unless there is an excessive blood loss, it is unlikely that you will suffer from any major complications owing to this.

C) Your worries post surgery

Q26. How will I be feeling immediately after the surgery?

Though you would still be under the influence of pain medications, severe soreness might be still felt. You might also be feeling the soreness at the site of the bone graft. In addition, you will still be under the influence of the anesthesia and would be feeling drugged from all the medication. Moreover, all the paraphernalia of tubes and catheters could unnerve you. Hence, it is important that you prepare yourself mentally beforehand for the same.

Q27. After how much time will I be able to walk?

If all has gone well with your surgery, the hospital staff might help you to walk a bit with a cane or walking stick on the 2nd or 3rd day after your operation. You will gradually be encouraged to walk greater distances (such as the corridor of your hospital) without straining your back. Moreover, you might also be instructed to continue the use of such walking aids for 4-6 weeks after your surgery. A physical therapist will treat you in the hospital; assist you with using an appropriate assistive device such as a cane or walker, instruct you in properly performing transitions and ambulation in order to ensure safety and protection of your back. They will also ensure that you are able to perform all necessary movements before you are released to your home.

Q28. How soon will I be able to eat or drink after surgery?

Most of the patients are able to take small sips of liquids as soon as after 4 to 5 hours of the surgery. Your doctors will gradually increase your intake and frequency in accordance with your health.

Q29. How soon can I take a shower after my surgery?

The minimum time stipulation for this is at least 72 hours, before which you will not be allowed to take a shower and will be bathed by a sponge bath. However, this time span can be longer if your wound is taking more time to heal. Under no circumstances you should ever wet a raw wound.

Q30. Will I need to have my stitches removed?

Nowadays, most surgeons only use dissolvable sutures beneath the skin. However, you will definitely need to have your stitches examined for any infection or a need for repeat dressing after around 10 days of your surgery.

Q31. *What is an average recovery schedule?*

Well, though the number of days and weeks might vary in different patients, the most common recovery schedule looks like this:

→ Hospital stay – Around 3 to 5 days
→ Being able to perform your daily routines yourself – Around 7 to 10 days
→ Back to school – Around 4 to 6 weeks
→ Being able to drive – 2 to 4 weeks
→ Lifting restrictions – For around 6 months
→ Full recovery – Approx 8 to 12 months

Q32.*When will I be able to live a normal life?*

Well, the complete process of fusion takes a minimum of 6 months. This implies that your body needs at least that much of time to heal and recover. You need to go slow on your physical activities and change your routines accordingly. For instance your doctor will put restrictions on the amount of weight you are allowed to lift for the first few months and so on.

Q33. *How independent will I be when I return home?*

You are going to need a major helping hand later. From moving around and cooking, to lifting and even changing positions in bed, you are going to need a good amount of help. Even if you are the type who prefers to do all of their work themselves, you cannot afford to strain your back post surgery and hence will need at least one family member, friend or a professional nurse to help you around. Ideally, experts suggest having someone with you for at least 3-4 weeks after your surgery.

Adding on, you are likely to recover and be independent much sooner if you are young, healthy, energetic and especially if you've had an active life before the surgery.

Q34. Will I be able to pick up and lift something easily later?

With some constraints and care, you should be able to lift something off the ground with ease. However, since you now have a straightened spine, you will have to learn to lift by bending your knees and squatting.

Q35. Will I gain any height?

Most likely, yes. Since your spine has become straighter, you are likely to add at least 3/8 to ¾ of an inch to your height.

Q36. Will I need to do any exercises to facilitate recovery from the surgery?

Once you are deemed fit for it, your surgeon will refer you to a physiotherapist who will prescribe a certain set of exercises to be performed everyday to expedite your recovery. The most common type of exercises advised post surgery will include:

→ Back strengthening exercises
→ Core strengthening exercises
→ Regular walking regimen
→ Breathing exercises to strengthen your pulmonary function

Your physiotherapist will prescribe a specific set of exercises keeping in mind your age and health status.

Q37. Will the unevenness in my shoulders/chest totally vanish?

Foremost, the surgery will reduce the protruding ribs below the breasts on the side of scoliosis. Though a major cosmetic improvement is expected, it is possible for some of the unevenness to still remain.

Q38. Will I need to make any major lifestyle changes?

Yes, of course. In fact, the preparation for this stage would have started much before your surgery. To begin with, you will need to change how things are placed in your house. You will need to keep everything at an accessible height so that you don't have to bend too low or reach too high for anything. You might also need to alter the placement of electrical switches and have an easy-to-reach bed switch nearby. You will need to make alternate arrangements for cooking and driving around and so on. In short, you will need to look at each of the aspects of your daily routine and see where all are you required to make preparations beforehand so that you are comfortable later. For instance you might realize that you need to have a chair that has a proper back and arm rests post surgery for full support and so on.

Q39. Will I need to change my mattress after the surgery?

Not really. All that you will need is a firm mattress that will adequately support your back, especially for the first 3-4 weeks after your surgery.

Q40. Will I need to make any major changes to my diet after the surgery?

Yes, certainly. You will need to make a few important changes, which include the below:

→ Having small, frequent meals
→ Keeping your food menu light, non-spicy and low-caloric
→ Totally abstaining from alcohol and smoking
→ Having specific foods that will aid recovery

Q41. Will the curve reoccur?

Well, in most of the cases, the fusion is permanent and the chances of the recurrence of the curve are not very high, unless you are old and suffer from major degeneration. However, a very minor hump or unevenness in the appearance might still remain.

Q42. Will the hardware in my back be visible?

Such an occurrence is very rare. Research shows that the hardware inserted into your back is almost never visible to the naked eye, except if you are extraordinarily lean or thin.

Q43. Will the instruments that are left inside damage my body later?

This is mostly not the case. These rods and other instruments have been scientifically designed to stay in the human body and offer adequate support. However, in some cases, the rods start causing some discomfort and pain after sometime, which is usually addressed with pain medication. However, in severe cases, an additional surgery might be required to remove these rods and other instrumentation.

Q44. Will the scar remain for long? Will it look ugly?

Usually, the site of incision in a scoliosis surgery is at places that are usually covered by clothing. Unless you go in for a major corrective cosmetic surgery, the scar is going to be staying with you for a lifetime. If you are the type to experiment, you can probably get some cosmetic add-on done around your scar. However, make sure you seek your surgeon's advice so that none of these adversely affect the health of your scar and the wound.

Q45. What is the crankshaft phenomenon?

The crankshaft phenomenon is a complication associated with the use of the Harrington procedure and is more common in younger children having immature skeletal systems. After the spinal fusion has been done, the front portion of the fused spine will still continue to grow. As the fused spine can't grow any longer, it will eventually start to twist and develop an additional curvature.

Q46. What is the flat back syndrome?

This one is also associated with the use of the Harrington procedure. In this condition, the patient's lower back loses its normal inward curve (lordosis). Consequently, after a few years, the disk will degenerate below the point of fusion, making it difficult for the patient to stand erect and also cause a lot of pain.

Q47. What is a wake-up test and why is it performed?

The Stagnara wake-up test is one of the many intra-operative (during the operation) tests done to detect any possible nerve damage which might happen during the surgery.

Q48. How much medication will I be given post surgery?

This one is a concern, especially for the patients who are allergic to certain medications. Immediately after the surgery, you feel be put on a heavy dosage of patient controlled analgesia (PCA) which means that the amount of medication can be controlled in accordance with the pain. In addition to this, you are likely to be on pain management medications and infection-fighting drugs for quite some time after the surgery. Hence, it important that you discuss any such factors with your surgeon beforehand.

Q49. Will I feel very weak after I return home?

Well, it all depends on how nicely you take care of yourself. You will definitely feel weak and vulnerable for quite some time after the surgery. However, if you have been following a healthy and active lifestyle before surgery, you are likely to re-gain your strength much faster.

Q50. When is a revision surgery required?

A revision surgery is quite a rare requirement and will be needed in one or more of the following cases:

→ Major recurrence of the curve
→ Severe discomfort or pain caused due to rods/other instruments
→ If spinal realignment is required
→ If your surgeon had used any obsolete techniques such as the Harrington instrumentation
→ If any major accident or trauma affects the fusion process
→ If hardware failure or pseudarthrosis has occurred

Real Scoliosis Stories: The pain went on...

The outcomes of a scoliosis surgery vary amongst different individuals and the experience of one might not be same as the other.

Claudia was diagnosed with a 25-degree scoliosis when she was eleven. She was immediately put on to a brace to help halt the progression of her curve. Since she was in her growing up years, Claudia felt all the discomfort and awkwardness a teenager usually goes through when she looks different from others.

Unfortunately, by the age of 12, her curve had already progressed to 59 degrees in spite of the brace. At this stage, she had a surgery to fuse the upper third of her spine to a bone graft from the hip. Long after the surgery was over, Claudia continued to be in pain and discomfort. When she was 19, Claudia had to undergo another surgery to remove some of the screws and hardware that were causing her discomfort.

However, even after trying a series of pain control methods, Claudia reports of constant pain in her back and also reports a serious loss of efficiency in her overall routine due to scoliosis and the surgery.

Final Words

The world of medicine can often be a perplexing one. A layman generally finds all the technical jargon quite ambiguous and is usually unable to understand any of the terminology without help.

However, in a world with millions of living organisms, it is virtually impossible to remain disease-free. However, it is also interesting to observe that being diseased is not the same as being unhealthy. Even the healthiest of individuals are inflicted by life-threatening disorders and diseases. All that is required to counter the impact of such illnesses is a healthy lifestyle, a strong immune system and above all, a positive attitude.

Being healthy is a state of being we can consciously maintain over a long period of time. Few of the important dictates of such a healthy mind and body includes a balanced diet, regular exercise, being stress-free and positive and above all, having a robust immune system.

When we have such an optimum state of physical and mental health, we are well-equipped to fight diseases and deformities like scoliosis. Basically a disease of misalignment, scoliosis creates an imbalance in your original spinal structure. It takes a series of steps starting from diagnosis and analysis to well-researched treatment options to restore the body's original balance. It is on this road to treatment that you need to re-educate yourself on the importance of making your choices with a great insight. *'Your Plan for Natural Scoliosis Prevention and Treatment'* will act as your righteous guide as you attempt to treat your scoliosis in a natural way.

Medicine, surgery and therapy are your essential companions as you forge ahead on the path of your scoliosis treatment. However, while some of you might just manage with the conservative, non-invasive approach, the ones with more severe conditions might have to resort to surgery.

Just remember to speak to your surgeon about all of the possible complications associated with the surgery to keep yourself mentally prepared. Get equipped with all the essential information about the surgery, its process, the equipment used and so on. For all you know, you and your doctor might collectively decide that you are better off living with a moderate curve instead of facing the hazards associated with a surgery. If you are in the elderly age group or already suffer from a more debilitating disease, this would usually be the case!

Remember, your health is *really* in your own hands. Do your research, speak to experts and make sure you are doing your best to treat and manage your curve. Eat right, exercise as you can and seek support. In case you do opt for surgery, you will need to make all possible modifications at home and workplace and also garner enough support. Spot out a handful of family members or friends who can attend to you in the hospital and more importantly, once you are back home. Considering that you will need help to even get up from a chair, there is a lot of preparation you should be doing in this regard.

After you've read the book, please forward any recommendations or feedback that you might have at scoliosis.feedback@gmail.com. You are also welcome to go through the wealth of information in the following informative books:

- Your Plan for Natural Scoliosis Prevention and Treatment
- Your Natural Scoliosis Treatment Journal
- An Essential Guide for Scoliosis and a Healthy Pregnancy

While the 'Scoliosis Exercises for Prevention and Correction' DVD can be a helpful audio-visual aid, the following Apps are just right for the tech-friendly generation of today:

- ScolioTrack for iPhone and Android
- Scoliometer for iPhone and Android
- Scoliometer Pro for iPad

You can also learn more about each of these and much more at www.HIYH.info.

It would be a pleasure to hear from you and your suggestions make my work all the more worthwhile. The time to act is now. Take your life in your own hands and progress your way to a healthier life.

Dr. Kevin Lau D.C.

References

1. Coventry MB. Anatomy of the intervertebral disk. Clin Orthop 67:9-15, 1969.

2. Jinkins JR: MRI of enhancing nerve roots in the unoperated lumbosacral spine. AJNR 14:193-202, 1993.

3. Langenskio¨ ld A, Michelsson JE. "Experimental progressive scoliosis in the rabbit," J Bone Joint Surg [Br] 1969;43:116–20.

4. Yamada K, Ikata I, Yamamoto H, et al. "Equilibrium function in scoliosis and active plaster jacket for the treatment.,"Tokushima J Exp Med 1969;16:1–7.

5. Yamada K, Yamamoto H, Nakagawa Y, et al. "Etiology of idiopathic scoliosis," Clin Orthop 1984;184:50–7.

6. Piggott, H.: "The natural history of scoliosis in myelodysplasia," J. Bone Jt Surg. 62: 54-58 (1980).

7. Kinetic Imbalance due to Suboccipital Strain Newborns. The Journal of Manual Medicine

8. Ikuyo Kou, Yohei Takahashi, Todd A Johnson, Atsushi Takahashi, Long Guo, Jin Dai, Xusheng Qiu, Swarkar Sharma, Aki Takimoto, Yoji Ogura, Hua Jiang, Huang Yan, Katsuki Kono, Noriaki Kawakami, Koki Uno, Manabu Ito, Shohei Minami, Haruhisa Yanagida, Hiroshi Taneichi, Naoya Hosono, Taichi Tsuji, Teppei Suzuki, Hideki Sudo, Toshiaki Kotani, Ikuho Yonezawa, Douglas Londono, Derek Gordon, John A. Herring, Kota Watanabe, Kazuhiro Chiba, Naoyuki Kamatani, Qing Jiang, Yuji Hiraki, Michiaki Kubo, Yoshiaki Toyama, Tatsuhiko Tsunoda, Carol A. Wise, Yong Qiu, Chisa Shukunami, Morio Matsumoto, and Shiro Ikegawa.

9. "Genetic variants in GPR126 are associated with adolescent idiopathic scoliosis"

10. Nature Genetics (2013)

11. Wynne–Davies R. "Familial (idiopathic) scoliosis. A family survey," J Bone Joint Surg [Br] 1968;50:24–30.

12. Cowell HR, Hall JN, MacEwen GD. "Genetic aspects of idiopathic scoliosis," Clin Orthop 1972;86:121–31.

13. Scoliosis & Epigenetics, Written by Dr. A. Joshua Woggon, Copyright 2012.

14. New York Times - http://health.nytimes.com/health/guides/disease/scoliosis/causes.html

15. Scoliosis as a Neurologic Condition: 4 Points on Two New Genes Making the Connection. Becker's Orthopedic, Spine and Pain Management Review. © Copyright ASC COMMUNICATIONS 2011.

16. Machida M, Dubousset J, Imamura Y, et al. "An experimental study in chickens for the pathogenesis of idiopathic scoliosis," Spine 1993;18:1609–15.

17. Scoliosis Associated With Typical Mayer-Rokitansky-Küster-Hauser Syndrome. Keri Fisher, PA-S, Richard H. Esham, MD, Ian Thorneycroft, PhD, MD, Departments of Physicians Assistant Studies, Medicine, and Obstetrics and Gynecology University of South Alabama, Mobile. Posted: 02/01/2000; South Med J. 2000;93(2) © 2000 Lippincott Williams & Wilkins.

18. Arai S, Ohtsuka Y, Moriya H, et al. "Scoliosis associated with syringomyelia," Spine 1993; 18: 1591-2.

19. Emery E, Redondo A, Rey A. "Syringomyelia and Arnord Chiari in scoliosis initially classified as idiopathic: Experience with 25 patients," Eur Spine J 1997; 6: 158-62.

20. Harrenstein RJ. Die Skoliose bei, Sauglingen und ihre Behandlung. Z Orthop Chir 1 930;52:1.

21. Lloyd-Roberts GC, Pilcher MF. "Structural idiopathic scoliosis in infancy,". J Bone Joint Surg [Br] 1965;47-B:520-23.

22. Juvenile Idiopathic Scoliosis. Curve Patterns and Prognosis in One Hundred and Nine Patients. C. M. ROBINSON, B.MED.SCI., F.R.C.S.†; M. J. MCMASTER, M.D., F.R.C.S.†, EDINBURGH, SCOTLAND. The Journal of Bone & Joint Surgery.1996; 78:1140-8. Copyright © The Journal of Bone and Joint Surgery, Inc.

23. Cobb JR: Outline for the study of scoliosis. Instructional course lectures. American Academy of Orthopedic Surgeons 5:261–275, 1948

24. Pritchett JW, Bortel DT: "Degenerative symptomatic lumbar scoliosis," Spine 18:700–703, 1993

25. O'Brien MF, Newman, PO, "Nonsurgical Treatment of Idiopathic Scoliosis," Surgery of the Pediatric Spine, ed. Daniel H. Kim et al. (Thieme Medical Publishers, 2008), 580. books.google.com.

26. Good CR, "The Genetic Basis of Idiopathic Scoliosis," Journal of the Spinal Research Foundation, 2009:4:1:13-5, www.spinemd.com.

27. Pearsall, D.J., Reid, J.G., and D.M. Hedden. (1992). "Comparison of three noninvasive methods for measuring scoliosis," Physical Therapy 72(9):648-657.

28. Wong, H., Hui, J.H.P., Rajan, U., and H. Chia. (2005). "Idiopathic scoliosis in Singapore schoolchildren," SPINE 30(10):1188-1196.

29. Yawn, B.P., Yawn, R.A., Hodge, D., Kurland, M., Shaughnessy, W.J., Ilstrup, D., and S.J. Jacobsen. (1999). "A population-based study of school scoliosis screening," JAMA 282(15):1427-1432.

30. Screening for adolescent idiopathic scoliosis. Policy statement. US Preventive Services Task Force. JAMA. 1993;269:2664–6.

31. Yawn BP, Yawn RA, Hodge D, Kurland M, Shaughnessy WJ, Ilstrup D, et al. "A population based study of school scoliosis screening," JAMA. 1999;282:1427–32.

32. Karachalios T, Sofianos J, Roidis N, Sapkas G, Korres D, Nikolopoulos K. "Ten-year follow-up evaluation of a school screening program for scoliosis," Is the forward-bending test an accurate diagnostic criterion for the screening of scoliosis? Spine. 1999;24:2318–24.

33. Screening for adolescent idiopathic scoliosis. Policy statement. US Preventive Services Task Force. JAMA. 1993;269:2664–6.

34. Hagan, J.F., Shaw, J.S., and P.M. Duncan, eds. 2008. Bright Futures: Guidelines for Health

35. Bunnell, W.P. (2005). Selective screening for scoliosis. Clinical Orthopaedics and Related Research 434:40-45.

36. Negrini S, Minozzi S, Bettany-Saltikov J, et al. "Braces for idiopathic scoliosis in adolescents," Spine (Phila Pa 1976). 2010;35(13):1285-1293. 10.1097/BRS.0b013e3181dc48f4.

37. Karachalios, T., Sofianos, J., Roidis, N., Sapkas, G., Korres, D., and K. Nikolopoulos.

38. (1999). "Ten-year follow-up evaluation of a school screening program for scoliosis," SPINE 24(22):2318-2324.

39. Karachalios, T., Sofianos, J., Roidis, N., Sapkas, G., Korres, D., and K. Nikolopoulos. (1999). "Ten-year follow-up evaluation of a school screening program for scoliosis. SPINE 24(22):2318-2324.

40. An evaluation of the Adams forward bend test and the scoliometer in a scoliosis school screening setting. Grossman TW, Mazur JM, Cummings RJ. Department of Orthopaedics, Naval Hospital, Great Lakes, Illinois, USA. J Pediatr Orthop. 1995 Jul-Aug;15(4):535-8.

41. Amendt, L.E., Ause-Ellias, K.L., Eybers, J.L., Tadsworth, C.T., Nielsen, D.H., and S.L. Weinstein. (1990). "Validity and reliability testing of the scoliometer," Physical Therapy 70(2):108-117.

42. Spine: Affiliated Society Meeting Abstracts: 23–26 September 2009 - Volume 10 - Issue - p 204 Electronic Poster Abstracts. What Does a Scoliometer Really Measure?: E☐Poster #73. Cahill, Patrick J. MD (Shriners' Hospital for Children); Ranade, Ashish MD; Samdani, Amer MD; Asghar, Jahangir MD; Antonacci, Darryl M. MD; Clements, David H. MD; MD; Betz, Randal R. MD. © 2009 Lippincott Williams & Wilkins, Inc.

43. Bunnell, W.P. (1984). "An objective criterion for scoliosis screening," J. Bone & Joint Surgery 66(9):1381-1387.

44. Reamy BV, Slakey JB. "Adolescent idiopathic scoliosis: review and current concepts," Am Fam Physician. 2001;64(1):111-116.

45. Lenssinck ML, Frijlink AC, Berger MY, Bierman-Zeinstra SM, Verkerk K, Verhagen AP. "Effect of bracing and other conservative interventions in the treatment of idiopathic scoliosis in adolescents: a systematic review of clinical trials," Phys Ther. 2005;85(12):1329-1339.

46. June 13, 2010: Interview with Dr. Alain Moreau, creator of Scoliosis blood test (http://www.scoliosis.org/forum/showthread.php?10705-Interview-with-Dr.-Alain-Moreau-creator-of-Scoliosis-blood-test)

47. Kane WJ. "Scoliosis prevalence: a call for a statement of terms," Clin Orthop. 1997;126:43–6.

48. Scoliosis Surgery, The Definitive Pateint's Reference. David K. Wolpen

49. Shea KG, Stevens PM, Nelson M, Smith JT, Masters KS, Yandow S. "A comparison of manual versus computer-assisted radiographic measurement: Intraobserver measurement variability for Cobb angles," Spine. 1998; 23:551-555.

50. Variability in Cobb angle measurements in children with congenital scoliosis, RT Loder; A Urquhart; H Steen; G Graziano; RN Hensinger; A Schlesinger; MA Schork; and Y Shyr. 1995 British Editorial Society of Bone and Joint Surgery

51. Chen YL. Vertebral centroid measurement of lumbar lordosis compared with the Cobb technique. Spine, Sept. 1, 1999:24(17), pp1786-1790.

52. J Bone Joint Surg Am. 1984 Sep;66(7):1061-71.The prediction of curve progression in untreated idiopathic scoliosis during growth. Lonstein JE, Carlson JM.

53. Cobb, J.R.: Outlines for the study of scoliosis measurements from spinal roentgenograms. Physical Therapy, 59: 764–765, 1948.

54. Table Peterson, Nachemson JBJS 1995; 77A:823-7

55. Spine (Phila Pa 1976). 2009 Apr 1;34(7):697-700. Curve progression in idiopathic scoliosis: follow-up study to skeletal maturity.

56. The pathogenesis of adolescent idiopathic scoliosis. A systematic review of the literature Kouwenhoven JWM Castelein RM.

57. Bull Acad Natl Med. 1999;183(4):757-67; discussion 767-8. [Idiopathic scoliosis: evaluation of the results]

58. Several factors may predict scoliosis progression Wu H. Eur Spine J. doi:10.1007/s00586-010-1512-9.

59. Assessment of curve progression in idiopathic scoliosis. Soucacos PN, Zacharis K, Gelalis J, Soultanis K, Kalos N, Beris A, Xenakis T, Johnson EO. Source: Department of Orthopedic Surgery, University of Ioannina, School of Medicine, Greece. Eur Spine J. 1998;7(4):270-7.

60. Roach JW. Adolescent idiopathic scoliosis. Orthop Clin North Am. 1999;30:353–65.

61. Nykoliation JW, Cassidy JD, Arthur BE, et al: An Algorithm for the Managemment of Scoliosis. J. Manipulative Physiol Ther 9:1, 1986

62. Spine (Phila Pa 1976). 2006 Aug 1;31(17):1933-42. Progression risk of idiopathic juvenile scoliosis during pubertal growth.

63. Kesling KL, Reinker KA. Scoliosis in twins. A meta-analysis of the literature and report of six cases. Spine. 1997;22:2009–14.

64. Cho KJ, Suk SI, Park SR, Kim JH, Kim SS, Choi WK, et al. Complications in posterior fusion and instrumentation for degenerative lumbar scoliosis. Spine (Phila Pa 1976) 2007;32:2232–7.

65. Brooks HL, Azen SP, Gerberg E, Brooks R, Chan L. Scoliosis: a prospective epidemiological study. J Bone Joint Surg Am 1975;57:968–72.

66. Specific exercises in the treatment of scoliosis--differential indication. Weiss HR, Maier-Hennes A.Source: Asklepios Katharina Schroth Spinal Deformities Rehabilita.tion Centre, Korczakstr. 2, 55566 Bad Sobernheim, Germany. hr.weiss@asklepios.com

67. The postural stability control and gait pattern of idiopathic scoliosis adolescents. Po-Quang Chen, Jaw-Lin Wang, Yang-Hwei Tsuang, Tien-Li Liao, Pei-I Huang, Yi-Shiong Hang. Section of Spinal Surgery, Department of Orthopedic, National Taiwan University Hospital, Taipei, Taiwan, ROC.

68. Relations Between Standing Stability and Body Posture Parameters in Adolescent Idiopathic Scoliosis Nault, Marie-Lyne BSc,*†; Allard, Paul PhD, PEng,*†; Hinse, Sébastien MSc,*†; Le Blanc, Richard PhD,†; Caron, Olivier PhD,‡; Labelle, Hubert MD,§; Sadeghi, Heydar PhD*†.

69. "Influence of Different Types of Progressive Idiopathic Scoliosis on Static and Dynamic Postural Control," Gauchard, Gérome C. PhD*†; Lascombes, Pierre MD‡; Kuhnast, Michel MD§; Perrin, Philippe P. MD, PhD*†. Spine: 1 May 2001 - Volume 26 - Issue 9 - pp 1052-1058.

70. Weiss HR: "The effect of an exercise programme on VC and rib mobility in patients with IS," Spine 1991, 16:88-93.

71. Worthington V, Shambaugh P: "Nutrition as an environmental factor in the etiology of idiopathic scoliosis,"

72. J Manipulative Physiol Ther 1993, 16(3):169-73.

73. Heijmans BT, Tobi EW, Lumey LH, Slagboom PE: "The epigenome: archive of the prenatal environment," Epigenetics 2009, 4(8):526-31.

74. Correction of Spinal Curvatures by Transcutaneous Electrical Muscle Stimulation AXELGAARD, JENS MS, PhD; NORDWALL, ANDERS MD; BROWN, JOHN C. MD.

75. Surface Electrical Stimulation Versus Brace in Treatment of Idiopathic Scoliosis. DURHAM, JOHN W. MD; MOSKOWITZ, ALAN MD; WHITNEY, JOHN BS.

76. http://sciencestage.com/d/573038/transcutaneous-electrical-stimulation-tces-for-the-treatment-of-adolescent-idiopathic-scoliosis-prel.html

---

77. "Transcutaneous electrical muscle stimulation for the treatment of progressive spinal curvature deformities," 1984, Vol. 6, No. 1 , Pages 31-46. Rancho Los Amigos Rehabilitation Engineering Center, Rancho Los Amigos Hospital, University of Southern California.

78. Morningstar, Mark W. "Outcomes for adult scoliosis patients receiving chiropractic rehabilitation: a 24-month retrospective analysis," Journal of Chiropractic Medicine. January 2011; 10: 179-184.

79. Blount, W. P.; Moe, J. H.: The Milwaukee Brace. Baltimore, Williams & Wilkins, 1973.

80. Goldberg, C. J.; Moore, D. P.; Fogarty, E. E.; Dowling, F. E.: "Adolescent idiopathic scoliosis: the effect of brace treatment on the incidence of surgery," Spine, 26(1):42-47, 2001.

81. Braces for idiopathic scoliosis in adolescents Negrini S, Minozzi S, Bettany-Saltikov J, Zaina F, Chockalingam N, Grivas TB, Kotwicki T, Maruyama T, Romano M, Vasiliadis ES - See more at: http://summaries.cochrane.org/CD006850/braces-for-idiopathic-scoliosis-in-adolescents#sthash.8CQkzUrl.dpuf

82. Nachemson, A.; Peterson, L. E.; and members of the Brace Study Group of the Scoliosis Research Society: "Effectiveness of treatment with a brace in girls who have adolescent idiopathic scoliosis. A prospective, controlled study based on data from the Brace Study of the Scoliosis Research Society," J. Bone and Joint Surg., 77-A: 815-822, June 1995.

83. Effectiveness of the Charleston Night-time Bending Brace in the Treatment of Adolescent Idiopathic Scoliosis. Lee CS, Hwang CJ, Kim DJ, Kim JH, Kim YT, Lee MY, Yoon SJ, Lee DH. Scoliosis Center, Asan Medical Center, College of Medicine, University of Ulsan, Seoul, Korea.J Pediatr Orthop. 2012 Jun;32(4):368-72.

84. Rowe, D. E.; Bernstein, S.M.; Riddick, M. F.; Adler, F.; Emans, J. B.; Gardner-Bonneau, D.: "A meta-analysis of the efficacy of non-operative treatments for idiopathic scoliosis," JBJS, 79A-5:664-674, 1997.

85. The estimated cost of school scoliosis screening Spine 2000 Sep 15;25(18):2387-91 Yawn & Yawn. Department of Research, Olmsted Medical Center, Rochester, Minnesota 55904, USA. Spine (Phila Pa 1976). 2000 Sep 15;25(18):2387-91.

86. Patil CG, Santarelli J, Lad SP, et al. Inpatient complications, mortality, and discharge disposition after surgical correction of idiopathic scoliosis: a national perspective. *Spine J.* 2008 Mar 19 [Epub ahead of print]

87. Risks for Complications After Scoliosis Surgery Identified. Complications after scoliosis surgery more likely in nonambulatory patients, large pre-op curve. Spine. Publish date: Apr 1, 2011

88. The estimated cost of school scoliosis screening Spine 2000 Sep 15;25(18):2387-91 Yawn & Yawn. Department of Research, Olmsted Medical Center, Rochester, Minnesota 55904, USA. Spine (Phila Pa 1976). 2000 Sep 15;25(18):2387-91.

89. http://www.europeanmedicaltourist.com/spine-surgery/scoliosis.html

90. Sharrock NE. Anesthesia. In: Callaghan JJ, Rosenberg AG, Rubash HE, eds. The Adult Hip Philadelphia: Lippincott - Raven Publishers, 1998.

91. [Anesthesia for scoliosis surgery: preoperative assessment and risk screening of patients undergoing surgery to correct spinal deformity]. Rev Esp Anestesiol Reanim. 2005 Jan;52(1):24-42; quiz 42-3, 47.

92. Engelhardt T, Webster NR. Pulmonary aspiration of gastric contents in anaesthesia. Br J Anaesth 1999; 83: 453–60

93. Genever EE. Suxamethonium□induced cardiac arrest in unsuspected pseudohypertrophic muscular dystrophy. Br J Anaesth 1971; 43: 984–6

94. Kafer ER.Review article: Respiratory and cardio vascular functions in scoliosis and the principles of anesthetic management. Anesthesiology 1980; 52:339-351.

95. Peterson DO, Drummond DC, Todd MM. Effects of halothane, enflurane, isoflurane and nitrous oxide on somatosensory evoked potentials in humans. Anesthesiology 1986; 65: 35–40

96. Pelosi L, Stevenson M, Hobbs GJ, et al. Intraoperative motor evoked potentials to transcranial electrical stimulation during two anesthetic regimens. Clin Neurophysiol 2001; 112: 1076–87

97. Anterior approach to the thoracolumbar spine: technical considerations. Burrington JD, Brown C, Wayne ER, Odom J., Arch Surg. 1976 Apr;111(4):456-63.

98. Posterior vertebrectomy in kyphosis, scoliosis and kyphoscoliosis due to hemivertebra. Aydogan M, Ozturk C, Tezer M, Mirzanli C, Karatoprak O, Hamzaoglu A. Istanbul Spine Center, Florence Nightingale Hospital, Istanbul, Turkey. J Pediatr Orthop B. 2008 Jan;17(1):33-7.

99. Combined anterior and posterior instrumentation in severe and rigid idiopathic scoliosis, Viola Bullmann, Henry F. H. Halm, Tobias Schulte, Thomas Lerner, Thomas P. Weber, Ulf R. Liljenqvist. European Spine Journal April 2006, Volume 15, Issue 4, pp 440-448

100. Posterior only versus combined anterior and posterior approaches to lumbar scoliosis in adults: a radiographic analysis. Pateder DB, Kebaish KM, Cascio BM, Neubaeur P, Matusz DM, Kostuik JP. Department of Orthopaedic Surgery, Johns Hopkins Hospital, Johns Hopkins University School of Medicine, Baltimore, MD, USA.Spine[2007, 32(14):1551-1554]

101. Vendoscopic Anterior Surgery for Idiopathic Thoracic Scoliosis; Preliminary Report on Pre-operative CT Examination and Small Thoracotomy for Safe and Accurate Screw Insertion.Authors: KAMIMURA M (Shinshu Univ. School Of Medicine) KINOSHITA T (Shinshu Univ. School Of Medicine) ITOH H (Shinshu Univ. School Of Medicine) YUZAWA Y (Shinshu Univ. School Of Medicine) TAKAHASHI J (Shinshu Univ. School Of Medicine). Journal Title: Spinal Deformity. Journal Code: L0113A.

102. MECHANICAL COMPLICATIONS DURING ENDOSCOPIC SCOLIOSIS SURGERY. J.R. Crawford, M.T. Izatt, C.J. Adam,R.D. Labrom and G.N. Askin.

103. Thoracoplasty in thoracic adolescent idiopathic scoliosis. Thoracoplasty in thoracic adolescent idiopathic scoliosis.

104. Se-Il Suk, Jin-Hyok Kim, Sung-Soo Kim, Jeong-Joon Lee, Yong-Tak Han. Seoul Spine Institute, Inje University Sanggye Paik Hospital, Seoul, Korea.

105. U.S. Army Medical Department Center and School, Fort Sam Houston, Texas. Spine[1994, 19(14):1636-1642]. Geissele AE, Ogilvie JW, Cohen M, Bradford DS.

106. Surgical technique: modern Luqué trolley, a self-growing rod technique. Ouellet J. Division of Orthopaedic Surgery, McGill University Health Centre, Montreal Children Hospital, 2300 Tupper Street, Montreal, QC H3H 1P3, Canada. jean.ouellet@muhc.mcgill.ca. Clin Orthop Relat Res. 2011 May;469(5):1356-67.

107. Hardware complications in scoliosis surgery. Bagchi K, Mohaideen A, Thomson JD, Foley LC. Present address: 5302 Bishop's View Circle, Cherry Hill, NJ 08002, USA. Pediatr Radiol. 2002 Jul;32(7):465-75. Epub 2002 Apr 4.

108. Scoliosis surgery : correction not correlated with instrumentation, quality of life not correlated with correction or instrumentation. Rolf SOBOTTKE, Jan SIEWE, Jan HOKEMA, Ulf SCHLEGEL, Thomas ZWEIG, Peer EYSEL. The University of Cologne, Germany, and the University of Bern, Switzerland.

109. Segmental pedicle screw instrumentation in idiopathic thoracolumbar and lumbar scoliosis. Halm H, Niemeyer T, Link T, Liljenqvist U. Center for Spine Surgery and Scoliosis Center, Klinikum Neustadt, Germany. Eur Spine J. 2000 Jun;9(3):191-7.

110. Comparative analysis of pedicle screw versus hook instrumentation in posterior spinal fusion of adolescent idiopathic scoliosis. Kim YJ, Lenke LG, Cho SK, Bridwell KH, Sides B, Blanke K. Washington University School of Medicine, Department of Orthopaedic Surgery and Shriners Hospitals for Children, St. Louis Unit, St. Louis, MO, USA. Spine (Phila Pa 1976). 2004 Sep 15;29(18):2040-8.

111. Pedicle screw instrumentation for adult idiopathic scoliosis: an improvement over hook/hybrid fixation. Rose PS, Lenke LG, Bridwell KH, Mulconrey DS, Cronen GA, Buchowski JM, Schwend RM, Sides BA. Spine (Phila Pa 1976). 2009 Apr 15;34(8):852-7; discussion 858. doi: 10.1097/BRS.0b013e31818e5962.

112. Pedicle screw instrumentation in adolescent idiopathic scoliosis (AIS), Se-Il Suk, Jin-Hyok Kim, Sung-Soo Kim, Dong-Ju Lim. European Spine Journal. January 2012, Volume 21, Issue 1, pp 13-22

113. Comparative analysis of pedicle screw versus hook instrumentation in posterior spinal fusion of adolescent idiopathic scoliosis. Kim YJ, Lenke LG, Cho SK, Bridwell KH, Sides B, Blanke K. Washington University School of Medicine, Department of Orthopaedic Surgery and Shriners Hospitals for Children, St. Louis Unit, St. Louis, MO, USA. Spine (Phila Pa 1976). 2004 Sep 15;29(18):2040-8.

114. Square-lashing technique in segmental spinal instrumentation: a biomechanical study. Eur Spine J. 2006 July; 15(7): 1153–1158. Published online 2006 February 10. doi: 10.1007/s00586-005-0010-y

115. Cobalt chromium sublaminar wires for spinal deformity surgery. Spine (Phila Pa 1976). 2006 Sep 1;31(19):2209-12. Cluck MW, Skaggs DL. University Hospitals of Cleveland Spine Institute, Cleveland, OH, USA.

116. Safety of sublaminar wires with Isola instrumentation for the treatment of idiopathic scoliosis. Girardi FP, Boachie-Adjei O, Rawlins BA. Scoliosis Service, Hospital for Special Surgery, New York, New York, USA.

117. Use of the Universal Clamp for deformity correction and as an adjunct to fusion: preliminary results in scoliosis. J Child Orthop. 2010 February; 4(1): 73–80. Published online 2009 November 28. doi: 10.1007/s11832-009-0221-6

118. Use of the Universal Clamp for deformity correction and as an adjunct to fusion: preliminary results in scoliosis. Jean-Luc Jouve, Jérôme Sales de Gauzy, Benjamin Blondel, Franck Launay, Franck Accadbled, Gérard Bollini. Journal of Children's Orthopaedics. February 2010, Volume 4, Issue 1, pp 73-80

119. Analysis of complications in scoliosis surgery. Xu RM, Sun SH, Ma WH, Liu GY, Gu YJ, Huang L, Ying JW, Jiang WY. Department of Orthopedics, the Sixth Hospital of Ningbog, Ningbo 315040, Zhejiang, China.

120. Scoliosis Research Society Morbidity and Mortality of Adult Scoliosis Surgery. Sansur, Charles A.; Smith, Justin S.; Coe, Jeff D.; Glassman, Steven D.; Berven, Sigurd H.; Polly, David W. Jr.; Perra, Joseph H.; Boachie-Adjei, Oheneba; Shaffrey, Christo.

121. Complications of scoliosis surgery in Prader-Willi syndrome. Accadbled F, Odent T, Moine A, Chau E, Glorion C, Diene G, de Gauzy JS. Spine (Phila Pa 1976). 2008 Feb 15;33(4):394-401. doi: 10.1097/BRS.0b013e318163fa24.

122. Results of surgical treatment of adults with idiopathic scoliosis. J Bone Joint Surg Am 1987 Jun;69(5):667-75

123. Sponseller PD, Cohen MS, Nachemson AL, Hall JE, Wohl ME.

124. Intraoperative blood loss during different stages of scoliosis surgery: A prospective study. Hitesh N Modi, Seung-Woo Suh*, Jae-Young Hong, Sang-Heon Song and Jae-Hyuk Yang

125. Complications and risk factors of primary adult scoliosis surgery: a multicenter study of 306 patients. Charosky S, Guigui P, Blamoutier A, Roussouly P, Chopin D; Study Group on Scoliosis. Spine (Phila Pa 1976). 2012 Apr 15;37(8):693-700. doi: 10.1097/BRS.0b013e31822ff5c1.

126. Complications of pedicle screw fixation in scoliosis surgery: a systematic review. Hicks JM, Singla A, Shen FH, Arlet V. Spine (Phila Pa 1976). 2010 May 15;35(11):E465-70. doi: 10.1097/BRS.0b013e3181d1021a.

127. Hardware complications in scoliosis surgery. Bagchi K, Mohaideen A, Thomson JD, Foley LC. Pediatr Radiol. 2002 Jul;32(7):465-75. Epub 2002 Apr 4.

Index

Scoliosis Exercises for Prevention and Correction DVD is a careful selection of exercises that you can do to reverse scoliosis in the comfort of your own home.

Broken down into three easy-to-digest sections, the DVD will take you through the various steps in order to start rebuilding and rebalancing your spine. The comprehensive sections cover everything from Body Balancing Stretches to Building Your Core and a number of different Body Alignment Exercises that have all been carefully designed and selected by Dr Kevin Lau.

For anyone who suffers scoliosis, the main advantages of the DVD are:

- A 60-minute concise expansion of the scoliosis exercises from Your Plan for Natural Scoliosis Prevention and Treatment.
- Body Balancing Exercises in the DVD explains in detail the correct stretching techniques for scoliosis sufferers to relieve stiffness.
- The Building Your Core section focuses on strengthening the muscles that give stability to your spine.
- Body Alignment Exercises will improve the overall alignment of your spine.
- All the exercises that feature in the DVD are suitable for pre and post-operative rehabilitation for scoliosis conditions.
- Safe even for those in pain or post-scoliosis surgery.
- All exercises covered in the Health In Your Hands DVD can be practiced at home, and with no special equipment required.

Cookbook

Strengthen your spine, one meal at a time!

Treating scoliosis requires a comprehensive approach, one which will restore your body's natural alignment, along with preventing the inevitable spinal degeneration that comes with age.

'Your Scoliosis Treatment Cookbook' – a one of its kind, never-before guide to customizing your diet and a vast collection of delicious, healthy recipes to suit your palette and treat scoliosis, all at the same time! The book brings to you the amazing and time-tested secrets of the optimal nutrition for spinal health in the form of an easy-to-follow guide. Just follow our step-by-step instructions on how to find out your own Paleo Type. Once you are done, all you need to do is to pick up the recipe to suit your taste buds and choose the ingredients according to the results of your Paleo Type.

What to expect:

- Reduce pain related to scoliosis
- Enhance spinal growth and development
- Strengthen your muscles
- Relax muscle tightness
- Improved sleep

- Rebalance your hormones
- Boost you energy levels
- Prevent spinal degeneration
- Help you achieve your ideal body size
- Strengthen your immune system

Journal

A day-by-day companion for 12-weeks to a straighter and stronger spine!

In this companion resource to the Amazon.com bestseller 'Your Plan for Natural Scoliosis Prevention and Treatment', Dr. Kevin Lau offers you the nuts-and-bolts knowledge you need to succeed on your 12-week health experience. Simply follow step-by-step as you're guided towards improved spinal health.

Step One: Identify your personal scoliosis condition

Step Two: Identify your unique dietary needs and metabolic type

Step Three: Stay motivated with Dr. Lau's proven exercise program, which includes comprehensive exercise charts and fitness resources

Step Four: Feel focused and inspired as you track your progress each day

Step Five: Watch and wait as your scoliosis improves, your pain decreases and your back becomes stronger

Surgery

An In-Depth and Unbiased Look Into What to Expect Before and During Scoliosis Surgery

Scoliosis surgery doesn't have to be a daunting, problematic and anxiety-ridden experience. In fact, with the proper information, advice and knowledge you can have the ability to make confident and informed decisions about the best and most suitable treatment options.

Dr. Kevin Lau's latest book will help you to discover current and crucial information that will guide you in making informed decisions about your future spinal health.

You will:

- **Learn more about the details of scoliosis surgery** – Including understanding components of the surgery itself such as why the rods put inside in your body during surgery (fusion) are meant to remain there.
- **Uncover the sobering facts** – For instance, you will learn that after surgery, there is a chance you may not return to full normalcy, in appearance or in activity level.
- **Discover** the factors that determine your long-term prognosis, including detailed case studies.
- **Learn** how to properly evaluate the risks associated with the many types of scoliosis surgery.
- **Get great tips** on how to afford your surgery and how to choose the best time, place and surgeon for your needs.
- **Discover** over 100 illustrations to help make it as easy to read and understand.

Pregnancy

Complete, easy-to-follow guide for managing your scoliosis during pregnancy!

"An Essential Guide for Scoliosis and a Healthy Pregnancy" is a month-by-month guide on covering everything you need to know about taking care of your spine and your baby. The book supports your feelings and empathizes with you throughout your amazing journey towards delivering a healthy baby.

This book provides answers and expert advice for pregnant women suffering from scoliosis. Full of information to cope with the physical and emotional upheavals of pregnancy during scoliosis. From conception to birth and beyond, this guide will hold your hand until you become a happy and proud mother of a healthy newborn baby.

ScolioTrack

Scoliotrack is a safe and innovative way to track one's scoliosis condition. The device allows the user to track the progress of the abnormal spinal curves that occur in scoliosis. With the touch of an iPhone or Android phone the user is easily able to track their month to month progression. This easy-to-use program is suitable for scoliosis sufferers of all ages. Its high degree of accuracy makes this application suitable for professional such as Medical Doctors, Chiropractors or Physiotherapist and simple enough for personal use at home.

Features of the App:

- Tracks and saves a person's Angle of Trunk Rotation (ATR), a key measurement in screening for and planning treatment of scoliosis.
- Tracks a person's height and weight, ideal for growing teenagers with scoliosis or adults who are health conscious.
- Scoliosis data is graphed making it easy to read month to month changes to a person's scoliosis.
- Camera function takes a photo of the person's back to notice any changes to the back visually such as rib humps, hip protrusion, body alignment or spinal deviation and compare it easily with previous photo records.

Scoliometer

A Convenient Scoliosis Screening Tool: Scoliometer App

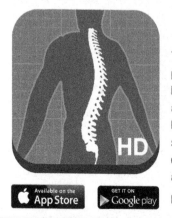

The scoliometer App is a useful and highly innovative tool for medical professionals, doctors and those who want to take scoliosis checkups at home. We can provide an always available, highly accurate replacement for a much more affordable price. Doctors and other medical professionals looking for a simple, fast and elegant way to measure the curvature of the spine can use this accurate tool. Doctors have used scoliometers as an effective tool in screening scoliosis for many years, and now with you can also have one conveniently on your phone.

Easy to use, clean and fast with accurate measurements for scoliosis.

For more information for the DVD, ScolioTrack or books visit: **www.HIYH.info**

Stay Connected

Stay connected with the latest health tips, news and updates from Dr. Lau with the following social media sites. Join the Health In Your Hands page on Facebook to have the opportunity to ask Dr. Kevin Lau questions about the book, general questions about their scoliosis, iPhone App called ScolioTrack or the exercise DVD:

   www.facebook.com/HealthInYourHands

   www.youtube.com/DrKevinLau

   www.DrKevinLau.blogspot.com

   www.twitter.com/DrKevinLau

Linked in   http://sg.linkedin.com/in/DrKevinLau